— AMERICA'S —
TEST KITCHEN

ALSO BY THE EDITORS AT AMERICA'S TEST KITCHEN

The America's Test Kitchen New Family Cookbook

The Complete Vegetarian Cookbook

The Complete Cooking for Two Cookbook

The Cook's Illustrated Meat Book

The Cook's Illustrated Baking Book

The Cook's Illustrated Cookbook

The Science of Good Cooking

Pressure Cooker Perfection

The America's Test Kitchen Cooking School Cookbook

The America's Test Kitchen Menu Cookbook

The America's Test Kitchen Quick Family Cookbook

The America's Test Kitchen Healthy Family Cookbook

The America's Test Kitchen Family Baking Book

THE AMERICA'S TEST KITCHEN LIBRARY SERIES

The Make-Ahead Cook

The How Can It Be Gluten Free Cookbook

Healthy Slow Cooker Revolution

Slow Cooker Revolution Volume 2:
The Easy-Prep Edition

Slow Cooker Revolution

The 6-Ingredient Solution

Comfort Food Makeovers

The America's Test Kitchen D.I.Y. Cookbook

Pasta Revolution

Simple Weeknight Favorites

The Best Simple Recipes

THE TV COMPANION SERIES

The Complete Cook's Country TV Show Cookbook

The Complete America's Test Kitchen TV Show
Cookbook 2001–2015

America's Test Kitchen: The TV Companion Cookbook
(2009 and 2011–2015 Editions)

Behind the Scenes with America's Test Kitchen

Test Kitchen Favorites

Cooking at Home with America's Test Kitchen

America's Test Kitchen Live!

Inside America's Test Kitchen

Here in America's Test Kitchen

The America's Test Kitchen Cookbook

AMERICA'S TEST KITCHEN ANNUALS

The Best of America's Test Kitchen
(2007–2015 Editions)

Cooking for Two (2010–2013 Editions)

Light & Healthy (2010–2012 Editions)

THE COOK'S COUNTRY SERIES

From Our Grandmothers' Kitchens

Cook's Country Blue Ribbon Desserts

Cook's Country Best Potluck Recipes

Cook's Country Best Lost Suppers

Cook's Country Best Grilling Recipes

The Cook's Country Cookbook

America's Best Lost Recipes

THE BEST RECIPE SERIES

The New Best Recipe

More Best Recipes

The Best One-Dish Suppers

Soups, Stews & Chilis

The Best Skillet Recipes

The Best Slow & Easy Recipes

The Best Chicken Recipes

The Best International Recipe

The Best Make-Ahead Recipe

The Best 30-Minute Recipe

The Best Light Recipe

The Cook's Illustrated Guide to Grilling and Barbecue

Best American Side Dishes

Cover & Bake

Italian Classics

American Classics

FOR A FULL LISTING OF ALL OUR BOOKS
OR TO ORDER TITLES

CooksIllustrated.com

AmericasTestKitchen.com

or call 800-611-0759

PRAISE FOR OTHER AMERICA'S TEST KITCHEN TITLES

"The perfect kitchen home companion . . . The practical side of things is very much on display . . . cook-friendly and kitchen-oriented, illuminating the process of preparing food instead of mystifying it."
THE WALL STREET JOURNAL ON *THE COOK'S ILLUSTRATED COOKBOOK*

"Carnivores with an obsession for perfection will likely have found their new bible in this comprehensive collection."
PUBLISHERS WEEKLY (STARRED REVIEW) ON *THE COOK'S ILLUSTRATED MEAT BOOK*

"This encyclopedia of meat cookery would feel completely overwhelming if it weren't so meticulously organized and artfully designed. This is Cook's Illustrated at its finest."
THE KITCHN.COM ON *THE COOK'S ILLUSTRATED MEAT BOOK*

"This book is a comprehensive, no-nonsense guide . . . a well-thought-out, clearly explained primer for every aspect of home baking."
THE WALL STREET JOURNAL ON *THE COOK'S ILLUSTRATED BAKING BOOK*

"The 21st-century Fannie Farmer Cookbook or The Joy of Cooking. If you had to have one cookbook and that's all you could have, this one would do it."
CBS SAN FRANCISCO ON *THE NEW FAMILY COOKBOOK*

"Buy this gem for the foodie in your family, and spend the extra money to get yourself a copy too."
THE MISSOURIAN ON *THE BEST OF AMERICA'S TEST KITCHEN 2015*

"This book upgrades slow cooking for discriminating, 21st-century palates—that is indeed revolutionary."
THE DALLAS MORNING NEWS ON *SLOW COOKER REVOLUTION*

"The go-to gift book for newlyweds, small families or empty nesters."
ORLANDO SENTINEL ON *THE COMPLETE COOKING FOR TWO COOKBOOK*

"Some 2,500 photos walk readers through 600 painstakingly tested recipes, leaving little room for error."
ASSOCIATED PRESS ON *THE AMERICA'S TEST KITCHEN COOKING SCHOOL COOKBOOK*

"Ideal as a reference for the bookshelf . . . will be turned to time and again for definitive instruction on just about any food-related matter."
PUBLISHERS WEEKLY ON *THE SCIENCE OF GOOD COOKING*

"A one-volume kitchen seminar, addressing in one smart chapter after another the sometimes surprising whys behind a cook's best practices . . . You get the myth, the theory, the science and the proof, all rigorously interrogated as only America's Test Kitchen can do."
NPR ON *THE SCIENCE OF GOOD COOKING*

"The sum total of exhaustive experimentation . . . anyone interested in gluten-free cookery simply shouldn't be without it."
NIGELLA LAWSON ON *THE HOW CAN IT BE GLUTEN FREE COOKBOOK*

"Even ultra-experienced gluten-free cooks and bakers will learn something from this thoroughly researched, thoughtfully presented volume."
PUBLISHERS WEEKLY ON *THE HOW CAN IT BE GLUTEN FREE COOKBOOK*

"If this were the only cookbook you owned, you would cook well, be everyone's favorite host, have a well-run kitchen, and eat happily every day."
THECITYCOOK.COM ON *THE AMERICA'S TEST KITCHEN MENU COOKBOOK*

"There are pasta books . . . and then there's this pasta book. Flip your carbohydrate dreams upside down and strain them through this sieve of revolutionary, creative, and also traditional recipes."
SAN FRANCISCO BOOK REVIEW ON *PASTA REVOLUTION*

"The entire book is stuffed with recipes that will blow your dinner-table audience away like leaves from a sidewalk in November."
SAN FRANCISCO BOOK REVIEW ON *THE COMPLETE COOK'S COUNTRY TV SHOW COOKBOOK*

"Rely on this doorstopper for explicit and comprehensive takes on recipes from basic to sophisticated."
TOLEDO BLADE ON *THE COMPLETE AMERICA'S TEST KITCHEN TV SHOW COOKBOOK*

THE BEST
Mexican
RECIPES

KITCHEN-TESTED RECIPES PUT THE
Real Flavors of Mexico WITHIN REACH

BY THE EDITORS AT
America's Test Kitchen

AMERICA'S TEST KITCHEN 17 Station Street, Brookline, MA 02445

Library of Congress Cataloging-in-Publication Data

The best Mexican recipes: kitchen-tested recipes put the real flavors of Mexico within reach / by the editors at America's Test Kitchen.
  pages cm
 Includes bibliographical references and index.
 ISBN 978-1-936493-97-5 (alk. paper)
1. Cooking, Mexican. I. America's Test Kitchen (Firm)
 TX716.M4.B4265 2015
 641.5972--dc23
                              2014046398

Manufactured in the United States of America
10 9 8 7 6 5 4 3 2 1

Paperback: $26.95 US
Distributed by America's Test Kitchen
17 Station Street, Brookline, MA 02445

EDITORIAL DIRECTOR: Jack Bishop

EDITORIAL DIRECTOR, BOOKS: Elizabeth Carduff

EXECUTIVE FOOD EDITOR: Julia Collin Davison

SENIOR EDITOR: Dan Zuccarello

ASSOCIATE EDITOR: Danielle DeSiato

ASSISTANT EDITOR: Melissa Herrick

EDITORIAL ASSISTANTS: Kate Ander and Samantha Ronan

TEST COOKS: Lawman Johnson, Sebastian Nava, and Russell Selander

DESIGN DIRECTOR: Amy Klee

ART DIRECTOR: Greg Galvan

ASSOCIATE ART DIRECTOR: Taylor Argenzio

DESIGNER: Jen Kanavos Hoffman

PHOTOGRAPHY DIRECTOR: Julie Cote

ASSOCIATE ART DIRECTOR, PHOTOGRAPHY: Steve Klise

STAFF PHOTOGRAPHER: Daniel J. van Ackere

ADDITIONAL PHOTOGRAPHY: Keller + Keller and Carl Tremblay

FOOD STYLING: Catrine Kelty and Marie Piraino

PHOTO SHOOT KITCHEN TEAM:

    ASSOCIATE EDITOR: Chris O'Connor

    TEST COOK: Dan Cellucci

    ASSISTANT TEST COOK: Cecelia Jenkins and Matthew Fairman

PRODUCTION DIRECTOR: Guy Rochford

SENIOR PRODUCTION MANAGER: Jessica Quirk

PRODUCTION MANAGEMENT SPECIALIST: Christine Walsh

PRODUCTION AND IMAGING SPECIALISTS: Heather Dube, Dennis Noble, Lauren Robbins, and Jessica Voas

PROJECT MANAGER: Britt Dresser

COPY EDITOR: Cheryl Redmond

PROOFREADER: Elizabeth Emery

INDEXER: Elizabeth Parson

PICTURED ON FRONT COVER: Shredded Beef Tacos with Cabbage-Carrot Slaw (page 83)

PICTURED OPPOSITE TITLE PAGE: Gorditas with Chicken with Pickled Onion and Cabbage Filling (page 111)

PICTURED ON BACK COVER: Tamales (page 116), Beef Enchiladas (page 142), Mushroom and Swiss Chard Quesadillas (page 138), Sopes (page 109), Sinaloa-Style Grill-Roasted Chickens (page 180), and Meatball Soup with Rice and Cilantro (page 58)

Contents

WELCOME TO AMERICA'S TEST KITCHEN

This book has been tested, written, and edited by the folks at America's Test Kitchen, a very real 2,500-square-foot kitchen located just outside of Boston. It is the home of *Cook's Illustrated* magazine and *Cook's Country* magazine and is the Monday-through-Friday destination for more than four dozen test cooks, editors, food scientists, tasters, and cookware specialists. Our mission is to test recipes over and over again until we understand how and why they work and until we arrive at the "best" version.

We start the process of testing a recipe with a complete lack of conviction, which means that we accept no claim, no theory, no technique, and no recipe at face value. We simply assemble as many variations as possible, test a half-dozen of the most promising, and taste the results blind. We then construct our own hybrid recipe and continue to test it, varying ingredients, techniques, and cooking times until we reach a consensus. The result, we hope, is the best version of a particular recipe, but we realize that only you can be the final judge of our success (or failure). As we like to say in the test kitchen, "We make the mistakes, so you don't have to."

All of this would not be possible without a belief that good cooking, much like good music, is indeed based on a foundation of objective technique. Some people like spicy foods and others don't, but there is a right way to sauté, there is a best way to cook a pot roast, and there are measurable scientific principles involved in producing perfectly beaten, stable egg whites. This is our ultimate goal: to investigate the fundamental principles of cooking so that you become a better cook. It is as simple as that.

If you're curious to see what goes on behind the scenes at America's Test Kitchen, check out our daily blog, AmericasTestKitchenFeed.com, which features kitchen snapshots, exclusive recipes, video tips, and much more. You can watch us work (in our actual test kitchen) by tuning in to *America's Test Kitchen* (AmericasTestKitchen.com) or *Cook's Country from*

America's Test Kitchen (CooksCountryTV.com) on public television. Tune in to America's Test Kitchen Radio (AmericasTestKitchen.com) on public radio to listen to insights, tips, and techniques that illuminate the truth about real home cooking. And find information about subscribing to *Cook's Illustrated* magazine at CooksIllustrated.com or *Cook's Country* magazine at CooksCountry.com. Both magazines are published every other month. However you choose to visit us, we welcome you into our kitchen, where you can stand by our side as we test our way to the best recipes in America.

FACEBOOK.COM/AMERICASTESTKITCHEN

TWITTER.COM/TESTKITCHEN

YOUTUBE.COM/AMERICASTESTKITCHEN

INSTAGRAM.COM/TESTKITCHEN

PINTEREST.COM/TESTKITCHEN

AMERICASTESTKITCHEN.TUMBLR.COM

GOOGLE.COM/+AMERICASTESTKITCHEN

PREFACE

In 1963, we took a family vacation to Mexico and I still remember lunch at an outdoor restaurant, one with strutting peacocks and an excess of waiters. Most of the guests were tourists, I suppose, but what I remember most is the taste of cilantro. It was a clear sign that I was somewhere foreign, a new place, and, more than an afternoon bullfight or the choked streets of Mexico City, cilantro was my gateway to this new world.

Since then, I have cooked out of Diana Kennedy's marvelous books, I have eaten at Rick Bayless's magnificent Chicago restaurants including Frontera Grill and Xoco, the best lunch spot in the world, and I've traveled to the Yucatán (Mérida, Cancún, Cozumel) as well as the Pacific Coast of Mexico. I have also had mediocre Mexican American food at countless restaurants, from suburban eateries to a few decent spots in Texas.

This preface is one way of saying that I have experienced the highs and lows of Mexican cooking, from the complex authenticity of Kennedy and Bayless to the forgettable "cheese and chiles" approach of lesser establishments.

What I really need is for someone to go through the entire Mexican repertoire—the usual suspects (tacos, fajitas, and burritos), street foods (*sopes* and gorditas), and authentic regional dishes, as well as Mexican-inspired foods—and pull out what makes sense for the American home cook, then test it endlessly so I know it is going to work. That, in a sentence, is why we have published *The Best Mexican Recipes*.

Of course, we start with great test kitchen recipes such as Ancho-Orange Pork Burritos, Soup of the Seven Seas, Shredded Beef Tacos with Cabbage-Carrot Slaw, Mexican Beef Stew, Yucatán-Style Barbecued Pork, and Sinaloa-Style Grill-Roasted Chickens. We've also included some slightly different offerings such as Meatballs in Chipotle Sauce, comfort food in the form of Spicy Chilaquiles with Fried Eggs, and an array of street foods made with a simple masa-based shell with a variety of fillings.

But *The Best Mexican Recipes* isn't just about the recipes, it's also about the techniques—understanding the essence of Mexican cuisine so you can become a better, more interesting cook. Many Mexican recipes depend on a puree of tomatoes, chiles, tomatillos, nuts, and aromatics as a flavor base instead of a broth. Roasting vegetables (this is easily done under a broiler instead of using the traditional *comal*) is also a classic technique for building flavor. And understanding the Mexican pantry (most items are widely available in supermarkets) is also key.

Ultimately, what most home cooks want is not every recipe in the Mexican repertoire, but the best recipes. We define "best" this way—these are the recipes that translate well to the American home kitchen and the American supermarket.

Of course, applying the test kitchen methodology helps, too. Making a pork burrito 20 or 30 times makes it easier for us to help you find success in your own kitchen.

On one of my trips to the Yucatán, I found myself at the top of a pyramid in the jungle. It was late afternoon. I climbed down and discovered a woman cooking and selling tamales wrapped in corn husks. Oddly enough, we were alone and it was quiet. The tamales were totally different than anything I had eaten before—a little smoky perhaps, some new spices—altogether foreign but comforting. It could have been at the height of the Mayan period or yesterday but the food was the connection.

I hope that *The Best Mexican Recipes* provides that connection for you, that its recipes will take you to a new place and time and that it changes how you see yourself and expands the possibilities of your home kitchen.

CHRISTOPHER KIMBALL
Founder and Editor,
Cook's Illustrated and *Cook's Country*
Host, *America's Test Kitchen* and
Cook's Country from America's Test Kitchen

Getting Started

Introduction

It is hardly surprising that Mexico, with its proximity to many American border towns, has had a huge and enduring influence on the American food scene. Millions of immigrants have brought with them their passion for regional specialties like empanadas and mole poblano, recipes that are now virtually household names in our country.

Some dishes—guacamole and salsa, to name two—are now so mainstream that we forget their origins. And tacos are the new pizza, found everywhere from fast food outlets and food trucks to white tablecloth restaurants.

So with this book, we set out to tell the story of Mexican cooking in the United States through a collection of foolproof recipes that range from little-known authentic dishes and Tex-Mex favorites to fresh, modern dishes inspired by the flavors of Mexico. As with any great cuisine, Mexican cooking is incredibly diverse. The history of some dishes dates back to pre-Columbian times. The cuisine blends the complex history of the diverse peoples native to Mexico along with those who came to Mexico from Spain and other parts of Europe, as well as Africa and Asia.

Because Mexico is such a huge country with a varied climate and topography, the range of cooking is amazing. This book represents a small sampling of Mexico's regional cuisines, highlighting the spicy fish preparations of the Yucatán (many infused with the flavors of the tropics) as well as heartier beef dishes from the north and the complex moles of Puebla and Oaxaca.

There's plenty of familiar fare, dishes like burritos and enchiladas that have long been part of the American repertoire. But we've also included dozens of authentic regional specialties you rarely see in restaurants north of the border, dishes like *poc chuc* (grilled citrus-marinated pork) or Soup of the Seven Seas (a spicy seafood soup made with fish, shellfish, and vegetables). And this book features uniquely American creations born in sunny California, where Mexican flavors have blended with the fresh sensibilities of contemporary cooking to produce Grilled Tequila Chicken with Orange, Avocado, and Pepita Salad, as well as Grilled Salmon Steaks with Lime-Cilantro Sauce.

We think this book presents the very best of Mexican cooking put through the filter of what makes sense for the American home kitchen. No incredibly exotic local ingredients or complicated techniques best left to chefs. This is home cooking at its finest.

The test kitchen's approach is always to teach and explain, and this book is no exception. We start at the supermarket, where the influence of Mexico has been so very noticeable. Even the most remote supermarket, far from our southern border, stocks an array of chiles, both fresh and dried. We demystify the world of anchos and poblanos and explain how to shop for other Mexican staples, everything from tomatillos to Cotija cheese.

We have paid particular attention to technique, so throughout this book we show you core Mexican cooking processes, spelling out both the hows and the whys so you can truly understand why something is best done one way versus another. More than 200 step photos, many organized into comprehensive "Learn How" lessons, will teach you the essentials—everything from making your own corn tortillas to assembling the best enchiladas.

So if you have long wanted to re-create your favorite Mexican dishes at home or are eager to try your hand at making some authentic specialties you have yet to encounter, this book will guide you every step of the way. Many dishes, like Mexican Beef Stew or Chicken with Ancho-Peanut Sauce, are surprisingly easy, but remarkable in the flavor they deliver. Others, like tamales or the delicious filled tortilla tarts known as *sopes*, demand a little more time—but we've made sure your efforts will deliver great results.

Chiles 101

Chiles, both fresh and dried, are the backbone of Mexican cuisine, with their unique flavors that range from mild and fresh to acidic and spicy to rich and deeply toasty. Some chiles are used for their heat, while others are used to provide flavor to sauces, stews, and spice rubs. Fresh chiles often have vegetal or grassy flavors, with clean, punchy heat. Dried chiles tend to have deeper, fruitier flavors, with nutty or even smoky undertones. Chiles get their heat from a compound called capsaicin, which is concentrated mostly in the inner whitish pith (called ribs), with progressively smaller amounts in the seeds and flesh. If you like a lot of heat, you can use the entire chile when cooking. If you prefer a milder dish, remove the ribs and seeds. Keep in mind, though, that even among chiles of the same variety, heat levels can vary. Here are some of the most common chiles we use in this book, as well as others that are popular in Mexican cooking.

Fresh Chiles

When shopping for fresh chiles, look for those with bright colors and tight, unblemished skin. Be aware that the same chiles can go by different names in different parts of the country, and can even vary in color.

	CHILE	APPEARANCE AND FLAVOR	HEAT	SUBSTITUTIONS
	Poblano	Large, triangular, green to red-brown; crisp, vegetal	🌶	Bell pepper, Anaheim
	Anaheim	Large, long, skinny, yellow-green to red; mildly tangy, vegetal	🌶🌶	Poblano
	Jalapeño	Small, smooth, shiny, green or red; bright, grassy	🌶🌶½	Serrano
	Serrano	Small, dark green; bright, citrusy	🌶🌶🌶	Jalapeño
	Habanero	Bulbous, bright orange to red; deeply floral, fruity	🌶🌶🌶🌶	Thai

Dried Chiles

When shopping for dried chiles, look for those that are pliable and smell slightly fruity. For most recipes, we find that the flavor of whole chiles is far superior to commercial chile powder.

	CHILE	APPEARANCE AND FLAVOR	HEAT	SUBSTITUTIONS
	Ancho (dried poblano)	Wrinkly, dark red; rich, with raisiny sweetness	🌶	Pasilla, mulato *You can use 1 table-spoon powder in place of 1 chile.*
	Mulato (dried smoked poblano)	Wrinkly, deep brown; smoky with hints of licorice and dried cherry	🌶	Ancho
	Pasilla	Long, wrinkled, purplish or dark brown; rich grapey, herby flavor	🌶🌶	Ancho, mulato
	Chipotle (dried smoked jalapeño)	Wrinkly, brownish red; smoky and chocolaty with tobacco-like sweetness	🌶🌶	*You can use 1 teaspoon powder or 1 teaspoon minced chipotle in adobo sauce in place of 1 chile.*
	Cascabel	Small, round, reddish brown; nutty, woodsy	🌶🌶	New Mexican
	New Mexican	Smooth, brick red; bright with smoky undertones	🌶🌶	Cascabel
	Guajillo	Wrinkly, dark red; mild, fruity, smoky	🌶🌶	New Mexican
	Arbol	Smooth, bright red; bright with smoky undertones	🌶🌶🌶	Pequín
	Pequín	Small, round, deep red; bright, citrusy	🌶🌶🌶🌶	Arbol

LEARN HOW **PREPARING CHILES**

Whole chiles, both fresh and dried, add not just spice but also layers of complex flavor to many of the dishes in this book. Use caution when working with chiles; the compound that makes them taste spicy, called capsaicin, can easily be rubbed off onto your hands (and then onto whatever you touch), causing a burning sensation. Wash your hands, cutting boards, and any other surfaces thoroughly after preparing chiles. We recommend wearing latex gloves when handling very hot chiles.

FRESH CHILES

To prepare fresh chiles, we usually cut the chiles in half and remove the ribs and seeds. To make a dish spicier, include some or all of the ribs and seeds.

1. Cut the chile in half lengthwise with a chef's knife.

2. Starting opposite the stem end, scrape out the ribs and seeds using the edge of a teaspoon.

3. To mince, cut the chile into thin strips, then cut the strips crosswise into small pieces.

DRIED CHILES

Dried chiles can have dirt or dust on the outside, so be sure to clean them gently with a damp towel before using. We tear dried chiles into ½-inch pieces to make them easier to puree into sauces and soups or grind into powder. Toasting deepens their flavor significantly. To make a dish spicier, include the seeds.

1. Stem and seed the chile using your hands.

2. Tear the chile into ½-inch pieces.

3. Toast the pieces in a dry skillet over medium-high heat until fragrant, 2 to 6 minutes.

Corn 101

Corn is a staple ingredient in Mexican cooking. It is used in a wide variety of forms and in dishes as diverse as tacos and tamales, soups and stews, and even sauces.

Fresh Corn

Fresh corn is used in salsas, soups, and fillings for dishes like enchiladas. We recommend buying the freshest corn you can find. Peel back the husks to check for brown spots and to make sure the kernels are firm.

Cornmeal

Cornmeal is available either white or yellow. It is made from dried corn that is milled into a fine, medium, or coarse grind. We use coarse-ground cornmeal in our tamale pie toppings.

Corn Husks

Dried corn husks are traditionally used to wrap and steam tamales. (Although some regions of southern Mexico use banana leaves, we use corn husks in this book.) When shopping for corn husks, we find it is a good idea to buy a few extras in case some are cracked, small, or otherwise unusable. We soak the husks in hot water before using them, which both softens them and removes any dirt that was trapped in the package.

Grits

While not a traditional Mexican ingredient, we add grits to the masa harina in our tamale dough to give the dough a deeper corn flavor. The coarse meal is made from ground dried hominy; it's available in old-fashioned, quick cooking, and instant varieties.

Hominy

Hominy, which is often added to soups and is perhaps most well known for its inclusion in posole, is made from dried corn kernels that have been soaked or cooked in an alkali solution (usually made with slaked lime or calcium hydroxide) to remove the germ and hull. Whole hominy is available both dried and canned; in this book, we use canned hominy in our posole.

Masa

Masa is a dough made from hominy that is finely ground. Traditionally, it's used to make tortillas, tamales, sopes, gorditas, and more. Masa is highly perishable and can be difficult to find in some parts of the United States.

Masa Harina

Literally meaning "corn flour," masa harina is a fine-textured flour made from dried masa. We add water to masa harina to make the dough for corn tortillas and tamales. We also use it to thicken sauces like Amarillo Sauce. Our favorite brand is **Maseca**.

Corn Tortillas

Although homemade tortillas and tostadas taste great, we don't always have time to make them from scratch and often rely on the convenience of store-bought. If possible, look for fresh, locally made tortillas (choose the thinnest brand your market sells). Our favorite corn tortillas, **Maria and Ricardo's Handmade Style Soft Corn Tortillas**, are tender yet substantial. The addition of wheat gluten keeps them soft and pliable. (If you prefer wheat-free tortillas, try **Mission White Corn Tortillas, Restaurant Style**.) As for store-bought tostadas, we like **Mission Estilo Casero Tostadas**, which are crunchy and have good corn flavor.

Herbs and Spices

ANNATTO: Annatto, called *achiote* in Mexico, is a very hard brick-red seed from the annatto tree. It is used both for color and for its subtle, earthy flavor in spice rubs and sauces. Look for annatto alongside the other Mexican spices at your market; these spices are often sold in a separate location from the other spices.

CAYENNE: Although you wouldn't know from its name, this spice usually contains not only fiery red cayenne pepper, but also a variety of other ground dried chiles. We use it to add kick to food or to enhance other flavors. The volatile oils in cayenne lose potency within a few months, so be sure to replenish regularly.

CILANTRO: Cilantro is nearly ubiquitous in Mexican cuisine. Sprinkled on meat or fish or stirred into salsa or soup, it finishes many a dish with a bright, herbal note. Cilantro is the fresh leaves and stems of the coriander plant. The flavorful stems can be chopped and used along with the leaves. Because it loses much of its flavor when cooked, we almost always add it after we take dishes off the heat. Store it with its stems in water or wrap it in damp paper towels and store it in a plastic bag in the crisper drawer of your refrigerator.

CINNAMON: Known in Mexico as *canela*, Mexican cinnamon is also called Ceylon cinnamon. Most cinnamon sold in the United States is actually cassia, not true cinnamon. Ceylon cinnamon tends to be milder than cassia, with floral and vanilla notes. It's used in Mexican chocolate as well as in savory applications like warm-spiced stews and sauces—many moles get their characteristic warm spice notes from the addition of cinnamon.

CHILI POWDER: Chili powder is a seasoning blend made from ground dried chiles and an assortment of other ingredients such as cumin, garlic, and oregano. It's an easy way to add spicy depth to chilis and sauces; rather than calling for minuscule amounts of several spices and chiles in a simple sautéed chicken recipe, for example, we use a bit of chili powder. Chili powder varies from brand to brand; our favorite, from **Morton & Bassett**, has a deep, complex flavor and just the right amount of heat.

CORIANDER: Coriander appears in a huge variety of recipes, from meat-heavy stews to spicy seafood dishes. The light brown spherical seeds are the dried fruit of the coriander plant. Coriander possesses a sweet, almost fruity flavor with just a hint of the soapy-metallic character of mature cilantro.

CUMIN: Cumin is among a handful of spices that appear again and again in Mexican cooking. Its earthy, warm flavor pairs well with many common Mexican ingredients, from fresh vegetables to roast chicken. When possible, buy whole seeds and grind them yourself; the flavor is more potent.

EPAZOTE: A common herb in Mexican cooking, epazote has a distinctive savory, earthy flavor. It's a key ingredient in our Toasted Corn with Epazote, but can be difficult to find in some parts of the United States; we find that a combination of fresh oregano and fresh cilantro makes an acceptable substitute.

OREGANO: Mexican oregano is different from Italian oregano; although they share the same basic, earthy flavor, Mexican oregano has notes of citrus and mild licorice. If you can't find dried Mexican oregano, use fresh Mediterranean oregano.

Fruits and Vegetables

AVOCADO: There is hardly a Mexican recipe that doesn't call for a garnish of chopped avocado or guacamole. When buying avocados, look for the small, dark, pebbly-skinned Hass variety. A ripe avocado should yield slightly to a gentle squeeze; if in doubt, try to remove the small stem. It should flick off easily and reveal green underneath. Underripe avocados will ripen unevenly if left on the counter; it's better to ripen them in the refrigerator (although it will take a couple days longer). Ripe avocados stored in the refrigerator can last up to five days. For information on how to prepare avocados, see page 22.

JÍCAMA: Jícama is a bulbous root vegetable that is generally eaten raw in slaws and salads. It tastes like a combination of apple and water chestnut, and it makes a refreshing accompaniment to spicy taco fillings. To prepare jícama, peel away the tough skin with a vegetable peeler or paring knife to reveal the milky white flesh. Once peeled, jícama can be shredded on a box grater, cut into thin rounds, sliced into matchsticks, or cut into chunks.

LIMES: A squeeze of lime juice brightens up many a Mexican dish. Although Key limes are often used in Mexico, we prefer regular Persian limes since they're widely available and easier to work with. Store limes in a sealed zipper-lock bag in the crisper drawer of your refrigerator.

PLANTAINS: Particularly popular in southern coastal Mexico, plantains are a large, starchy variety of banana. They ripen from green to yellow to black, and are usually peeled before cooking. Plantains are often cut into strips and fried or incorporated into soups and stews.

SOUR ORANGES: Also known as bitter or Seville oranges, sour oranges are used throughout Mexico. Their tart, acidic juice is often used for sauces, like the one for Carnitas, or in marinades, as in Yucatán-Style Barbecued Pork. Because sour oranges are hard to come by in many parts of the Unites States, we substitute a combination of orange and lime juices.

TOMATILLOS: Called *tomates verdes* in much of Mexico, small green tomatillos have a tangier, more citrusy flavor than true green tomatoes. When choosing tomatillos, look for pale green orbs with firm flesh that fills and splits open the fruit's papery outer husk, which must be removed before cooking. While we prefer the flavor and texture of fresh tomatillos, we have found that you can substitute one 12-ounce can of tomatillos, drained and rinsed, for every 8 ounces of fresh tomatillos. For information on how to prepare tomatillos, see page 20.

TOMATOES: Fresh and canned tomatoes are an integral part of Mexican cooking. Fresh tomatoes are used for salsas and garnishes, while canned tomatoes form the basis of many soups, stews, sauces, and braises. When it comes to canned tomatoes, we find that it pays to shop carefully; brand matters. If using canned diced tomatoes, we prefer **Hunt's. Muir Glen** makes the best tomato puree as well as the best canned whole tomatoes. And when it comes to tomato paste, we prefer **Goya**.

Nuts and Seeds

PEANUTS: Peanuts are grown and eaten throughout Mexico and are a vital ingredient in many mole sauces, for which they are ground up and simmered with chiles, chocolate, and other nuts and seeds to make a rich, dark sauce. Peanuts are also used to make simpler sauces and are often eaten as a snack.

SESAME SEEDS: Sesame seeds were introduced to Mexico by the Spanish, and have since become an integral part of many moles and sauces. In Mexico, they're often used unhulled. We use hulled sesame seeds in our recipes, since they're more widely available in the United States.

PUMPKIN SEEDS: Sold both as unhulled seeds and as hulled green pepitas, pumpkin seeds are native to Mexico. Unhulled, toasted pumpkin seeds give Pumpkin Seed Dip its signature texture and flavor, while pepitas are a common choice for mole-style pumpkin seed sauces. They can also simply be roasted and eaten as a snack.

MEXICAN CREMA

Thick, slightly tangy Mexican *crema* is a popular way to impart a touch of richness to many dishes. Drizzled atop creamy Spicy Pinto Bean Soup, it adds a bright finishing touch, and dishes like Baja Fish Tacos with Pickled Onion and Cabbage just don't seem complete without it. Similar in flavor and texture to crème fraîche, Mexican crema is quite simple to make at home. We've developed two versions: a more authentic version that is cultured overnight, and a quick version that tastes great and takes only a few minutes to make.

Overnight Mexican Crema

MAKES ABOUT 1 CUP

Avoid ultrapasteurized cream, which has been heated to higher temperatures, killing enzymes and bacteria and even altering the cream's protein structure, making it hard to achieve the right texture.

- 1   **cup cream**
- 2   **tablespoons buttermilk**
- ⅛   **teaspoon salt**
- 2   **teaspoons lime juice**

Stir together cream and buttermilk in container. Cover and place in warm location (75 to 80 degrees is ideal; lower temperatures will lengthen fermentation time) until mixture is thickened but still pourable, 12 to 24 hours. Dissolve salt in lime juice and add to mixture. Refrigerate for up to 2 months.

Quick Mexican Crema

MAKES ABOUT 1¼ CUPS

- ½   **cup mayonnaise**
- ½   **cup sour cream**
- 2   **tablespoons lime juice**
- 2   **tablespoons milk**

Whisk all ingredients together in bowl. (Sauce can be refrigerated for up to 2 days.)

Other Ingredients

FLOUR TORTILLAS: Flour tortillas are most often found in northern Mexico, and used for dishes like burritos, quesadillas, flautas, and fajitas. Our favorite brand is **Old El Paso 6-Inch Flour Tortillas.**

BEANS: In Mexico, beans are a staple food; pinto beans and black beans are the most common, although garbanzo beans are also used. We use both canned and dried beans in this book. Try to buy dried beans from a store with high turnover, as old beans will not soften as well. Before cooking them, we often soak dried beans overnight in a saltwater solution, which results in a creamier texture and fewer burst beans. Refried beans, which are traditionally cooked in lard and mashed, are one of the most popular Mexican bean preparations. Refried beans are simple to make at home, but if you prefer the convenience of canned refried beans, we like **Taco Bell Home Originals Refried Beans.**

COTIJA CHEESE: Cotija is a tangy, salty, aged cheese that is commonly crumbled and used as a garnish for finished dishes. If you can't find Cotija, feta makes a good substitute.

QUESO FRESCO: *Queso fresco* is a soft, fresh cheese that, like Cotija, is used most often as a garnish since it does not melt well. It has a mildly salty flavor that is comparable to mild feta, which you can use as a substitute if you can't find queso fresco.

QUESO DE OAXACA: This specialty of the Oaxacan region is an excellent melting cheese, often used in dishes like Queso Fundido. If you can't find it, we recommend using Monterey Jack as a substitute.

CHORIZO: The sausage known as chorizo comes in several styles. Fresh Mexican chorizo, which is what we use in this book, is made from finely ground pork. It has a pronounced spicy tanginess from chili powder and vinegar. We usually remove it from its casing before cooking. Spanish chorizo is made from more coarsely ground pork and is sold dry-cured and fully cooked. It is bright red with smoky flavor (from smoked paprika) and can be sweet or spicy. Both Mexican and Spanish chorizo are sold at well-stocked supermarkets 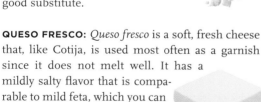 and specialty stores.

LARD: Often used as a cooking fat in Mexico, lard is a traditional ingredient in tamale dough. We found that lard gave our tamales a rich flavor that vegetable shortening simply couldn't match. Lard is available in butcher's shops or well-stocked supermarkets.

MEXICAN CHOCOLATE: Mexican chocolate has a grainier texture than other chocolates due to the fact that it is often stone-ground in the traditional manner. Sweetened Mexican chocolate (which is often ground with cinnamon and other flavorings like almond or vanilla) tastes of molasses and/or dried fruit. It's often used in a drink similar to American hot chocolate and in some types of mole sauces.

TEQUILA: Real tequila is made from the juice of the blue agave plant, and can be produced only in certain regions of Mexico. (Tequila that is not made from 100 percent blue agave is called *mixto*, and can be produced outside of Mexico. Tequila made from 100 percent agave will say so on the bottle.) Tequila is used for more than just margaritas: It's also an ingredient in sauces like *salsa borracha* and is incorporated into dishes like Drunken Beans.

Equipment

If you have a well-stocked kitchen, you're probably well equipped to cook many authentic Mexican dishes. But if you plan on doing a lot of Mexican cooking, we recommend having a few key items on hand. While some of these are essential, others simply make Mexican cooking easier and more foolproof.

TORTILLA PRESS: Corn tortillas are easy to make at home, especially if you use a tortilla press (instead of a rolling pin) to flatten the balls of masa, or dough, into disks. Tortillas made in a tortilla press will be thinner and more uniform than those made with a rolling pin. Our winner, the handsome **La Mexicana Tortilladora de Madera Barnizada/Mesquite Tortilla Press**, is weighty enough to make pressing effortless. It made even tortillas, and its ample pressing surface ensured that the dough wouldn't ooze out the sides. It's on the expensive side, though; for a less expensive option, we recommend the **Imusa Cast Iron Tortilla Press**.

SPICE GRINDER: The volatile flavor compounds in spices turn dull over time, a process that accelerates once the spices are ground. Since Mexican food relies on lots of spices and ground chiles, we find that the flavor enhancement from grinding your own spices is well worth the small effort. Although Mexican cooks traditionally grind their spices and dried chiles using a *molcajete*, a stone mortar and pestle, we find that the best results come from a good coffee grinder. Our winner, the **Krups Fast-Touch Coffee Mill**, makes a fine, even-textured powder and is easy to use and clean. (We recommend designating separate grinders for coffee and spices.)

BLENDER: In traditional Mexican cooking, home cooks use a *metate* (a rectangular piece of stone with a depression in the center) and a *mano* (a smaller, cylindrical stone that crushes the food against the metate) for grinding corn, making chile pastes, and processing smooth sauces and stews. Luckily, making smooth pastes is much easier with the right blender. Our favorite blender, the **Vitamix 5200**, is an investment, but the **Breville The Hemisphere Control** also excels on most tasks.

FOOD PROCESSOR: A food processor is great for tasks that can be difficult or time-consuming to achieve by hand. We use it to finely chop vegetables for things like Mexican-Style Picadillo, to mix dough for dishes like tamales, and to process chunky sauces, like the tomatillo sauce for Chicken Enchiladas Verdes. We recommend the **Cuisinart Custom 14-Cup Food Processor**, which is efficient, sturdy, and easily handles even small amounts of food.

SKILLET: Whether you're toasting chiles, browning meat, or making a complete meal like rice and beans, a good skillet is invaluable. It's helpful to have both traditional and nonstick skillets in multiple sizes (even better if they're ovensafe). Our favorite traditional skillet is the **All-Clad 12-Inch Stainless Fry Pan**; our favorite nonstick is the **T-fal Professional Nonstick Fry Pan, 12.5 Inches.**

SAUTÉ PAN: These midheight, midweight, lidded vessels have straight sides that are perfect for shallow frying. They're also handy when a recipe requires browning and then adding liquid, like our Sopes or Gorditas. We like sauté pans that are at least 10 inches in diameter. Look for one that has an aluminum core with layers of stainless steel. Our favorite is the **Viking Stainless 7-Ply 3-Quart Sauté Pan**.

BAKING SHEET: Traditional Mexican recipes often call for charring vegetables or chiles on a *comal*, a flat, usually cast-iron, griddle. We re-create the same effect using the broiler and a good rimmed baking sheet. We also use baking sheets to bake tostada shells, quesadillas, empanadas, burritos, and more. Look for thick, light-colored sheets like our winner, the **Wear-Ever Half Size Heavy Duty Sheet Pan (13 gauge) by Vollrath**.

WIRE RACK: We use wire racks to allow air to circulate while foods like our Stuffed Jalapeños are cooking; this helps the chiles cook evenly on all sides. We also keep finished foods with crisp exteriors, like the fried fish for Baja Fish Tacos with Pickled Onion and Cabbage, on a wire rack in a warm oven until ready to serve; this helps to preserve its crunchy coating. Look for a rack with a woven grid (as opposed to bars that run in just one direction) and that measures 17 by 12 inches, so it will fit snugly inside a standard rimmed baking sheet. We prefer the **CIA Bakeware 12-Inch x 17-Inch Cooling Rack**.

GLASS BAKING DISH: This versatile dish is ideal for baking enchiladas and casseroles, marinating large steaks, or transporting piles of loaded skewers out to the grill. We recommend having a 13 by 9-inch glass **Pyrex Bakeware** dish. It's sturdy and dishwasher-safe, and the thick, tempered glass retains plenty of heat to ensure deep, even browning. Plus, it's naturally scratch-resistant so you can cut and serve straight from the dish.

STEAMER BASKET: We use a steamer basket set inside a large Dutch oven to make tamales. The basket lifts the tamales out of the liquid, leaving enough room below for the simmering water. Our preferred model, the **OXO Good Grips Pop-Up Steamer**, is roomy and fits nicely into a Dutch oven.

DUTCH OVEN: From frying fish to braising meat and everything in between, a Dutch oven is one of the most useful and versatile tools you can have in your kitchen. Built for both oven and stovetop use, a good Dutch oven should be big and wide (with at least a 6- to 8- quart capacity) with a heavy, tight-fitting lid. Our favorites are the **All-Clad Stainless 8-Quart Stockpot** and the **Le Creuset 7¼-Quart Round French Oven**. For a less expensive option, the **Lodge Color Enamel 6-Quart Dutch Oven** also performs well.

The Building Blocks of Mexican Cooking

Traditional Mexican cuisine relies on a variety of cooking techniques, some of which are unique to Mexican cooking, and others that may look familiar to the average American cook. The methods below are the building blocks for many of the recipes throughout this book.

MAKING SAUCES

One of the most distinctive features of Mexican cuisine is its sauces. Used not only as serving sauces, but often as cooking mediums, Mexican sauces are as much a part of the dish as the meat and vegetables. Unlike the thin, broth-based pan sauces that are common in French cooking, Mexican sauces are often vegetable-based. Ingredients like fresh and dried chiles, tomatoes, tomatillos, nuts, seeds, and aromatics are blended into a smooth puree before or after cooking. This puree is then used as a base for sauces like moles or pumpkin seed sauces. This technique is also used for soups and stews, where the puree is commonly fried in oil to deepen its flavor before building the soup.

USING MARINADES AND RUBS

MARINADES: Many Mexican dishes, like Sinaloa-Style Grill-Roasted Chickens, Grilled Fish Tacos, or Yucatán-Style Barbecued Pork, get their flavor from a bold marinade. Mexican marinades range from simple mixtures of salt and lime juice to cooked combinations of chiles, garlic, and other aromatic ingredients. We find that most marinades, however, don't go more than skin-deep. Here in the test kitchen, we pump up flavor as well as juiciness by creating marinades with lots of seasonings and flavorings but also a healthy dose of salt. Salt, unlike most other flavorings, can penetrate deep into meat to season it throughout and also increases juiciness. When using acidic ingredients like lime juice, we make sure not to marinate the meat for too long to ensure that the meat doesn't become mushy. We also add oil to most marinades, since most of the herbs and spices we add to marinades are oil-soluble, meaning they only release their full flavor when mixed into oil. Sometimes we also slash or score meat before marinating it to allow the marinade to penetrate even further into the meat. We also recommend flipping or stirring meat as it marinates to ensure that all of the meat gets equal exposure to the marinade. Finally, for a burst of fresh flavor, we often reserve some marinade to toss with the meat at the end of cooking.

RUBS: Mexican cuisine relies heavily on spices, and sometimes, meat or fish gets a flavor boost from a spice rub, like Chile-Rubbed Roast Chicken or Spicy Grilled Beef and Chorizo Kebabs. We find that spice rubs are preferable to marinades when a dry surface is needed, such as in Carne Asada. Many of the spice rubs in this book include dried chiles, which are toasted and ground to a powder. These chile powders get depth and nuance from the addition of warm and earthy spices and herbs like cumin, coriander, cinnamon, nutmeg, and oregano. We prefer to use whole spices and chiles and grind them ourselves, since whole spices have a deeper, more potent flavor than preground varieties.

TOASTING, ROASTING, AND CHARRING

You will see many recipes in this book that call for roasting fresh chiles and other vegetables like tomatoes, tomatillos, and onions to deepen their flavor. Mexican cooks achieve good char on vegetables using a *comal*, a flat, heavy cast-iron griddle. Since most American cooks don't own a comal, we achieve the same deep char by using the broiler in recipes like Tomatillo Salsa or Pumpkin Seed Dip. When working with dried chiles, nuts, and seeds, we often toast them to bring out their flavors, as we do in many of our mole sauces; this is easy to do in a dry skillet or, when working with a larger amount, on a baking sheet in the oven.

COOKING WITH TORTILLAS

Tortillas are, of course, used as a serving vessel for tacos and tostadas, and served on the side of countless other Mexican dishes. But when they are incorporated into a dish, such as enchiladas, they are often softened by briefly frying them, one at a time, in hot oil. This helps to make the tortillas pliable and decreases the risk that they'll crack or fall apart in the sauce. Since frying tortillas one at a time is time-consuming and messy, we often warm the tortillas all at once in the microwave instead. In some recipes, such as *pastel Azteca*, we opt to toast the tortillas to both deepen their flavor and help them hold together when covered in sauce.

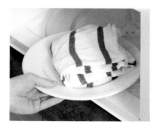

BRAISING AND SHREDDING MEAT

One of the key techniques of Mexican cuisine is long, slow cooking, which allows meat to become ultratender and infused with flavor. Oftentimes meat is braised and then shredded and combined with a sauce and used as a filling for tamales, tacos, enchiladas, and more. We frequently cook the meat directly in the sauce, which infuses both the sauce and the meat with lots of flavor. For this purpose, choosing the right cut is essential. Beef chuck-eye roast, beef short ribs, pork shoulder, and chicken thighs are some of our favorite braising cuts, since their plentiful fat and connective tissue turn meltingly tender when cooked for an extended time. In the test kitchen, we have found that the most foolproof (and hands-off) method of braising is to cook in a covered pot in the oven. While the direct heat of the stovetop increases the risk of scorching the bottom of the pot, using the oven results in more even cooking and less need to stir.

FRYING BRAISED MEAT: Although braising works to produce ultratender, moist meat, achieving crisp edges or a crunchy crust is nearly impossible. In some cases, Mexican cooks braise a large cut of meat, shred it, and then fry the shreds, like in Carnitas. We often broil rather than fry the pieces of meat, since it's easier in a home kitchen.

FINISHING AND SERVING

Fresh garnishes are a hallmark of Mexican cuisine. Creamy avocado, Mexican crema, crunchy radishes, fresh cilantro, or a squeeze of lime juice help to complete and round out many a dish, especially those that are heavily spiced or richly sauced. In Mexico, the midday meal is traditionally the largest meal of the day and consists of multiple elements—soup, rice, beans, generously sauced meat, tortillas. The garnishes add textural interest and a welcome layer of freshness to the meal.

STUFFED JALAPEÑOS

Appetizers
and Drinks

Fresh Tomato Salsa

Makes about 3 cups

✓ **WHY THIS RECIPE WORKS:** Brightly flavored, relish-like *salsa fresca* (or *salsa cruda*) accompanies a wide variety of Mexican dishes, so we set out to create a versatile, chunky salsa that emphasized the tomatoes. To solve the problem of watery salsa, we drained diced tomatoes in a colander. For a stream-lined mixing process, we layered the other ingredients on top of the tomatoes while they drained, then stirred everything together in a bowl. We finished the salsa with lime juice (which tasted more authentic—and better—than lemon juice), salt, and sugar. Serve with homemade chips (see page 21).

1½   **pounds tomatoes, cored and cut into ½-inch pieces**
½   **cup finely chopped red onion**
¼   **cup chopped fresh cilantro**
1   **large jalapeño chile, stemmed, seeds reserved, and minced**
1   **small garlic clove, minced**
2   **teaspoons lime juice, plus extra for seasoning**
   Salt and pepper
   Sugar

Place tomatoes in colander and let drain for 30 minutes. As tomatoes drain, layer onion, cilantro, jalapeño, and garlic on top. Shake colander to drain excess juice, then transfer vegetables to serving bowl. Stir in lime juice. (Salsa can be refrigerated for up to 3 hours.) Add reserved jalapeño seeds to increase heat as desired. Season with salt, pepper, sugar, and extra lime juice to taste before serving.

Slow-Roasted Tomato Salsa

Makes about 2 cups

✓ **WHY THIS RECIPE WORKS:** To achieve the smoky-sweet flavor of traditional *salsa asada*, or "roasted salsa," we oven-roasted sliced tomatoes and garlic. Raw onion, jalapeño, cilantro, and lime juice gave our salsa pleasant heat and bright, tangy flavor. Serve with homemade chips (see page 21).

½   **cup extra-virgin olive oil**
4   **garlic cloves, sliced thin**
2   **pounds tomatoes, cored and sliced ½ inch thick**
   Salt and pepper
¼   **cup finely chopped red onion**
1   **jalapeño chile, stemmed, seeded, and minced**
2   **tablespoons minced fresh cilantro**
1   **tablespoon lime juice, plus extra for seasoning**

1. Adjust oven rack to middle position and heat oven to 325 degrees. Grease bottom of 13 by 9-inch baking dish with 2 tablespoons oil and sprinkle half of garlic into dish. Arrange tomato slices in dish, overlapping as needed to fit, then season with salt, sprinkle with remaining garlic, and drizzle with remaining 6 tablespoons oil. Roast tomatoes until slightly shriveled and most of their juices have been replaced with oil, 1½ to 2 hours.

2. Remove dish from oven and let tomatoes cool completely. Using slotted spoon, transfer tomatoes and garlic to cutting board and chop coarse; discard oil. Combine chopped tomatoes and garlic, onion, jalapeño, cilantro, and lime juice in serving bowl. (Salsa can be refrigerated for up to 2 days.) Season with salt, pepper, and extra lime juice to taste before serving.

Tomatillo Salsa

Makes about 2 cups

✔️ **WHY THIS RECIPE WORKS:** *Salsa verde* (literally meaning "green sauce") is perhaps more common on the authentic Mexican table than tomato-based salsa fresca. We wanted a tangy, well-balanced tomatillo salsa recipe that highlighted the green, citrusy notes of the fruit and paired nicely with a variety of Mexican dishes. While some salsa verde recipes use raw tomatillos, most cook them either by boiling or roasting. Cooking softens the fruit, which can be quite firm, and mellows its acidity. We found that charring half under the broiler and leaving the other half raw produced a salsa with a clean, fresh flavor and subtle, smoky nuances. We combined the tomatillos with the traditional salsa verde seasonings—jalapeño, onion, garlic, cilantro, lime juice, and salt—in the bowl of a food processor, and pulsed the salsa to a chunky consistency. Serve with homemade chips or as an accompaniment to grilled steaks, chicken, or fish.

1 **pound tomatillos, husks and stems removed, rinsed well and dried**
1 **teaspoon vegetable oil**
1 **small white onion, chopped**
1 **jalapeño chile, stemmed, halved, and seeded**
½ **cup fresh cilantro leaves**
2 **tablespoons lime juice**
1 **garlic clove, minced**
  Salt
2 **teaspoons extra-virgin olive oil**
  Sugar

1. Adjust oven rack 6 inches from broiler element and heat broiler. Line rimmed baking sheet with aluminum foil. Toss half of tomatillos with vegetable oil and transfer to prepared sheet. Broil until tomatillos are spotty brown and skins begin to burst, 7 to 10 minutes. Transfer tomatillos to food processor and let cool completely.

2. Halve remaining tomatillos and add to food processor with broiled tomatillos. Add onion, jalapeño, cilantro, lime juice, garlic, and ¼ teaspoon salt. Pulse until slightly chunky, 16 to 18 pulses. Transfer salsa to serving bowl, cover, and let sit at room temperature for at least 30 minutes. (Salsa can be refrigerated for up to 2 days.) Stir in olive oil and season with salt and sugar to taste before serving.

TEST KITCHEN TIP **PREPARING TOMATILLOS FOR SALSA**

1. Pull papery husks and stems off of tomatillos; discard.

2. Rinse tomatillos in colander to rid them of sticky residue from husks and dry.

3. Broil half of tomatillos until skins are spotty brown, leaving other half raw to add to salsa later.

Homemade Fried Tortilla Chips

Makes 4 ounces; serves 4

✔ **WHY THIS RECIPE WORKS:** Even the best store-bought chips can't compare to the fresh corn flavor and ultracrisp texture of homemade tortilla chips. Luckily, making tortilla chips at home is fairly simple. Since the tortillas are integral to the recipe, we found that quality was very important. We got the best results with fresh, locally made tortillas (choose the thinnest brand your market sells). We prefer the flavor of peanut oil when deep frying, but vegetable or corn oil will also work. We like the larger crystal size of kosher salt here because it's easy to sprinkle evenly over the chips and its small crunch is a nice addition. We prefer to use store-bought tortillas over homemade because their uniform size and thickness are easier to work with. The recipe can be doubled; be sure to fry the chips in four batches.

8   (6-inch) corn tortillas
5   cups peanut oil
    Kosher salt

1. Cut each tortilla into 6 wedges. Line 2 baking sheets with several layers of paper towels. Heat oil in Dutch oven over medium-high heat to 350 degrees.

2. Add half of tortillas and fry until golden and crisp around edges, 2 to 4 minutes. Transfer fried chips to prepared sheet, sprinkle lightly with salt, and let cool. Repeat with remaining tortillas. Serve. (Cooled chips can be stored at room temperature for up to 4 days.)

Homemade Baked Tortilla Chips

Makes 2½ ounces; serves 2 to 3

✔ **WHY THIS RECIPE WORKS:** Sometimes, you just don't want to heat up a big pot of oil to make homemade tortilla chips. But too often, baked versions turn out unevenly cooked, chewy, or just plain tasteless. For a baked chip recipe that's worth its salt, we found it was key to use a liberal amount of vegetable oil spray to coat the chips evenly and thoroughly before baking. We also made sure to bake them until they were completely crisp. You can substitute flour tortillas for the corn tortillas if desired. Flour tortillas come in a variety of sizes; if using tortillas larger than 6 inches, you will need fewer of them and will be able to cut more wedges out of each. We prefer to use store-bought tortillas over homemade because their uniform size and thickness are easier to work with.

5   (6-inch) corn tortillas
    Vegetable oil spray
    Kosher salt

1. Adjust oven rack to middle position and heat oven to 350 degrees. Spray both sides of tortillas liberally with oil spray, then cut each tortilla into 6 wedges. Season with salt and spread into single layer on baking sheet.

2. Bake tortillas, stirring occasionally, until golden and crisp, 15 to 20 minutes. Remove chips from oven and let cool before serving. (Cooled chips can be stored at room temperature for up to 4 days.)

Chunky Guacamole

Makes about 3 cups

✓ **WHY THIS RECIPE WORKS:** Traditional Mexican guacamole is usually quite simple: At its most basic, it consists of roughly mashed avocados mixed with lime juice and a sprinkle of salt. But the guacamole found in American restaurants often sacrifices the singular character of the avocado by adding too many other flavorings, and the texture of the guacamole is reduced to a listless, smooth puree. We wanted to highlight the dense, buttery texture and distinct flavor of the avocado in a chunky, hearty guacamole. For the best texture, we lightly mashed one avocado with the seasoning ingredients, then gently mixed in two more diced avocados. Just 2 tablespoons of chopped onion and two cloves of minced garlic provided a nice bite without overwhelming the avocados' flavor; a small amount of cumin provided a warm background note; and cilantro and minced jalapeño gave the guacamole a bright boost. Very ripe avocados are key in this recipe. To minimize the risk of discoloration, prepare the minced ingredients first so they are ready to mix with the avocados as soon as they are cut. Serve with homemade chips (see page 21).

3 ripe avocados
¼ cup minced fresh cilantro
1 jalapeño chile, stemmed, seeded, and minced
2 tablespoons finely chopped red onion
2 tablespoons lime juice
2 garlic cloves, minced
Salt
½ teaspoon ground cumin

1. Halve 1 avocado, remove pit, and scoop flesh into medium bowl. Add cilantro, jalapeño, onion, lime juice, garlic, ¾ teaspoon salt, and cumin and mash with potato masher (or fork) until mostly smooth.

2. Halve, pit, and dice remaining 2 avocados. Add cubes to bowl with mashed avocado mixture and gently mash until mixture is well combined but still coarse. (Guacamole can be refrigerated for up to 24 hours with plastic wrap pressed directly against its surface.) Season with salt to taste before serving.

TEST KITCHEN TIP **DICING AN AVOCADO**

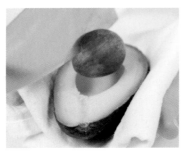

1. After slicing avocado in half around pit, lodge edge of knife blade into pit and twist to remove. Using wooden spoon, pry pit safely off knife.

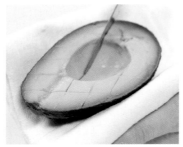

2. Make ½-inch crosshatch incisions in flesh of each avocado half with knife, cutting down to but not through skin.

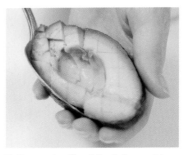

3. Separate diced flesh from skin with soupspoon inserted between skin and flesh, gently scooping out avocado cubes.

Black Bean Dip

Makes about 2 cups

✔ **WHY THIS RECIPE WORKS:** Black beans are native to Mexico and are a staple ingredient in Mexican cooking. We wanted to highlight black beans' rich flavor in a smooth and creamy appetizer dip. To keep this starter quick and easy, we turned to canned black beans. The secret to achieving a creamy and complex-tasting dip was to pair the starchy bean with a lighter vegetable—in this case, onion—and then infuse the mixture with aromatic spices. A combination of oregano, cumin, and chipotle in adobo provided earthy, spicy, and smoky notes. Garlic added much-needed depth, but raw garlic tasted harsh. We found that soaking the garlic in lime juice for at least 15 minutes mellowed its flavor. We combined everything in the food processor, which gave the dip a smooth, luxurious texture. Letting the dip rest at room temperature for at least 30 minutes ensured that all of the flavors melded nicely. A bit of fresh cilantro stirred in just before serving added a burst of freshness to our easy dip. Serve with homemade chips (see page 21).

- 2 tablespoons lime juice
- 1 garlic clove, minced
- 1 teaspoon minced fresh oregano
- 2 (15-ounce) cans black beans, rinsed
- ½ onion, chopped
- 1 tablespoon extra-virgin olive oil
- 1 teaspoon minced canned chipotle chile in adobo sauce
- ½ teaspoon ground cumin
- Salt
- 2 tablespoons minced fresh cilantro

1. Combine lime juice, garlic, and oregano in small bowl; set aside for at least 15 minutes.

2. Pulse beans, onion, oil, chipotle, cumin, ¼ teaspoon salt, and lime juice mixture in food processor until fully ground, 5 to 10 pulses. Scrape down sides of bowl with rubber spatula. Continue to process until uniform paste forms, about 1 minute, scraping down bowl twice.

3. Transfer dip to bowl, cover, and let sit at room temperature for at least 30 minutes. (Dip can be refrigerated for up to 24 hours; bring to room temperature before serving.) Stir in cilantro and season with salt to taste before serving.

TEST KITCHEN TIP MINCING FRESH HERBS

Place your hand on handle of chef's knife and rest fingers of your other hand on top of blade. Use rocking motion to evenly mince herbs, pivoting knife as you chop.

Pumpkin Seed Dip

Makes about 3 cups

✔ **WHY THIS RECIPE WORKS:** This traditional hummus-like dip is popular in the Yucatán peninsula. It is made from toasted pumpkin seeds and roasted tomatoes; the earthy, toasty flavors in the dip are complemented by the heat of a habanero chile and the bright freshness of lime juice and cilantro. The dip is traditionally made with unhulled pumpkin seeds, which are still encased in their white shells (or hulls). For due diligence, we tried making dips with both unhulled seeds and hulled green pepitas, but tasters unanimously preferred the coarser texture and deeper flavor of the dip made with the unhulled seeds. However, unhulled pumpkin seeds are almost always sold roasted and salted; to avoid an inedibly salty dip, we found it was crucial to rinse off the salt before we used the seeds. We then toasted the seeds in a hot oven until they turned a rich, golden color before processing them into the dip. A blender was crucial for reaching our desired consistency; a food processor did not break down the pumpkin seed hulls as well as the blender did. If using unsalted pumpkin seeds, you can skip the rinsing and drying in step 1 and go directly to toasting. Serve with homemade chips (see page 21).

1½   cups roasted, unhulled pumpkin seeds
1   pound tomatoes, cored and halved
¼   cup extra-virgin olive oil
1   onion, chopped
2   tablespoons lime juice
1   habanero chile, stemmed, seeded, and chopped
    Salt and pepper
2   ounces queso fresco, crumbled (½ cup)
2   tablespoons chopped fresh cilantro

1. Adjust 1 oven rack to middle position and second rack 6 inches from broiler element. Heat oven to 400 degrees. Rinse pumpkin seeds under warm water and dry thoroughly. Spread seeds on rimmed baking sheet, place sheet on lower rack, and toast seeds until golden brown, stirring occasionally, 12 to 15 minutes. Set aside to cool slightly and heat broiler.

2. Line second rimmed baking sheet with aluminum foil. Toss tomatoes with 1 tablespoon oil and arrange cut side down on prepared sheet. Place sheet on upper rack and broil until tomatoes are spotty brown, 7 to 10 minutes. Transfer tomatoes to blender and let cool completely.

3. Add onion, lime juice, habanero, pumpkin seeds, and remaining 3 tablespoon oil to blender and process until smooth, about 1 minute, scraping down sides of blender as needed. Transfer dip to serving bowl and refrigerate until completely chilled, at least 2 hours or up to 24 hours. Season with salt and pepper to taste. Sprinkle with queso fresco and cilantro before serving.

TEST KITCHEN TIP **TOASTING PUMPKIN SEEDS**

1. If salted, rinse pumpkin seeds, dry thoroughly, and spread on rimmed baking sheet.

2. Toast seeds in oven until golden brown, 12 to 15 minutes.

7-Layer Dip

Serves 8 to 10

☑ **WHY THIS RECIPE WORKS:** While seven-layer dip isn't a traditional Mexican dish, it does make appealing use of Mexican ingredients and flavors to create a truly party-worthy appetizer. But too often, the dip relies heavily on canned and processed ingredients and inevitably turns out messy and bland. We wanted to up the ante on this party classic. Rather than canned refried beans, we opted for a fresher layer made with canned black beans mashed with garlic, chili powder, and lime juice. To prevent the sour cream layer from becoming runny, we combined it with a generous amount of pepper Jack cheese. Homemade guacamole far surpassed store-bought. Tasters rejected store-bought salsa as well, so we made a quick, fresh pico de gallo with chopped tomatoes, jalapeños, cilantro, scallions, and lime juice. A layer of sliced scallions added bite and color. Our six layers were so packed with flavor, we decided to eliminate the usual canned black olives, finding their metallic flavor distracting. This recipe is usually served in a clear dish so you can see the layers. For a crowd, double the recipe and serve in a 13 by 9-inch glass baking dish. If you don't have time to make fresh guacamole as called for, simply mash three avocados with 3 tablespoons lime juice and ½ teaspoon salt. Serve with homemade chips (see page 21).

- **4 large tomatoes, cored, seeded, and chopped fine**
- **6 scallions (2 minced; 4, green parts only, sliced thin)**
- **2 jalapeño chiles, stemmed, seeded, and minced**
- **3 tablespoons minced fresh cilantro**
- **2 tablespoons plus 2 teaspoons lime juice (2 limes)**
   Salt
- **1 (15-ounce) can black beans, drained but not rinsed**
- **2 garlic cloves, minced**
- **¾ teaspoon chili powder**
- **1 pound pepper Jack cheese, shredded (4 cups)**
- **1½ cups sour cream**
- **1 recipe (3 cups) Chunky Guacamole (page 22)**

1. Combine tomatoes, minced scallions, jalapeños, cilantro, 2 tablespoons lime juice, and ⅛ teaspoon salt in bowl. Let sit until tomatoes begin to soften, about 30 minutes. Drain mixture, discard liquid, and return to bowl.

2. Meanwhile, pulse beans, garlic, chili powder, remaining 2 teaspoons lime juice, and ⅛ teaspoon salt in food processor to coarse paste, about 15 pulses. Spread bean mixture evenly into 8-inch square baking dish or 1-quart glass bowl.

3. In clean, dry workbowl, pulse 2½ cups pepper Jack and sour cream until smooth, about 15 pulses. Spread sour cream mixture evenly over bean layer. Top evenly with remaining 1½ cups pepper Jack, followed by guacamole and, finally, drained tomato mixture. (Dip can be refrigerated for up to 24 hours; bring to room temperature before serving.) Sprinkle with sliced scallion greens before serving.

Queso Fundido

Serves 6 to 8

✔ **WHY THIS RECIPE WORKS:** Spanish for "melted cheese," *queso fundido* is a hearty table dip of melted Mexican cheese topped with roasted poblano peppers and crispy chorizo sausage. Hot from the oven, this gooey, bubbling dip is perfect served with tortilla chips or warm, soft tortillas. Authentic versions are made with *queso de Oaxaca*, a firm Mexican cheese similar to mozzarella and prized for its melting ability and salty tang. Cubing the cheese worked better than shredding it; it melted more evenly and released less oil. We also noticed that the cheese was best if pulled from the oven as soon as it was melted—if given the chance to overcook, it released more oil, which pooled on top of the cheese. As for the chorizo-poblano topping, we cooked the chorizo in a hot skillet to render the fat, then added thinly sliced poblano and continued to cook until their skins turned spotty brown. Finally, we added some thinly sliced onion to round out the flavors, and drained the mixture to prevent the topping from turning the dish greasy. We spooned the topping over the cubed cheese and, after only 10 minutes in the oven, our queso fundido turned out velvety smooth. If you can't find fresh Mexican-style chorizo, chopped, cured Spanish-style may be substituted. While queso de Oaxaca makes an excellent queso fundido, we found that Monterey Jack is a perfectly acceptable (and more commonly available) substitute. Do not substitute preshredded Monterey Jack cheese; it is coated with anticaking agents that will cause the melted cheese to harden as soon as it is removed from the oven. Take care not to overcook the cheese or it will begin to leach oil.

1 teaspoon vegetable oil

4 ounces Mexican-style chorizo sausage, casings removed

1 poblano chile, stemmed, seeded, and sliced thin

½ small onion, sliced thin

8 ounces queso de Oaxaca, cut into ½-inch pieces

6 (8-inch) corn or flour tortillas, warmed and cut into wedges

1. Adjust oven rack to lower-middle position and heat oven to 375 degrees. Heat oil in 12-inch nonstick skillet over medium-high heat until shimmering. Add chorizo and cook, breaking up meat with wooden spoon, until fat begins to render, about 1 minute. Stir in poblano and onion and cook until chorizo and vegetables are well browned, 5 to 7 minutes. Drain chorizo mixture in colander.

2. Spread queso Oaxaca evenly into 9-inch pie plate, then sprinkle with drained chorizo mixture. Transfer pie plate to oven and bake until cheese is just melted, 8 to 10 minutes. Serve immediately with tortillas.

TEST KITCHEN TIP

REMOVING CASING FROM CHORIZO

To remove casing from Mexican chorizo, hold sausage firmly at 1 end and squeeze meat out of opposite end.

Molletes

Serves 6

✔ **WHY THIS RECIPE WORKS:** In Mexico, *molletes* are a popular snack or appetizer that can be found at many restaurants and coffee shops, as well as many street food stalls. Somewhat akin to Italian bruschetta, molletes are a simple combination of toasted bread, refried beans, melted cheese, and fresh salsa. Individual *bolillo* rolls (similar to small French baguettes) are the most common type of bread used for molletes, but they are hard to find in U.S. supermarkets. A standard loaf of French bread was easier to come by and, for our simple appetizer recipe, one long loaf was easier to handle than several small rolls. We removed some of the interior crumb so that the bread would cradle the beans and cheese, helping the finished molletes hold together. As for the cheese, *Chihuahua*—a good melting cheese that's similar to mild white cheddar—is commonly used in Mexico, but it can be hard to find in American stores. We opted for mild cheddar instead. To build our molletes, we first buttered and toasted the hollowed-out bread, then spread it with refried beans and a generous handful of cheese. Once the cheese was just melted, we topped the loaves with fresh homemade pico de gallo. To make sure the salsa wouldn't make the bread soggy, we eliminated excess moisture by salting the chopped tomatoes and letting them drain for 30 minutes. A minced jalapeño, a squeeze of lime juice, and some fresh cilantro rounded out our pico de gallo. The fresh, raw salsa provided the perfect contrast to the rich, melty cheese and creamy beans. We prefer the thinner, more delicate crust of French or Italian bread here; avoid using rustic loaves with thick crusts. Any type of refried beans will work well here. If you can find Chihuahua cheese, substitute it for the cheddar cheese for a more authentic flavor.

3   **tomatoes, cored and chopped**
    Salt and pepper
½   **cup finely chopped onion**
½   **cup fresh cilantro leaves**
1   **jalapeño chile, stemmed, seeded, and minced**
1   **garlic clove, minced**
2   **tablespoons lime juice**
1   **(16-inch) loaf French or Italian bread**
4   **tablespoons unsalted butter, softened**
1   **cup refried beans**
8   **ounces mild cheddar cheese, shredded (2 cups)**

1. Toss tomatoes with ¼ teaspoon salt in colander and let drain for 30 minutes. As tomatoes drain, layer onion, cilantro, jalapeño, and garlic on top. Shake colander to drain off and discard excess tomato juice. Transfer mixture to bowl, stir in lime juice, and season with salt and pepper to taste.

2. Adjust oven rack to middle position and heat oven to 400 degrees. Line baking sheet with aluminum foil. Slice bread in half horizontally, then remove all but ¼ inch of interior crumb; reserve removed crumb for another use. Spread butter evenly inside hollowed bread and place cut side up on prepared sheet. Bake until lightly toasted and browned, about 8 minutes.

3. Let bread cool slightly, spread refried beans evenly inside toasted bread and top with cheese. Bake until cheese is just melted, 5 to 7 minutes. Transfer bread to cutting board, top with salsa, and slice crosswise into 2-inch pieces. Serve warm.

TEST KITCHEN TIP **HOLLOWING OUT BREAD**

Slice bread in half horizontally. Using your fingers, remove all but ¼ inch of interior crumb. (Reserve excess bread for another use, such as fresh bread crumbs.)

Ultimate Beef Nachos

Serves 4 to 6

☑ **WHY THIS RECIPE WORKS:** Nachos are a crave-worthy pleasure—warm tortilla chips mingling with melted cheese, piquant salsa, luxurious guacamole, and spicy beef. But despite their widespread appearance on restaurant menus, finding a good plate of nachos can be a challenge. Most versions are plagued by tasteless jarred salsa, packaged guacamole, and unnaturally fluid "cheese." We wanted to eliminate the stale prefab ingredients for nachos that would actually be worth eating. First up for repair: the cheese. Four cups of shredded cheese proved to be just the right amount; any less left some chips neglected while more just about drowned them. We tested a wide variety of cheeses, including cheddar, Monterey Jack, pepper Jack, and even gouda and Muenster. In the end, tasters preferred the potent flavor of cheddar. Preshredded cheese turned out dry and dull; we opted to shred our own from a block. Layering the chips with the cheese guaranteed even distribution. Thinly sliced jalapeños, layered in with the cheese, were a welcome spicy addition. As for the beef, we seasoned it with garlic, onion, chili powder, and a host of other spices, and layered it into the chips with the cheese, first sautéing it quickly to ensure that it was cooked through. Salsa livened up our nachos, as did guacamole, and simply dolloping them along the edges made the nachos easy to pick up and eat. A last-minute sprinkle of fresh scallions and a squeeze of lime brightened up our nachos. Homemade Fresh Tomato Salsa and Chunky Guacamole are key to making this recipe above average, but if you are short on time you can use your favorite store-bought varieties.

2   teaspoons vegetable oil
1   small onion, chopped fine
1   tablespoon chili powder
1   garlic clove, minced
1   teaspoon minced fresh oregano
     or ¼ teaspoon dried
½   teaspoon ground cumin
½   teaspoon ground coriander
¼   teaspoon cayenne pepper
⅛   teaspoon salt
8   ounces 90 percent lean ground beef
8   ounces tortilla chips
1   pound cheddar cheese, shredded (4 cups)
2   large jalapeño chiles, stemmed and
     sliced thin
2   scallions, sliced thin
1½   cups Chunky Guacamole (page 22)
1   cup Fresh Tomato Salsa (page 19)
½   cup sour cream
     Lime wedges

1. Adjust oven rack to middle position and heat oven to 400 degrees. Heat oil in 12-inch skillet over medium heat until shimmering. Add onion and cook until softened, about 3 minutes. Stir in chili powder, garlic, oregano, cumin, coriander, cayenne, and salt and cook until fragrant, about 30 seconds. Add ground beef and cook, breaking up meat with wooden spoon, until beef is no longer pink, about 5 minutes.

2. Spread half of tortilla chips evenly into 13 by 9-inch baking dish. Sprinkle 2 cups cheddar evenly over chips, then top evenly with half of beef mixture, followed by half of jalapeño slices. Repeat layering with remaining chips, cheddar, beef mixture, and jalapeños. Bake until cheese is melted and just beginning to brown, 7 to 10 minutes.

3. Let nachos cool for 2 minutes, then sprinkle with scallions. Drop scoops of guacamole, salsa, and sour cream around edges of nachos. Serve immediately, passing lime wedges separately.

Tomatillo and Pinto Bean Nachos

Serves 4 to 6

✓ **WHY THIS RECIPE WORKS:** We wanted a vegetarian option for nachos that delivered big, bold flavor—not just a pile of chips, cheese, and beans. For a hearty topping, we chopped fresh tomatillos and sautéed them with corn (frozen kernels were ideal for year-round convenience). Bold seasonings like garlic, oregano, and coriander provided an aromatic backbone and made the fresh flavor of the tomatillos pop. To avoid soggy chips, we cooked the tomatillo mixture until all the moisture had evaporated and we sprinkled the cheese on the chips first so it would act as a protective layer. While cheddar cheese worked best for our beef nachos (page 30), we found that we liked the flavor of spicy pepper Jack for this version. We also wanted to add a bean component to our vegetarian nachos, but refried beans added too much moisture to the mix. We opted for whole canned pinto beans instead, and sprinkled them between each layer of filling. Fresh jalapeños added another layer of flavor and texture to our nachos; we simply laid thin slices over the beans. Once we had layered in all of our ingredients, it took just 10 minutes in the oven to melt the cheese—any more and the chips became soggy. Once the nachos came out of the oven, we added sliced radishes for fresh, cooling crunch. Homemade Fresh Tomato Salsa and Chunky Guacamole are key to making this recipe above average, but if you are short on time you can use your favorite store-bought varieties.

- 1 tablespoon vegetable oil
- 1 onion, chopped fine
- 3 garlic cloves, minced
- 1 teaspoon ground coriander
- 1 teaspoon salt
- 2 teaspoons minced fresh oregano or ½ teaspoon dried
- 12 ounces tomatillos, husks and stems removed, rinsed well, dried, and cut into ½-inch pieces
- 1 cup frozen corn, thawed
- 8 ounces tortilla chips
- 12 ounces pepper Jack cheese, shredded (3 cups)
- 1 (15-ounce) can pinto beans, rinsed
- 2 jalapeño chiles, stemmed and sliced thin
- 3 radishes, trimmed and sliced thin
- 1½ cups Chunky Guacamole (page 22)
- 1 cup Fresh Tomato Salsa (page 19)
- ½ cup sour cream
    Lime wedges

1. Adjust oven rack to middle position and heat oven to 400 degrees. Heat oil in 12-inch nonstick skillet over medium heat until shimmering. Add onion and cook until softened, about 5 minutes. Stir in garlic, coriander, salt, and oregano and cook until fragrant, about 30 seconds. Add tomatillos and corn, reduce heat to medium-low, and cook until tomatillos have released all their moisture and mixture is nearly dry, about 10 minutes. Let cool slightly.

2. Spread half of tortilla chips evenly into 13 by 9-inch baking dish. Sprinkle 1½ cups pepper Jack evenly over chips, then top evenly with half of tomatillo mixture, followed by half of beans and, finally, half of jalapeños. Repeat layering with remaining chips, pepper Jack, tomatillo mixture, beans, and jalapeños. Bake until cheese is melted and just beginning to brown, 7 to 10 minutes.

3. Let nachos cool for 2 minutes, then sprinkle with radishes. Drop scoops of guacamole, salsa, and sour cream around edges of nachos. Serve immediately, passing lime wedges separately.

Stuffed Jalapeños

Serves 6 to 8

✓ **WHY THIS RECIPE WORKS:** A cousin of traditional Mexican chiles rellenos (stuffed green chiles), these Tex-Mex appetizers are a party favorite. The heat of the jalapeños is perfectly tempered by the cream cheese filling, and a fried coating gives them appealing crunch. But the process of making these two-bite treats at home is labor-intensive, and many recipes turn out unremarkable results. We wanted a recipe for stuffed jalapeños that would eliminate the fuss and play up the flavor. We decided to skip the breading and deep-frying, since this technique was time-consuming and messy. To adjust our stuffed jalapeño recipe to work in the oven, we cut the chiles in half, scooped out the ribs and seeds, and par-cooked them in a hot oven. This slightly softened their flesh and drove off extra moisture. For our filling, we combined cream cheese with mild cheddar, Monterey Jack, bread crumbs, and an egg yolk for a creamy yet stable texture. Bacon, cilantro, scallions, lime juice, and cumin rounded out the flavor of the filling. Once stuffed, the jalapeños needed only about 10 more minutes in the oven to become perfectly browned and tender. See the photo on page 16.

6 slices bacon
12 jalapeño chiles, halved lengthwise with
     stems left intact, seeds and ribs removed
     Salt
4 ounces mild cheddar cheese, shredded
     (1 cup)
4 ounces Monterey Jack cheese, shredded
     (1 cup)
4 ounces cream cheese, softened
2 scallions, sliced thin
3 tablespoons minced fresh cilantro
2 tablespoons panko bread crumbs
1 large egg yolk
2 teaspoons lime juice
1 teaspoon ground cumin

1. Adjust oven rack to upper-middle position and heat oven to 500 degrees. Set wire rack in rimmed baking sheet. Cook bacon in 12-inch nonstick skillet over medium heat until crisp, 7 to 9 minutes. Using slotted spoon, transfer bacon to paper towel–lined plate. When bacon is cool enough to handle, chop fine and set aside.

2. Season jalapeños with salt and place cut side down on prepared rack. Bake until just beginning to soften, about 5 minutes. Remove jalapeños from oven and reduce oven temperature to 450 degrees. When cool enough to handle, flip jalapeños cut side up.

3. Mix cheddar, Monterey Jack, cream cheese, scallions, cilantro, panko, egg yolk, lime juice, cumin, and bacon together in bowl until thoroughly combined. Divide cheese mixture among jalapeños, pressing into cavities. (Filled jalapeños can be covered and refrigerated for up to 24 hours.)

4. Bake jalapeños until tender and filling is lightly browned, 9 to 14 minutes. Let cool for 5 minutes. Serve.

TEST KITCHEN TIP **SEEDING JALAPEÑOS**

To remove ribs and seeds from jalapeño, cut pepper in half lengthwise, then use teaspoon to scoop down inside of each half.

Bean and Beef Taquitos

Serves 4 to 6

✔ **WHY THIS RECIPE WORKS:** *Taquito* literally means "little taco," but these filled and fried tortillas have outsize appeal. We set out to streamline the work-intensive process. First, we replaced long-braised chuck with spiced ground beef. To prevent the filling from falling out of the open ends of the taquitos, we thickened it with mashed pinto beans. Microwaving the tortillas made them pliable enough to roll. A quick egg wash helped to seal the taquitos, and switching from deep-frying to shallow frying allowed us to start cooking the taquitos seam-side-down, guaranteeing that the rolls held together. For more information on how to roll taquitos, see steps 2 and 3 on page 135. Serve with Avocado Sauce (page 135).

1	cup plus 4 teaspoons vegetable oil
8	ounces 90 percent lean ground beef
1	cup canned pinto beans, rinsed
1	onion, halved and sliced thin
2	jalapeño chiles, stemmed, seeded, and minced
3	garlic cloves, minced
1	teaspoon ground cumin
1	teaspoon chili powder
1	(8-ounce) can tomato sauce
½	cup water
3	tablespoons minced fresh cilantro
	Salt and pepper
12	(6-inch) corn tortillas
1	large egg, lightly beaten

1. Heat 1 teaspoon oil in 12-inch nonstick skillet over medium-high heat until just smoking. Add ground beef and cook, breaking up meat with wooden spoon, until no longer pink, about 5 minutes. Drain beef in colander. In separate bowl, mash beans to paste with potato masher.

2. Heat 1 tablespoon oil in now-empty skillet over medium heat until shimmering. Add onion and cook until softened and lightly browned, 5 to 7 minutes. Stir in jalapeños, garlic, cumin, and chili powder and cook until fragrant, about 30 seconds. Stir in tomato sauce, water, cilantro, ½ teaspoon salt, ½ teaspoon pepper, drained beef, and mashed beans. Cook, stirring often, until mixture has thickened and begins to sizzle, about 10 minutes. Season with salt and pepper to taste, transfer to bowl, and let cool for 20 minutes.

3. Adjust oven rack to middle position and heat oven to 200 degrees. Line rimmed baking sheet with parchment paper. Set wire rack in second rimmed baking sheet. Stack 6 tortillas, wrap in damp dish towel, and place on plate; microwave until warm and pliable, about 1 minute.

4. Working with 1 tortilla at a time, brush edges of top half with beaten egg. Spread 3 tablespoons filling in tight row across lower half of tortilla, fold bottom of tortilla over filling, then pull back on tortilla to tighten around filling. Roll tightly, place seam side down on parchment-lined sheet, and cover with second damp towel. Microwave remaining 6 tortillas and repeat with remaining filling. (Taquitos can be covered with damp towel, wrapped tightly in plastic wrap, and refrigerated for up to 24 hours.)

5. Add remaining 1 cup oil to clean, dry 12-inch nonstick skillet and heat over medium-high heat to 350 degrees. Using tongs, place 6 taquitos, seam side down, in oil. Fry taquitos until golden on all sides, about 8 minutes, turning as needed and adjusting heat as needed to maintain oil temperature between 300 and 325 degrees. Transfer to prepared wire rack and place in oven to keep warm while repeating with remaining 6 taquitos. Serve.

Empanadas

Makes 24 empanadas

✓ **WHY THIS RECIPE WORKS:** Prevalent throughout Mexico, empanadas are filled pastries similar to turnovers. Since the dough is an essential element, we turned our attention to it first. Although the traditional method of making dough calls for mixing melted lard or vegetable shortening with flour, we found that this approach created dough that was greasy and tough. Instead, we employed a method more often used for pie dough: Cut cold butter into flour, then mix gently with ice water until a dough forms. This produced a tender, flaky dough. Next we turned to the fillings. Empanadas can be made with a wide variety of fillings, depending on the region and on personal tastes. We decided to develop two simple fillings: a basic beef and cheese filling and a poblano chile and corn filling. For our beef filling, 85 percent lean ground chuck was ideal for its beefy flavor. We bloomed our seasonings—onion, tomato paste, garlic, oregano, cumin, cloves, and cayenne—in a bit of oil, which brought out their flavors. As for the cheese, Monterey Jack worked well for its meltability and mild tang. For our second flavorful empanada filling, we liked the mildly spicy, vegetal flavor of poblano chiles combined with sweet corn (frozen kernels tasted great and kept the process simple). Some aromatic spices, scallions, and two kinds of cheese rounded out the flavor of the filling. There should be plenty of dough to cut out and make 24 empanadas without having to reroll any dough scraps; we found the rerolled scraps of dough to be very tough.

3¾ cups (18¾ ounces) all-purpose flour
1 tablespoon sugar
1½ teaspoons salt
12 tablespoons unsalted butter, cut into ½-inch
    pieces and chilled
1¼ cups ice water
1 recipe filling (page 38), chilled
2 tablespoons extra-virgin olive oil

1. Process flour, sugar, and salt together in food processor until combined, about 3 seconds. Scatter butter pieces over flour mixture and pulse until mixture resembles coarse cornmeal, about 16 pulses. Transfer mixture to large bowl. Working with ¼ cup ice water at a time, sprinkle water over flour mixture and, using stiff rubber spatula, stir and press dough together until dough sticks together and no small bits of flour remain (you may not need to use all of water).

2. Turn dough onto clean, dry counter and gently press into cohesive ball. Divide dough into 2 even pieces. Turn each piece of dough onto sheet of plastic wrap, flatten into 6-inch disks, wrap tightly, and refrigerate for 1 hour. Let chilled dough sit on counter to soften slightly, about 10 minutes, before rolling.

3. Adjust oven racks to upper-middle and lower-middle positions and heat oven to 425 degrees. Line 2 baking sheets with parchment paper. Roll 1 dough disk into 18-inch circle, about ⅛ inch thick, on lightly floured counter. Using 4-inch round biscuit cutter, cut out 12 rounds, discarding dough scraps. Place 1 tablespoon filling in center of each dough round. Brush edges of dough with water and fold dough over filling. Press to seal, and crimp edges with tines of fork. Transfer to 1 prepared sheet, cover, and refrigerate. Repeat with remaining dough disk and remaining filling. (Filled empanadas can be wrapped tightly in plastic wrap and refrigerated for up to 24 hours or frozen for up to 1 month. After empanadas are completely frozen, about 8 hours, they can be transferred to zipper-lock freezer bags to save space in freezer. Transfer back to parchment paper-lined sheet before baking. Increase baking time by about 5 minutes.)

4. Brush tops of empanadas with oil and bake until golden brown, 20 to 30 minutes, switching and rotating sheets halfway through baking. Let cool for 5 minutes before serving.

EMPANADA FILLINGS

Both of our empanada fillings are ultraflavorful, yet simple to put together. Be sure to make the filling well in advance of when you plan to serve the empanadas; it is important that the filling is thoroughly chilled when you use it. Each filling makes enough for 24 empanadas.

Beef and Cheese Filling

1	tablespoon extra-virgin olive oil
1	onion, chopped fine
3	garlic cloves, minced
1	tablespoon tomato paste
1	teaspoon minced fresh oregano or ¼ teaspoon dried
1	teaspoon ground cumin
⅛	teaspoon ground cloves
⅛	teaspoon cayenne pepper
12	ounces 85 percent lean ground beef
½	cup beef broth
	Salt and pepper
4	ounces Monterey Jack cheese, shredded (1 cup)
2	tablespoons minced fresh cilantro

Heat oil in 12-inch skillet over medium heat until just shimmering. Add onion and cook until softened, about 5 minutes. Stir in garlic, tomato paste, oregano, cumin, clove, and cayenne and cook until fragrant, about 1 minute. Add ground beef and cook, breaking up meat with wooden spoon, until beef is no longer pink, about 5 minutes. Stir in broth, bring to simmer, and cook until mixture is moist but not wet, about 8 minutes. Season with salt and pepper to taste. Transfer mixture to bowl, let cool slightly, then cover and refrigerate until completely cool, about 1 hour. Stir in Monterey Jack and cilantro. (Filling can be refrigerated for up to 2 days.)

Poblano and Corn Filling

2	tablespoons unsalted butter
12	ounces (2 to 3) poblano chiles, stemmed, seeded, and chopped fine
3	scallions, white parts minced, green parts sliced thin
2	garlic cloves, minced
1	teaspoon minced fresh oregano or ¼ teaspoon dried
1	teaspoon ground cumin
1	teaspoon ground coriander
	Salt and pepper
¾	cup frozen corn, thawed
4	ounces pepper Jack cheese, shredded (1 cup)
4	ounces queso fresco, crumbled (1 cup)

Melt butter in 12-inch skillet over medium heat. Add poblanos and scallion whites and cook until softened and lightly browned, about 8 minutes. Stir in garlic, oregano, cumin, coriander, and ¼ teaspoon salt and cook until fragrant, about 30 seconds. Stir in corn and season with salt and pepper to taste. Transfer mixture to bowl, let cool slightly, then cover and refrigerate until completely cool, about 1 hour. Stir in pepper Jack, queso fresco, and scallion greens. (Filling can be refrigerated for up to 2 days.)

LEARN HOW **EMPANADAS**

Empanadas make a great appetizer, but only if the flavorful filling stays securely inside the dough and doesn't burst out during cooking. Getting a perfect seal can be tricky, but our multi-pronged approach guarantees that the filling stays where it belongs—inside the flaky pastry pockets.

1. CUT OUT DOUGH ROUNDS:
After rolling out the dough, use a 4-inch biscuit cutter to make 12 rounds. Cut the rounds as close together as possible to get the correct number of rounds without needing to reroll the scraps. Rerolled dough turns tough when baked.

2. SPOON FILLING ONTO DOUGH:
Place about 1 tablespoon of the chilled filling on each dough round. It is important not to overstuff the empanadas or they will not seal properly.

3. BRUSH EDGES WITH WATER:
Using either your finger or a pastry brush, moisten the edge of each dough round with water. This encourages a tight seal on the empanadas so the filling won't ooze out.

4. SEAL EMPANADAS: Fold the dough round in half over the filling to make a half-moon shape. Pinch the seams closed. This gives the empanadas their trademark shape.

5. CRIMP EDGES: Using a fork, crimp the edge of each empanada. The crimped edges not only look decorative but also completely seal the empanadas.

6. BRUSH WITH OIL AND BAKE:
Brush the empanadas with oil and bake until the crusts turn golden brown. To ensure the empanadas cook evenly, be sure to switch and rotate the baking sheets halfway through baking.

Mexican-Style Shrimp Cocktail

Serves 6

☑ **WHY THIS RECIPE WORKS:** Mexican *coctel de camarones* bears little resemblance to American shrimp cocktail. Rather, this cool, elegant appetizer marries tender shrimp with chunks of fresh tomato, cucumber, avocado, and onion, all in a gently spicy, tomato-based sauce. To start, we used a tried-and-true test kitchen poaching method to ensure that our shrimp were both flavorful and perfectly cooked: We simmered them in seasoned water for about 10 minutes, then took the pot off the stovetop and covered it so the shrimp could gently finish cooking without risk of drying out. Since the vegetables are eaten raw, we only needed to determine the best way to cut them. We liked the textural contrast of ½-inch chunks of cucumber, tomato, and avocado; the onion we chopped fine. As for the thin sauce, we stuck with tradition and combined Clamato juice, which provided robust seafood notes, and ketchup, which gave the sauce a sweet-savory flavor and allowed it to nicely coat the shrimp and vegetables. Just a splash of lime juice and hot sauce rounded out our boldly flavored, full-bodied base. Look for Clamato juice next to the tomato juice in the grocery store. If you can't find Clamato juice, substitute a combination of 1½ cups V8 juice, ½ cup water, and 1 teaspoon sugar. Serve in individual goblets or glasses with homemade chips (see page 21).

1½	pounds medium shrimp (41 to 50 per pound), peeled, deveined, and tails removed
¼	cup chopped fresh cilantro, stems reserved
1	teaspoon black peppercorns
1	tablespoon sugar
	Salt and pepper
3	tomatoes, cored and cut into ½-inch pieces
1	cucumber, peeled, halved lengthwise, seeded, and cut into ½-inch pieces
1	small red onion, chopped fine
2	cups Clamato juice
½	cup ketchup
2	tablespoons lime juice, plus lime wedges for serving
1	tablespoon hot sauce
1	avocado, halved, pitted, and cut into ½-inch pieces

1. Combine shrimp, 3 cups water, cilantro stems, peppercorns, sugar, and 1 teaspoon salt in large saucepan. Place saucepan over medium heat and cook, stirring occasionally, until shrimp are pink and firm to touch, 8 to 10 minutes (water should be just bubbling around edge of saucepan and register 165 degrees). Remove saucepan from heat, cover, and let shrimp sit in cooking liquid for 2 minutes.

2. Meanwhile, fill large bowl with ice water. Drain shrimp into colander, discarding cilantro stems and spices. Immediately transfer shrimp to ice water to stop cooking and chill thoroughly, about 3 minutes. Remove shrimp from ice water and thoroughly pat dry with paper towels.

3. Mix tomatoes, cucumber, onion, Clamato juice, ketchup, lime juice, and hot sauce together in serving bowl. Stir in shrimp, cover, and refrigerate for at least 30 minutes. (Shrimp cocktail can be refrigerated for up to 24 hours; let sit at room temperature for 10 minutes before serving.) Stir in avocado and chopped cilantro and season with salt and pepper to taste. Serve.

TEST KITCHEN TIP SEEDING CUCUMBERS

Peel and halve cucumber lengthwise. Run small spoon inside each cucumber half to scoop out seeds and surrounding liquid.

Shrimp and Lime Ceviche

Serves 6

✔ **WHY THIS RECIPE WORKS:** Served as an appetizer with crunchy tortilla chips or used as a topping for tostadas, this simple seafood dish is refreshing and summery. Rather than using heat to cook the seafood, traditional ceviche relies on acidic juices, such as lime or lemon juice, to do the "cooking." Although there are many variations throughout Latin America, Mexican ceviche is often made with shrimp. We tested several combinations of acidic liquids, even white wine vinegar and cider vinegar, and settled on equal parts lime and lemon juice for the most well-rounded, balanced flavor. To bring the more-traditional lime flavor to the fore, we also added a bit of lime zest. We sliced each shrimp in half lengthwise, which helped all of the pieces to cook evenly and gave our ceviche a pleasant chunky texture. We rounded out the fresh flavor of the shrimp with a few seasoning ingredients: jalapeño, garlic, scallions, cilantro, and a pinch of sugar. We also liked the addition of tomato, which provided a welcome color and texture contrast to the shrimp. A bit of extra-virgin olive oil stirred in before serving helped to meld the flavors and add some depth. Be sure to pat the shrimp dry with paper towels so that any moisture does not water down the marinade. Serve with homemade chips (see page 21).

- 1   tomato, cored, seeded, and chopped fine
- ½   cup lemon juice (3 lemons)
- 1   jalapeño chile, stemmed, seeded, and minced
- 1   teaspoon grated lime zest plus ½ cup juice (4 limes)
- 1   garlic clove, minced
-     Salt and pepper

- 1   pound extra-large shrimp (21 to 25 per pound), peeled, deveined, tails removed, and halved lengthwise
- ¼   cup extra-virgin olive oil
- 4   scallions, sliced thin
- 3   tablespoons minced fresh cilantro
- ½   teaspoon sugar

1. Combine tomato, lemon juice, jalapeño, lime zest and juice, garlic, and ½ teaspoon salt in medium bowl. Stir in shrimp, cover, and refrigerate until shrimp are firm and opaque throughout, 45 minutes to 1 hour, stirring halfway through refrigerating.

2. Drain shrimp mixture in colander, leaving shrimp slightly wet, and transfer to serving bowl. Stir in oil, scallions, cilantro, and sugar. Season with salt and pepper to taste. Serve.

TEST KITCHEN TIP DEVEINING SHRIMP

1. Use paring knife to make shallow cut along back of shrimp to expose vein.

2. Use tip of knife to lift out vein. Discard vein by wiping blade on paper towel.

Fresh Margaritas

Makes about 4 cups; serves 4 to 6

✓ **WHY THIS RECIPE WORKS:** Too often, restaurant margaritas are cloyingly sweet or artifical-tasting. We wanted to develop the ideal version of this refreshing cocktail, with the perfect balance of sweet, sour, and tart flavors. Tests revealed that *reposado* or "rested" tequila, which is made from 100 percent blue agave and aged for 12 months or less, had a mellow flavor that blended perfectly with the other ingredients. Steeping lemon and lime zest in equal parts lemon and lime juice created a base with deep, citrus flavor. A little sugar mitigated any bitterness. Equal proportions of tequila, triple sec, and juice made for a well-balanced cocktail.

Classic Margaritas

We recommend steeping for the full 24 hours, if possible. If you need to serve margaritas immediately, omit the zest and skip the steeping process altogether.

4	teaspoons finely grated lime zest plus ½ cup juice (4 limes)
4	teaspoons finely grated lemon zest plus ½ cup juice (3 lemons)
¼	cup superfine sugar
	Pinch salt
2	cups crushed ice
1	cup 100 percent agave tequila, preferably reposado
1	cup triple sec

1. Combine lime zest and juice, lemon zest and juice, sugar, and salt in 2-cup liquid measuring cup; cover and refrigerate until flavors meld, at least 4 hours or up to 24 hours.

2. Divide 1 cup crushed ice among 4 to 6 margarita or double old-fashioned glasses. Strain juice mixture into 1-quart pitcher or cocktail shaker; discard solids. Add tequila, triple sec, and remaining 1 cup crushed ice; stir or shake until thoroughly combined and chilled, 20 to 60 seconds. Strain into ice-filled glasses and serve immediately.

Strawberry Margaritas

The strawberry flavor in this variation makes the zest and steeping process unnecessary.

5	ounces strawberries, hulled (1 cup)
½	cup lime juice (4 limes)
½	cup lemon juice (3 lemons)
¼	cup superfine sugar
	Pinch salt
2	cups crushed ice
1	cup 100 percent agave tequila, preferably reposado
1	cup triple sec
½	cup Chambord

1. Process strawberries, lime juice, lemon juice, sugar, and salt in blender until smooth, about 30 seconds.

2. Divide 1 cup crushed ice among 4 to 6 margarita or double old-fashioned glasses. Strain juice mixture into 1-quart pitcher or cocktail shaker; discard solids. Add tequila, triple sec, Chambord, and remaining 1 cup crushed ice; stir or shake until thoroughly combined and chilled, 20 to 60 seconds. Strain into ice-filled glasses and serve immediately.

TEST KITCHEN TIP ZESTING CITRUS

Rub fruit against holes of rasp-style grater, grating over same area of fruit only once or twice to avoid grating bitter white pith beneath skin.

Aguas Frescas
Each makes about 8 cups; serves 8 to 10

✔ WHY THIS RECIPE WORKS: *Agua fresca* is the catchall term for a wide variety of popular nonalcoholic beverages that are made by combining fruits, grains, seeds, or flowers with sugar and water. Literally meaning "fresh water," these beverages are served from large barrel-style glass jars, and make for a very colorful and appealing display. One of the most popular aguas frescas is the garnet-colored *agua de Jamaica* (ha-MIKE-ah), or hibiscus tea. Deep purple dried hibiscus flowers are steeped in water, producing a tart, cranberry-like flavor. Sugar is added to balance the tartness, and the refreshing tea is served very cold, over ice. We tested soaking the flowers overnight before boiling and cooling the mixture, but found that the flavor was only slightly more potent than stirring the flowers directly into boiled water and letting them steep for just 1 hour. (The soaked flowers also made a good snack; their sweet flavor and chewy texture were similar to dried fruit.) Once we had strained the mixture, we found that a cup of white sugar perfectly balanced the tartness of the liquid—any more, and it became sickly sweet. Tasters also liked the hibiscus tea very cold, so we made sure to refrigerate it for at least 2 hours. For a second refreshing agua fresca, we turned to a slightly different, though equally common, method: processing fruit and water in a blender and then straining out the pulp. We chose watermelon as our base, and accented it with fresh lime juice for a lightly sweet and tangy beverage. Just a little bit of agave syrup and a pinch of salt brought out the sweet and tart flavors in the drink.

Hibiscus Agua Fresca
You can find hibiscus flowers in some grocery stores and specialty markets. The soaked flowers can be saved and eaten; they have a texture similar to dried fruit. Keep the flowers refrigerated in an airtight container.

8   cups water
2   cups dried hibiscus flowers, rinsed
1   cup sugar
    Pinch salt

Bring 4 cups water to boil in medium saucepan. Off heat, stir in hibiscus flowers, cover, and let steep for 1 hour. Strain mixture into 2-quart pitcher; discard solids. Stir in sugar and salt until dissolved, then stir in remaining 4 cups water. Refrigerate until completely chilled, about 2 hours. Serve over ice. (Agua Fresca can be refrigerated for up to 5 days; stir to recombine before serving.)

Watermelon-Lime Agua Fresca
If you can't find seedless watermelon, remove as many seeds as possible before processing.

8   cups seedless watermelon, cut into
     1-inch pieces
2   cups water
⅓   cup lime juice (3 limes), plus extra
     as needed
2   tablespoons agave nectar or honey,
     as needed
⅛   teaspoon salt
     Mint leaves (optional)

Working in 2 batches, process watermelon and water in blender until smooth, about 30 seconds. Strain mixture through fine-mesh strainer into 2-quart pitcher; discard solids. Stir in lime juice, agave, and salt into watermelon mixture. Stir in extra lime juice and agave to taste. Serve over ice with mint, if using. (Agua Fresca can be refrigerated for up to 5 days; stir to recombine before serving.)

CHICKEN POSOLE VERDE

Soups, Stews, and Chilis

Chilled Tomato Soup

Serves 4

✔ **WHY THIS RECIPE WORKS:** In Mexico, soup is an integral part of *la comida*—the main meal of the day, generally eaten in the late afternoon. In fact, many feel that the meal isn't complete without a hot soup course. However, during the warmest months of the year, chilled soups provide a reprieve from the oppressive heat. A chilled tomato soup is a refreshing addition to a Mexican dinner, but only if it shines with bright tomato flavor. The key to deep, concentrated tomato flavor turned out to be salting: We tossed the chopped tomatoes with salt and let them drain for an hour. A slice of bread provided body and "creaminess" without the flavor-dulling effect of heavy cream, and for even more robust tomato flavor, we soaked the bread in the liquid released by the tomatoes. Processing the soup in a blender and then straining it through a fine-mesh strainer produced an emulsified, smooth texture. Fresh cilantro provided herbal notes while rich, tangy *crema* complemented the brightly-flavored soup. Be sure to use juicy, ripe tomatoes in this recipe. For the best flavor, allow the soup to sit in the refrigerator overnight before serving.

1. Toss tomatoes with ½ teaspoon salt and let drain in fine-mesh strainer, set over bowl to reserve drained liquid, for 1 hour. Toss drained tomatoes with shallot, garlic, and sugar in separate bowl. Add bread to drained tomato liquid, let soak for 1 minute, then stir into tomatoes.

2. Transfer half of mixture to blender and process for 30 seconds. With blender running, slowly drizzle in 3 tablespoons oil until completely smooth, about 2 minutes. Strain through fine-mesh strainer into large bowl, using rubber spatula to help pass soup through strainer. Repeat with remaining mixture and remaining 2 tablespoons olive oil; strain into bowl.

3. Stir in vinegar and season with salt and pepper to taste. Cover and refrigerate until chilled and flavors meld, at least 2 hours or up to 2 days.

4. Before serving, season soup with salt, pepper, extra sugar, and extra vinegar to taste. Stir in 2 tablespoons cilantro. Garnish individual portions with remaining 1 tablespoon cilantro and drizzle with crema.

3½	pounds tomatoes, cored and chopped coarse
	Salt and pepper
1	shallot, peeled and halved
1	garlic clove, quartered
1	teaspoon sugar, plus extra for seasoning
1	slice hearty white sandwich bread, crust removed, torn into 1-inch pieces
5	tablespoons extra-virgin olive oil
1	teaspoon sherry vinegar, plus extra for seasoning
3	tablespoons minced fresh cilantro
½	cup Mexican crema

TEST KITCHEN TIP
CORING AND CHOPPING TOMATOES

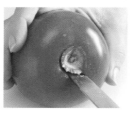

1. Remove core of tomato using paring knife.

2. Slice tomato crosswise. Stack several slices of tomato, then slice both crosswise and widthwise into pieces as desired.

Spicy Butternut Squash Soup with Chipotle

Serves 4 to 6

✅ **WHY THIS RECIPE WORKS:** Squash is a perennial favorite in Mexican cooking, so for a soup with intense squash flavor, we sautéed shallots and butter with the squash seeds and fibers, simmered the mixture in water, and then used the liquid to steam the unpeeled squash. We scooped the squash flesh from the skin once cooled, then pureed it with the reserved steaming liquid for a perfectly smooth texture and big squash flavor.

4   **tablespoons unsalted butter**
1   **large shallot, chopped fine**
1   **(3-pound) butternut squash, halved lengthwise and widthwise, seeds and fibers removed and reserved**
6   **cups water, plus extra as needed**
     Salt and pepper
½   **cup heavy cream**
1   **tablespoon honey**
2   **teaspoons minced canned chipotle chile in adobo sauce**
½   **teaspoon ground cumin**
2   **tablespoons minced fresh cilantro**
¼   **cup pepitas, toasted**

1. Melt 2 tablespoons butter in Dutch oven over medium heat. Add shallot and cook until softened, 2 to 3 minutes. Add squash seeds and fibers and cook, stirring occasionally, until butter turns orange, about 4 minutes.

2. Stir in water and 1 teaspoon salt and bring to boil. Reduce to simmer, place squash cut side down in steamer basket, and lower basket into pot. Cover and steam squash until it is completely tender, 30 to 40 minutes.

3. Using tongs, transfer cooked squash to rimmed baking sheet. When cool enough to handle, use large spoon to scrape cooked squash from skin; discard skin. Strain steaming broth through fine-mesh strainer into 4-cup liquid measuring cup. You should have at least 3 cups of broth; if short, add water.

4. Working in batches, puree cooked squash with 3 cups broth until smooth, 1 to 2 minutes. Return puree to clean pot. Stir in heavy cream, honey, chipotle, cumin, and remaining 2 tablespoons butter. Return to brief simmer, adding additional broth (or water) as needed to adjust soup's consistency. Stir in cilantro and season with salt and pepper to taste. Garnish individual bowls with pepitas before serving.

TEST KITCHEN TIP CUTTING UP A BUTTERNUT SQUASH

1. Drive chef's knife into center of squash; press down through end of squash. Repeat on opposite side.

2. Halve each piece squash widthwise, separating narrow top end from wider, seed-filled bottom end.

3. Scrape out seeds and fibers using spoon, and reserve.

Chicken and Chickpea Soup

Serves 6 to 8

✔ **WHY THIS RECIPE WORKS:** *Caldo tlalpeño* is a smoky, spicy soup laden with tender pieces of shredded chicken, meaty chickpeas, and savory bites of avocado in a broth rich with the smoky flavor and spice of chipotle chiles. While many traditional recipes called for soaking dried chipotle chiles, we were happily surprised to see that just as many used the canned alternative. This fast, convenient option packed a deep, smoky punch, so we turned our attention to replacing a tough-to-find Mexican herb called epazote. Tests showed that a mix of cilantro and oregano provided a good approximation. Although the herbs are traditionally steeped in the broth while cooking, we found that mincing and stirring them in just before serving provided a burst of freshness that the finished soup needed. We built our soup base by first browning bone-in, skin-on chicken breasts (a traditional cut for this soup), developing flavorful fond in the pan. After removing the browned breasts, we softened our aromatic ingredients in the rendered chicken fat before stirring in a bit of flour, which produced a rich, deeply flavored broth with great substance. Although nontraditional, zucchini, added along with the chickpeas, provided a fresh counterpoint to the rich soup. We shredded the chicken and added it back to the soup just a few minutes before serving to ensure that the delicate meat wouldn't overcook and turn tough. Serve with lime wedges, diced avocado, and/or sliced radishes.

1½   **pounds bone-in split chicken breasts, trimmed**
    Salt and pepper
1   **tablespoon vegetable oil**
2   **onions, chopped fine**
2   **carrots, peeled and sliced ½ inch thick**

5   **garlic cloves, minced**
2   **teaspoons minced canned chipotle chile in adobo sauce**
1½   **teaspoons minced fresh thyme or ½ teaspoon dried**
2   **tablespoons all-purpose flour**
8   **cups chicken broth**
2   **zucchini, cut into ½-inch pieces**
1   **(15-ounce) can chickpeas, rinsed**
3   **tablespoons minced fresh cilantro**
1   **teaspoon minced fresh oregano**

1. Pat chicken dry with paper towels and season with salt and pepper. Heat oil in Dutch oven over medium-high heat until just smoking. Brown chicken lightly, 2 to 3 minutes per side; transfer to plate.

2. Add onions and carrots to fat left in pot and cook over medium heat until softened and lightly browned, 8 to 10 minutes. Stir in garlic, chipotle, and thyme and cook until fragrant, about 30 seconds. Stir in flour and cook for 1 minute. Slowly whisk in broth, scraping up any browned bits, and bring to simmer.

3. Return browned chicken and any accumulated juices to pot, reduce heat to low, cover, and simmer gently until chicken registers 160 degrees, 15 to 20 minutes.

4. Transfer chicken to cutting board and let cool slightly. Using 2 forks, shred chicken into bite-size pieces; discard skin and bones. Meanwhile, stir zucchini and chickpeas into soup and simmer until zucchini is just tender, 5 to 10 minutes.

5. Stir shredded chicken into soup and simmer until heated through, about 2 minutes. Off heat, stir in cilantro and oregano and season with salt and pepper to taste. Serve.

Chicken Tortilla Soup

Serves 6 to 8

✓ **WHY THIS RECIPE WORKS:** We wanted a recipe for this popular soup (known in Mexico as *sopa Azteca*) with authentic flavor and a streamlined method. Typically, the vegetables are charred on a *comal* (griddle), then pureed and fried. To simplify, we made a puree from smoky chipotles, tomatoes, onion, garlic, and jalapeño, then fried the puree in oil. We poached chicken in store-bought broth infused with onion, garlic, cilantro, and oregano, which gave our base plenty of flavor without a from-scratch stock. We oven-toasted tortilla strips instead of frying them. For mild spiciness, trim the ribs and seeds from the jalapeño (or omit it altogether) and use 1 teaspoon chipotle chile pureed with the tomatoes in step 3. For a spicier soup, add up to 1 tablespoon adobo sauce in step 4 before you add the chicken. See Learn How on page 56.

SOUP

8	**(6-inch) corn tortillas, cut into ½-inch-wide strips**
2	**tablespoons vegetable oil**
	Salt
8	**cups chicken broth**
1	**large white onion, quartered**
4	**garlic cloves, peeled**
8	**sprigs fresh cilantro**
1	**sprig fresh oregano**
1½	**pounds bone-in split chicken breasts, trimmed**
2	**tomatoes, cored and quartered**
½	**jalapeño chile**
1	**tablespoon minced canned chipotle chile in adobo sauce**

GARNISHES

1	**ripe avocado, halved, pitted, and cut into ½-inch pieces**
8	**ounces Cotija cheese, crumbled (2 cups)**

Lime wedges
Fresh cilantro
Minced jalapeño chile
Mexican crema

1. Adjust oven rack to middle position and heat oven to 425 degrees. Toss tortilla strips with 1 tablespoon oil, spread onto rimmed baking sheet, and bake, stirring occasionally, until deep golden brown and crisp, about 14 minutes. Season lightly with salt and transfer to paper towel–lined plate.

2. Meanwhile, bring broth, 2 onion quarters, 2 garlic cloves, cilantro sprigs, oregano sprig, and ½ teaspoon salt to simmer in Dutch oven over medium-high heat. Add chicken, reduce heat to low, cover, and simmer gently until chicken registers 160 degrees, 15 to 20 minutes. Transfer chicken to cutting board and let cool slightly. Using 2 forks, shred chicken into bite-size pieces; discard skin and bones. Strain broth through fine-mesh strainer; discard solids.

3. Process tomatoes, jalapeño, chipotle, remaining 2 onion quarters, and remaining 2 garlic cloves in food processor until smooth, about 30 seconds, scraping down sides of bowl as needed. Heat remaining 1 tablespoon oil in now-empty pot over medium-high heat until shimmering. Add tomato-onion mixture and ⅛ teaspoon salt and cook, stirring frequently, until mixture has darkened in color and liquid has evaporated, about 10 minutes.

4. Stir in strained broth, scraping up any browned bits, and bring to simmer. Cook until flavors meld, about 15 minutes. Stir in shredded chicken and simmer until heated through, about 2 minutes. Off heat, season with salt and pepper to taste. Place some tortilla strips in bottom of individual bowls and ladle soup over top. Serve, passing garnishes separately.

LEARN HOW **CHICKEN TORTILLA SOUP**

Traditional Mexican tortilla soup is a full-flavored, satisfying meal in a bowl, but traditional versions call for homemade chicken stock, a charred-vegetable base, and fried tortilla strips. We streamlined the recipe for a faster but equally flavorful version.

1. BAKE TORTILLA STRIPS: Toss the tortilla strips with vegetable oil, then spread the strips on a rimmed baking sheet and bake until the strips are crisp and golden. Baking (rather than frying) is faster, and it produces tortilla strips that turn out less greasy and just as crispy.

2. POACH CHICKEN: Bring the broth, onion, garlic, herbs, and salt to a simmer. Add the chicken; simmer until the chicken is fully cooked. Convenient store-bought broth is enhanced by the aromatic ingredients and bone-in chicken.

3. STRAIN BROTH: Set the chicken aside to cool and then shred. Strain the broth through a fine-mesh strainer into a bowl or a large measuring cup. Discard the spent solids and set the broth aside.

4. MAKE SOUP BASE: Process the tomatoes, jalapeño, chipotle, onion, and garlic in a food processor until smooth, then sauté the puree until it is fragrant and darkened. Sautéing the puree concentrates flavor, while chipotle chile adds smokiness.

5. ADD BROTH, THEN CHICKEN: Stir the strained broth into the sautéed puree and cook to blend the flavors. Add the shredded chicken. Adding the chicken back to the soup at this point ensures that it doesn't overcook.

6. LAYER INGREDIENTS IN BOWL: Place the tortilla strips in individual serving bowls and ladle the soup over the top. Garnish with minced jalapeños, Cotija, Mexican *crema*, cilantro, avocado, and lime wedges. Each garnish brings another layer of flavor; we like to offer a wide variety.

Mexican Beef and Vegetable Soup

Serves 6 to 8

✓ **WHY THIS RECIPE WORKS:** Mexico's version of beef and vegetable soup, *caldo de res*, is rich with spices, tender chunks of meat, and vegetables like tomatoes, corn, and squash. Our goal was to develop the authentic flavors of this soup while eliminating the long cooking time required by traditional recipes. To streamline the process we eliminated bone-in cuts and focused on quicker-cooking boneless cuts. In the end, a beef chuck-eye roast proved to be our cut of choice—it was flavorful, tender, and juicy. We browned the meat and then set it aside while we sautéed garlic and onion. We found that sautéing some oregano and cumin along with our aromatics helped to bring out their flavors. We then added the broth (a combination of beef broth and chicken broth was best), returned the beef to the pot, and simmered everything until the meat was tender. Next, we considered which vegetables to add. Most authentic recipes called for chayote, a gourd-like fruit similar to a summer squash that is often used in Mexican cooking. Unfortunately, it is difficult to find in many parts of the United States, and we found its mild flavor disappointing. Zucchini lent a similar texture and had much more flavor. Tomatoes and corn are another mainstay in most caldo de res recipes. We found that canned diced tomatoes provided a more reliable flavor than fresh, but fresh corn on the cob was preferred over frozen kernels. We also included carrots and red potatoes, which contributed an earthiness that tasters felt enriched the overall flavor of the soup. To maintain the rustic feel of the soup, we cut the zucchini, corn, and potatoes into large pieces. With a host of complex flavors and contrasting textures, our soup was now much less work than the original, but still just as hearty and delicious. Serve with lime wedges and/or sliced radishes.

1   **pound boneless beef chuck-eye roast, trimmed and cut into 1-inch pieces**
     Salt and pepper
1   **tablespoon vegetable oil**
1   **onion, chopped**
5   **garlic cloves, minced**
1   **tablespoon minced fresh oregano or 1 teaspoon dried**
½   **teaspoon ground cumin**
4   **cups beef broth**
2   **cups chicken broth**
1   **(14.5-ounce) can diced tomatoes, drained**
2   **bay leaves**
2   **carrots, peeled and cut into ½-inch pieces**
10   **ounces red potatoes, unpeeled, cut into 1-inch pieces**
1   **zucchini, cut into ½-inch pieces**
2   **ears corn, husks and silk removed, cut into 1-inch rounds**
2   **tablespoons minced fresh cilantro**

1. Pat beef dry with paper towels and season with salt and pepper. Heat oil in Dutch oven over medium-high heat until just smoking. Brown beef on all sides, 5 to 7 minutes; transfer to bowl.

2. Add onion to fat left in pot and cook over medium heat until softened, about 5 minutes. Stir in garlic, oregano, and cumin and cook until fragrant, about 30 seconds. Stir in beef broth, chicken broth, tomatoes, and bay leaves, scraping up any browned bits, and bring to simmer. Stir in browned beef with any accumulated juices, reduce heat to low, cover, and simmer gently for 30 minutes.

3. Stir in carrots and potatoes and simmer, uncovered, until beef and vegetables are just tender, 20 to 25 minutes. Stir in zucchini and corn and simmer until corn is tender, 5 to 10 minutes.

4. Off heat, discard bay leaves. Stir in cilantro and season with salt and pepper to taste. Serve.

Meatball Soup with Rice and Cilantro

Serves 6 to 8

✓ **WHY THIS RECIPE WORKS:** This hearty soup known as *sopa de albondigas* features tender spiced meatballs and a complexly flavored broth. The meatballs traditionally contain rice, which, historically, supplemented the meat when it was scarce or pricey, making the dish more satisfying. When testing traditional methods for making this soup, we found that stirring raw rice into our meatball mix was not an option: When the rice was perfectly cooked, the meatballs were dry; when the meatballs were nicely tender and juicy, the rice was still inedibly crunchy. After testing a variety of types of rice including instant rice, parcooked rice, and long-grain converted rice, we discovered that the best solution was to use long-grain rice and parcook it for 8 minutes before stirring it into the meatball mix. Next, we took a closer look at the broth for our soup. We created a richly flavored base by sautéing a pureed mixture of tomatoes, onion, garlic, and jalapeño. This concentrated, roasty puree gave our finished soup a deeply complex flavor profile. Finally, we turned to the last key component in this soup: the vegetables. While many versions of this recipe are brothy, with large chunks of vegetables, we found that cutting our carrots and zucchini into slightly smaller pieces made for a more satisfying soup. We also incorporated rice directly into the broth to make the finished soup even heartier. Serve with lime wedges, sliced radishes, and/or thinly sliced jalapeños.

1	cup long-grain white rice
	Salt and pepper
8	ounces 90 percent lean ground beef
8	ounces ground pork
5	tablespoons minced fresh cilantro
1	large egg
3	garlic cloves, minced
1½	teaspoons minced fresh oregano or ½ teaspoon dried
¼	teaspoon ground cumin
2	tomatoes, cored and quartered
½	onion, quartered
½	jalapeño chile, stemmed, halved, and seeded
1	tablespoon vegetable oil
8	cups chicken broth
2	carrots, peeled and cut into ½-inch pieces
1	small zucchini, cut into ½-inch pieces

1. Bring 4 cups water to boil in Dutch oven. Add rice and ¾ teaspoon salt and cook, stirring occasionally, for 8 minutes. Drain rice through fine-mesh strainer, rinse with cold water, and drain again.

2. Using your hands, mix half of parcooked rice, ground beef, ground pork, 3 tablespoons cilantro, egg, one-third of garlic, oregano, cumin, 1 teaspoon pepper, and ½ teaspoon salt together in large bowl until thoroughly combined. Pinch off and roll mixture into 1-tablespoon-size meatballs (about 40 meatballs total) and arrange on rimmed baking sheet.

3. Process tomatoes, onion, jalapeño, and remaining garlic in food processor until smooth, about 30 seconds, scraping down sides of bowl as needed. Heat oil in now-empty pot over medium-high heat until shimmering. Add tomato-onion mixture and cook, stirring frequently, until mixture has darkened in color and liquid has evaporated, about 10 minutes.

4. Stir in broth and carrots, scraping up any browned bits, and bring to simmer. Cook until carrots are almost tender, about 10 minutes. Stir in zucchini and remaining parcooked rice, then gently add meatballs and simmer until meatballs are cooked through, 10 to 12 minutes. Off heat, stir in remaining 2 tablespoons cilantro and season with salt and pepper to taste. Serve.

Soup of the Seven Seas

Serves 6 to 8

✔ **WHY THIS RECIPE WORKS:** Traditionally prepared by Mexican fisherman, *caldo de siete mares*, or "soup of the seven seas," combined the freshest catch of the day along with a few vegetables in a spicy seafood broth. Today, the specific ingredients vary according to the region and the time of year, so for our version, we settled on a combination of mussels, catfish, and shrimp, all of which are native to the Gulf of Mexico. Cooking down a pureed mixture of toasted ancho chiles and aromatics gave us a complex base for our broth, but it lacked real seafood flavor. To remedy this, we created a quick seafood stock by cooking shrimp shells with our aromatic spice mixture, then simmering the mixture in a combination of clam juice and chicken broth. The addition of potatoes and corn, staples of the Mexican diet, made the soup feel hearty and satisfying. To ensure that every element was perfectly cooked, we simmered the corn, potatoes, and mussels in the fragrant broth until just cooked through, then removed them before adding the shrimp and catfish. If you can't find catfish, sole is a good substitute. Discard any mussel with an unpleasant odor or with a cracked or broken shell or a shell that won't close.

3   dried ancho chiles, stemmed, seeded, and torn into ½-inch pieces (¾ cup)
1   onion, quartered
3   garlic cloves, peeled
1   tablespoon dried oregano
2   teaspoons ground cumin
2   teaspoons sugar
2   bay leaves
    Salt and pepper
3   tablespoons vegetable oil
1   pound large shrimp (26 to 30 per pound), peeled, deveined, tails removed, and shells reserved
5   cups chicken broth
2   (8-ounce) bottles clam juice
2   ears corn, husks and silk removed, cut into 1-inch rounds
1   pound russet potatoes, peeled and cut into ½-inch pieces
1   pound mussels, scrubbed and debearded
1½ pounds skinless catfish fillets, cut into 2-inch pieces
2   tablespoons minced fresh cilantro
    Lime wedges

1. Toast anchos in Dutch oven over medium-high heat, stirring frequently, until fragrant, 2 to 6 minutes; transfer to food processor. Add onion, garlic, oregano, cumin, sugar, bay leaves, and 1 teaspoon pepper to processor and pulse until coarsely chopped, about 15 pulses.

2. Heat oil in now-empty pot over medium-high heat until shimmering. Add ancho mixture, shrimp shells, and ½ teaspoon salt and cook, stirring frequently, until mixture has darkened in color and shrimp shells have turned bright pink, 2 to 3 minutes. Stir in broth and clam juice, scraping up any browned bits, and bring to simmer. Cook until flavors meld, about 10 minutes. Strain broth through fine-mesh strainer; discard solids. Return strained broth to again-empty pot and bring to simmer.

3. Stir in corn and potatoes and simmer until potatoes are tender, 8 to 10 minutes. Increase heat to medium-high, stir in mussels, cover, and simmer briskly until most mussels have opened, 3 to 4 minutes (discard any unopened mussels). Using slotted spoon, transfer mussels, potatoes, and corn to individual bowls.

4. Return broth to gentle simmer over low heat. Add catfish and shrimp to pot, cover, and cook until catfish and shrimp are opaque throughout, about 3 minutes. Off heat, gently stir in cilantro and season with salt and pepper to taste. Ladle broth, shrimp, and catfish over mussels and vegetables. Serve with lime wedges.

Spicy Pinto Bean Soup

Serves 6

✔ **WHY THIS RECIPE WORKS:** This Mexican bean soup, called *sopa tarasca*, features deep chile flavor and a silky texture. Named after the Tarascos, an indigenous people of the southwestern state of Michoacán, this soup is generally a smooth puree of pinto beans heavily seasoned with dried ancho chiles. To re-create the complexity of this traditional soup, we turned to three diversely flavored chiles: Ancho chiles provided subtle sweetness, canned chipotle chiles in adobo contributed smoky, spicy flavor with a bit of acidity, and a fresh jalapeño offered bright vegetal notes. Pureeing our chiles along with tomatoes, onion, garlic, and oregano in a blender created a vibrant puree, which we cooked in hot oil to concentrate its flavor. We added our broth to this rich base, which allowed us to scrape up the flavorful browned bits on the bottom of the pot. Using this aromatic broth to cook our dried beans infused them with flavor. We found that using a standard amount of cooking liquid to beans resulted in a soup that was too thick and pasty once blended. Doubling the ratio of liquid to beans allowed us to achieve a light and creamy consistency while still highlighting the flavor of the beans. Serve with toasted pepitas, chopped fresh cilantro, and Mexican crema or sour cream.

    Salt and pepper
8 ounces (1¼ cups) dried pinto beans, picked over and rinsed
3 dried ancho chiles, stemmed, seeded, and torn into ½-inch pieces (¾ cup)
2 tomatoes, cored and quartered
1 onion, quartered
3 garlic cloves, peeled
1 jalapeño chile, stemmed, halved, and seeded
1 tablespoon minced canned chipotle chile in adobo sauce
1 tablespoon dried oregano
3 tablespoons vegetable oil
7 cups chicken broth, plus extra as needed
2 bay leaves

1. Dissolve 1½ tablespoons salt in 2 quarts cold water in large bowl or container. Add beans and soak at room temperature for at least 8 hours or up to 24 hours.

2. Drain beans and rinse well. Toast anchos in Dutch oven over medium-high heat, stirring frequently, until fragrant, 2 to 6 minutes; transfer to blender. Add tomatoes, onion, garlic, jalapeño, chipotle, and oregano and process until smooth, about 30 seconds.

3. Heat oil in now-empty pot over medium-high heat until shimmering. Add ancho mixture and 1 teaspoon salt and cook, stirring frequently, until mixture has darkened in color and liquid has evaporated, about 10 minutes. Stir in broth, scraping up any browned bits. Stir in beans and bay leaves and bring to simmer. Reduce heat to low, cover, and simmer gently until beans are tender, 1 to 1½ hours.

4. Discard bay leaves. Working in batches, process soup in clean, dry blender until smooth, 1 to 2 minutes. Return soup to again-empty pot, adjust consistency with extra broth as needed, and season with salt and pepper to taste. Serve.

Black Bean Soup

Serves 6

✓ **WHY THIS RECIPE WORKS:** Traditional Mexican black bean soup is redolent with smoky, spicy, and savory flavors, but classic recipes require soaking beans overnight, then simmering the beans for hours in from-scratch stock along with hard-to-find beef bones and smoked ham hocks. But quicker recipes developed for modern kitchens often produce watery, bland, and unattractive soups. We wanted a simplified procedure that would result in a rich, flavorful black bean soup. To start, we decided to use dried beans, which, unlike canned beans, released flavor into the broth as they cooked. We discovered that it was unnecessary to soak the beans overnight; when the beans were left unsoaked, a portion of them would burst, resulting in a thicker, creamier soup. We maximized the flavor of store-bought broth by including additional aromatics and ham steak for savory depth. To avoid the unappealing gray beans that plague so many versions of this soup, we stirred baking soda into the beans as they cooked, which kept their color intact and our soup vibrant. Dried beans tend to cook unevenly, so be sure to taste several beans to determine their doneness in step 1. For efficiency, you can prepare the soup ingredients while the beans simmer. Serve with lime wedges, chopped cilantro, chopped red onion, and/or sour cream.

5   cups water, plus extra as needed
1   pound (2½ cups) dried black beans,
    picked over and rinsed
4   ounces ham steak, trimmed
2   bay leaves
⅛   teaspoon baking soda
    Salt and pepper
3   tablespoons extra-virgin olive oil
2   large onions, chopped fine
1   large carrot, peeled and chopped fine
3   celery ribs, chopped fine
6   garlic cloves, minced

1½ tablespoons ground cumin
½   teaspoon red pepper flakes
6   cups chicken broth
2   tablespoons cornstarch
2   tablespoons water
2   tablespoons lime juice

1. Place water, beans, ham steak, bay leaves, and baking soda in large saucepan with tight-fitting lid. Bring to boil over medium-high heat, skimming foam from surface as needed. Stir in 1 teaspoon salt, reduce heat to medium-low, cover, and simmer briskly until beans are tender, 1¼ to 1½ hours (if after 1½ hours beans are not tender, add 1 cup more water and continue to simmer until tender); do not drain beans. Discard bay leaves. Transfer ham steak to cutting board, let cool slightly, then cut into ¼-inch pieces; set aside.

2. Heat oil in Dutch oven over medium-high heat until shimmering. Add onions, carrot, celery, and ½ teaspoon salt and cook, stirring occasionally, until vegetables are softened and lightly browned, 12 to 15 minutes. Reduce heat to medium-low, add garlic, cumin, and pepper flakes and cook, stirring constantly, until fragrant, about 3 minutes. Stir in broth, scraping up any browned bits. Stir in beans and bean cooking liquid, bring to simmer, and cook, stirring occasionally, until flavors meld, about 30 minutes.

3. Ladle 1½ cups beans and 2 cups liquid into food processor or blender, process until smooth, and return to pot. Stir together cornstarch and water in small bowl until combined, then gradually stir half of cornstarch mixture into soup. Bring to boil over medium-high heat, stirring occasionally, until fully thickened. If soup is still thinner than desired once boiling, stir remaining cornstarch mixture to recombine and gradually stir mixture into soup; return to boil to fully thicken. Off heat, stir in lime juice and ham. Season with salt and pepper to taste. Serve.

Lentil and Chorizo Soup

Serves 6 to 8

✔ **WHY THIS RECIPE WORKS:** Lentils were first brought to Mexico by the Spanish conquistadors in the 15th century. The Spaniards would often cook the legume along with salted, preserved meats to create a thick, meaty lentil soup. The people of Mexico eventually adapted the soup to their tastes by using sausage instead of salt pork. For our version, we opted for traditional Mexican chorizo, which has an intense flavor well suited to the earthy lentils. Browning the sausages first and then simmering them whole ensured that they didn't overcook and dry out while the lentils became tender. We soaked the lentils in a warm brine for 30 minutes to ensure that they were both well seasoned and that they didn't burst apart during cooking. Sweating onion, carrots, and cilantro in a covered pot along with the remaining fat from the chorizo provided a rich flavor base for our deeply flavorful soup ingredients. We found that cooking a combination of spices along with the aromatics allowed the flavors to bloom and provided a balanced heat that stood up well to the rich soup. A tablespoon of flour, stirred in along with the spices, thickened the broth to the perfect stew consistency. A bit of tart red wine vinegar offered welcome brightness. If you can't find fresh Mexican-style chorizo, cured Spanish-style may be substituted.

1	pound (2¼ cups) brown lentils, picked over and rinsed
	Salt and pepper
2	tablespoons extra-virgin olive oil
1½	pounds Mexican-style chorizo sausage, pricked with fork several times
1	onion, chopped fine
3	carrots, peeled and cut into ¼-inch pieces
3	tablespoons minced fresh cilantro
2	tablespoons ancho chile powder
3	garlic cloves, minced
1	teaspoon ground cumin
⅛	teaspoon ground cloves
1	tablespoon all-purpose flour
7	cups water
2	bay leaves
1	tablespoon red wine vinegar, plus extra for seasoning

1. Place lentils and 2 teaspoons salt in heatproof container. Cover with 4 cups boiling water and let soak for 30 minutes. Drain well.

2. Heat oil in Dutch oven over medium-high heat until just smoking. Brown chorizo on all sides, 6 to 8 minutes; transfer to plate. Reduce heat to low and add onion, carrots, 1 tablespoon cilantro, and 1 teaspoon salt to fat left in pot. Cover and cook, stirring occasionally, until vegetables are very soft but not brown, 15 to 20 minutes. If vegetables begin to brown, add 1 tablespoon water to pot.

3. Stir in chile powder, garlic, cumin, and cloves and cook until fragrant, about 2 minutes. Stir in flour and cook for 1 minute. Slowly whisk in water, scraping up any browned bits, and bring to simmer. Add browned chorizo with any accumulated juices and bay leaves, reduce heat to low, cover, and simmer gently until lentils are tender, 15 to 20 minutes.

4. Discard bay leaves. Transfer chorizo to cutting board, let cool slightly, then halve lengthwise and slice ¼ inch thick. Stir chorizo into soup and simmer until heated through, about 2 minutes. Off heat, stir in vinegar and remaining 2 tablespoons cilantro. Season with salt, pepper, and extra vinegar to taste. Serve.

Chicken Stew with Sweet Potato, Pineapple, and Plantains

Serves 6 to 8

✔ **WHY THIS RECIPE WORKS:** Rooted in the flavor profile of the classic Oaxacan mole called *manchamanteles* (literally, "tablecloth stainer"), this spicy, sweet, and savory stew is as flavorful as it is complex. Traditional manchamanteles consists of a vibrant red sauce made from chiles, nuts, and seeds, served over tender pieces of braised chicken, pineapple, plantains, sweet potatoes, and pinto beans. We set out to create a stew that would incorporate each of these elements and bring all of the flavors into focus. To re-create the traditional chile paste for the base of the stew, we ground toasted dried ancho chiles, a portion of our pineapple, onion, toasted peanuts and sesame seeds, garlic, and jalapeño in a blender until we had a smooth, rich puree. Sautéing this mixture before adding the broth gave us a heady medium for braising our chicken, sweet potatoes, and pinto beans. We found that using the oven was an ideal hands-off method for maintaining a gentle simmer while our stew cooked. Stirring ripe plantains and pieces of pineapple into the finished stew ensured that the tender fruit didn't turn to mush during cooking. A small amount of red wine vinegar helped to round out the deep chile flavor. If plantains are not available, ripe but firm bananas may be substituted; however, the flavor will be somewhat sweeter.

3   **dried ancho chiles, stemmed, seeded, and torn into ½-inch pieces (¾ cup)**
4½   **cups chicken broth**
2   **cups ½-inch pineapple pieces**
1   **onion, quartered**
¼   **cup unsalted dry-roasted peanuts**
3   **tablespoons sesame seeds, toasted, plus extra for serving**
3   **garlic cloves, peeled**
1   **jalapeño chile, stemmed**
3   **tablespoons vegetable oil**
    Salt and pepper
1   **pound sweet potatoes, peeled and cut into ½-inch pieces**
1   **(15-ounce) can pinto beans, rinsed**
4   **pounds bone-in chicken thighs, skin removed, trimmed**
2   **ripe plantains, peeled, quartered lengthwise and sliced 1 inch thick**
1   **tablespoon red wine vinegar**
4   **scallions, sliced thin**

1. Adjust oven rack to lower-middle position and heat oven to 300 degrees. Toast anchos in Dutch oven over medium-high heat, stirring frequently, until fragrant, 2 to 6 minutes; transfer to blender. Add ½ cup broth, 1 cup pineapple, onion, peanuts, sesame seeds, garlic, and jalapeño and process until smooth, about 60 seconds.

2. Heat oil in now-empty pot over medium-high heat until shimmering. Add ancho mixture and 1 teaspoon salt and cook, stirring frequently, until mixture has darkened in color and liquid has evaporated, about 10 minutes. Stir in remaining 4 cups broth, scraping up any browned bits. Stir in sweet potatoes and beans and bring to simmer. Season chicken with salt and pepper and nestle into pot. Cover, transfer pot to oven, and cook until chicken is tender, about 1 hour.

3. Remove pot from oven and transfer chicken to cutting board. Let chicken cool slightly, then, using 2 forks, shred into bite-size pieces; discard bones. Stir shredded chicken, plantains, and remaining 1 cup pineapple into stew and bring to simmer over medium heat. Stir in vinegar and season with salt and pepper to taste. Serve with scallions and extra sesame seeds.

Chicken Posole Verde

Serves 6 to 8

☑ **WHY THIS RECIPE WORKS:** Posole is the Mexican name for both hominy (dried field corn kernels treated with lime and boiled until tender but still chewy) and the full-flavored stew made with hominy and meat. The stew is made throughout Mexico in several distinct styles: white (made without chiles), red (made with dried red chiles), and green (made with cilantro, jalapeños, and tomatillos). We decided to create a green posole with chicken. We found that breast meat had a tendency to dry out and become stringy, while dark meat (thighs in particular) became perfectly tender. Using whole bone-in chicken thighs resulted in easy-to-shred meat, giving our stew a pleasant rustic texture. We quickly browned the chicken, then sautéed our aromatics after we removed the chicken from the pot, allowing us to incorporate the flavorful browned bits into our broth. When we returned our partially cooked chicken to the pot, we moved the cooking from the stove to the more even, gentle heat of the oven. Once the chicken was tender, we set it aside before stirring in the hominy. (Canned hominy proved to be an acceptable substitute for dried; the lightly sweet kernels were pleasantly chewy.) To give the stew its trademark tanginess, we made a vibrant puree of traditional, verdant ingredients: tomatillos, jalapeño, and fresh cilantro. Adding this mixture late in the cooking process allowed the flavors to meld without dulling the freshness of the puree. Finally, we returned the shredded chicken to the pot to warm briefly before serving. Serve with lime wedges, diced avocado, and/or sliced radishes. See the photo on page 48.

- **4** **pounds bone-in chicken thighs, trimmed**
  Salt and pepper
- **2** **tablespoons vegetable oil**
- **1** **onion, chopped fine**
- **3** **garlic cloves, minced**
- **1** **tablespoon chopped fresh oregano or 1 teaspoon dried**
- **4½** **cups chicken broth**
- **12** **ounces tomatillos, husks and stems removed, rinsed well, dried, and quartered**
- **2** **jalapeños, stemmed, halved, and seeded**
- **2½** **cups fresh cilantro leaves and stems, trimmed (2 bunches)**
- **2** **(15-ounce) cans white or yellow hominy, rinsed**

1. Adjust oven rack to lower-middle position and heat oven to 300 degrees. Pat chicken dry with paper towels and season with salt and pepper. Heat 1 tablespoon oil in Dutch oven over medium-high heat until just smoking. Brown half of chicken, about 5 minutes per side; transfer to plate. Repeat with remaining 1 tablespoon oil and remaining chicken. Let cool slightly, then remove skin.

2. Pour off all but 1 tablespoon fat from pot; add onion and ¼ teaspoon salt and cook over medium heat until softened, about 5 minutes. Stir in garlic and oregano and cook until fragrant, about 30 seconds. Stir in 4 cups broth, scraping up any browned bits, and bring to simmer. Nestle browned chicken into pot along with any accumulated juices. Cover, transfer pot to oven, and cook until chicken is tender, about 1 hour.

3. Remove pot from oven, transfer chicken to cutting board, and let cool slightly. Meanwhile, process tomatillos, jalapeños, cilantro, and remaining ½ cup broth in blender until smooth, about 30 seconds. Stir tomatillo mixture and hominy into stew, bring to simmer over medium heat, and cook until flavors meld, 10 to 15 minutes.

4. Using 2 forks, shred chicken into bite-size pieces; discard bones. Stir shredded chicken into stew and cook until heated through, about 2 minutes. Season with salt and pepper to taste. Serve.

Pork Posole Rojo

Serves 8 to 10

✔ **WHY THIS RECIPE WORKS:** Posole *rojo*, or red posole, is richer than its green cousin, with a deep and earthy flavor profile. Authentic versions are made with bones from the head, neck, shank, and feet of a pig, supplemented with some boneless meat from the shoulder or loin. The traditional bones provided rich, porky flavor and gave the stew body, but we discovered that we could simplify by using a bone-in pork butt roast. Splitting the roast into small chunks before cooking proved to be the easiest cooking method; the chunks cooked faster than a whole roast and were easier to shred than small cubes. To avoid firming up the texture of the meat (which would inhibit shredding), we skipped browning and instead parcooked the meat gently with onions and garlic to develop flavor in the broth. Chicken broth provided savory depth, while canned tomatoes added lively acidity and color. For the chiles, we liked the rich, slightly sweet flavor of anchos, which we soaked and pureed into a thick paste. We mixed most of the puree into the stew, saving the rest to add later for those who wanted extra heat. As in our green posole, we added the hominy only after the meat was cooked and removed from the pot; this gave the hominy enough time to absorb flavor from the broth but didn't allow it to become mushy. For an accurate measurement of boiling water, bring a full kettle of water to a boil and then measure out the desired amount. Serve with lime wedges, diced avocado, and/or sliced radishes.

1   **(5-pound) bone-in pork butt roast**
    Salt and pepper
2   **tablespoons vegetable oil**
2   **large onions, chopped coarse**
5   **garlic cloves, minced**
6   **cups chicken broth**
1   **(14.5-ounce) can diced tomatoes**

1   **tablespoon minced fresh oregano**
    or 1 teaspoon dried
3   **dried ancho chiles, stemmed and seeded**
1½ **cups boiling water**
3   **(15-ounce) cans white or yellow hominy,**
    rinsed

1. Adjust oven rack to lower-middle position and heat oven to 300 degrees. Trim thick skin and excess fat from meat and cut along muscles to divide roast into large pieces of various sizes; reserve bones. Season pork with salt and pepper.

2. Heat oil in Dutch oven over medium heat until shimmering. Add onions and ¼ teaspoon salt and cook until softened, about 8 to 10 minutes. Stir in garlic and cook until fragrant, about 30 seconds. Add pork and bones and cook, stirring often, until meat is no longer pink on outside, about 8 minutes. Stir in broth, tomatoes and their juice, oregano, and ½ teaspoon salt and bring to simmer, skimming foam from surface as needed. Cover, place pot in oven, and cook until pork is tender, about 2 hours.

3. Meanwhile, soak anchos in bowl with boiling water until softened, about 20 minutes. Process anchos and soaking liquid in blender until smooth, about 30 seconds. Strain through fine-mesh strainer into bowl, using rubber spatula to help pass chili mixture through strainer. Measure out and reserve ¼ cup ancho mixture for serving.

4. Remove pot from oven, transfer pork to cutting board, and let cool slightly; discard bones. While pork cools, stir hominy and remaining ancho mixture into pot and bring to simmer over medium heat. Reduce heat to low, cover, and simmer gently until flavors meld, about 30 minutes.

5. Using 2 forks, shred pork into bite-size pieces. Stir shredded pork into stew and cook until heated through, about 2 minutes. Season with reserved ancho mixture, salt, and pepper to taste. Serve.

Mexican Beef Stew

Serves 6 to 8

WHY THIS RECIPE WORKS: Ubiquitous throughout Mexico as well as parts of Texas, *carne guisada* (literally meaning "stewed meat") is the Mexican answer to beef stew. Chock-full of beef and vegetables in an aromatic tomato sauce, the consistency of the stew looks similar to classic American versions, but the flavor is distinctly Mexican. To start, we built a spicy base that included jalapeño, oregano, cumin, and cinnamon in addition to the traditional onions and garlic, but tasters wanted even deeper flavor. We found that toasting two dried ancho chiles and adding them to the pot as the beef simmered, then discarding them just before serving provided seasoning without adding too much heat. Adding the traditional potatoes and bell peppers halfway through cooking allowed them to soak up the flavor of the stew without becoming too soft. We also added briny green olives at the end of cooking so they would retain their firm texture. Cutting our meat and vegetables into large pieces gave the stew an appealingly rustic texture. Cilantro, stirred in just before serving, provided vibrant, fresh flavor. Satisfying by itself, carne guisada can also be served with rice and warm tortillas.

2 dried ancho chiles, stemmed and seeded
4 pounds boneless beef chuck-eye roast, pulled apart at seams, trimmed, and cut into 1½-inch pieces
   Salt and pepper
2 tablespoons vegetable oil
2 onions, chopped fine
3 garlic cloves, minced
1 jalapeño chile, stemmed, seeded, and minced
1 tablespoon dried oregano
1½ teaspoons ground cumin
¼ teaspoon ground cinnamon
2 tablespoons all-purpose flour
3 cups beef broth
1 (14.5-ounce) can diced tomatoes
1½ pounds red potatoes, unpeeled, cut into 1½-inch pieces
2 red or green bell peppers, stemmed, seeded, and cut into 1-inch pieces
1 cup pitted green olives, chopped coarse
¼ cup minced fresh cilantro

1. Adjust oven rack to lower-middle position and heat oven to 325 degrees. Toast anchos in Dutch oven over medium-high heat, stirring frequently, until fragrant, 2 to 6 minutes; transfer to bowl.

2. Pat beef dry with paper towels and season with salt and pepper. Heat 1 tablespoon oil in now-empty pot over medium-high heat until just smoking. Brown half of beef on all sides, 7 to 10 minutes; transfer to plate. Repeat with remaining 1 tablespoon oil and remaining beef.

3. Add onions and ¼ teaspoon salt to fat left in pot and cook over medium heat until softened, about 5 minutes. Stir in garlic, jalapeño, oregano, cumin, and cinnamon and cook until fragrant, about 30 seconds. Stir in flour and cook for 1 minute. Slowly whisk in broth, scraping up any browned bits. Stir in tomatoes and their juice and toasted anchos and bring to a simmer. Stir in browned beef and any accumulated juices, cover, transfer pot to oven, and cook for 1 hour.

4. Stir in potatoes and bell peppers, cover, and cook in oven until beef and potatoes are tender, 1 to 1½ hours.

5. Remove pot from oven and discard anchos. Stir in olives and let sit until heated through, 2 minutes. Adjust stew consistency with hot water as needed. Stir in cilantro and season with salt and pepper to taste. Serve.

White Chicken Chili

Serves 6 to 8

✓ **WHY THIS RECIPE WORKS:** The bold flavors of Mexican green chiles take the forefront in this alternative to meat-heavy chilis. We aimed to develop a rich stew-like chili with moist chicken, tender beans, and a complex flavor profile. A single type of chile made a one-dimensional stew; instead we used a combination of spicy jalapeños, mild Anaheims, and sweet poblanos. To avoid a bland, watery sauce, we tried thickening the chili with masa harina, but tasters disliked its noticeable texture and flavor. Instead, we pureed some of the chili base, which thickened the chili without compromising its flavor. A minced raw jalapeño stirred in before serving provided a shot of heat and color. If you can't find Anaheim chiles, add an additional poblano and jalapeño to the chili. Serve with lime wedges, sour cream, and tortilla chips.

3	poblano chiles, stemmed, seeded, and cut into 1-inch pieces
3	Anaheim chiles, stemmed, seeded, and cut into 1-inch pieces
1	pound onions, cut into 1-inch pieces
3	pounds bone-in split chicken breasts, trimmed
	Salt and pepper
2	tablespoons vegetable oil
3	jalapeño chiles, stemmed, seeded, and minced
6	garlic cloves, minced
1	tablespoon ground cumin
1½	teaspoons ground coriander
2	(15-ounce) cans cannellini beans, rinsed
3	cups chicken broth
3	tablespoons lime juice (2 limes)
¼	cup minced fresh cilantro
4	scallions, sliced thin

1. Pulse half of poblanos, half of Anaheims, and half of onions in food processor until consistency of chunky salsa, 10 to 12 pulses, scraping down sides of bowl as needed; transfer to medium bowl. Repeat with remaining poblanos, Anaheims, and onions; transfer to bowl (do not clean food processor).

2. Pat chicken dry with paper towels and season with salt and pepper. Heat 1 tablespoon oil in Dutch oven over medium-high heat until just smoking. Brown half of chicken, about 5 minutes per side; transfer to plate. Repeat with remaining 1 tablespoon oil and remaining chicken. Let cool slightly, then remove skin.

3. Pour off all but 2 tablespoons fat from pot and reduce heat to medium. Add chile mixture, two-thirds of jalapeños, garlic, cumin, coriander, and ¼ teaspoon salt. Cover and cook, stirring occasionally, until vegetables are softened, about 10 minutes. Remove pot from heat.

4. Transfer 1 cup cooked vegetable mixture to now-empty food processor. Add 1 cup beans and 1 cup broth and process until smooth, about 20 seconds. Add vegetable-bean mixture and remaining 2 cups broth to pot and bring to simmer over medium-high heat. Nestle browned chicken into pot along with any accumulated juices. Reduce heat to low, cover, and simmer gently until chicken registers 160 degrees, 15 to 20 minutes.

5. Transfer chicken to cutting board and let cool slightly. Meanwhile, stir remaining beans into chili and simmer, uncovered, until beans are heated through and chili has thickened slightly, about 10 minutes.

6. Using 2 forks, shred chicken into bite-size pieces; discard bones. Stir shredded chicken and remaining jalapeño into chili and cook until heated through, about 2 minutes. Off heat, stir in lime juice, cilantro, and scallions. Season with salt and pepper to taste. Serve.

Carne Adovada

Serves 6

✓ **WHY THIS RECIPE WORKS:** Popular in New Mexico, the chili called *carne adovada* contains tender chunks of pork braised in an intense, richly flavored red chile sauce. We set out to create a streamlined method for this satisfying dish. We started by browning cubes of well-marbled pork butt to build flavor and render fat. Next, we reached for a jar of chili powder, which typically includes dried ground chiles, cumin, oregano and garlic, all of which are used in most carne adovada recipes. By blooming the chili powder along with chipotle in adobo, extra oregano, and fresh minced garlic and onion, we were able to create a deeply flavorful base for our chili. To mirror the subtle sweetness of dried chiles, we added raisins, soaked in coffee instead of water to bring their sweetness into robust, bittersweet balance. Pureeing the sauce with chicken broth melded the flavors and provided a smooth base for our chili. Once we added the pork back to the sauce, we finished the cooking in the even, gentle heat of the oven. Cilantro, lime juice, and lime zest added after cooking provided a balanced brightness. Pork butt roast is often labeled Boston butt in the supermarket. You can substitute 1½ teaspoons ground espresso powder dissolved in ½ cup boiling water for the brewed coffee if desired. Serve with lime wedges, sliced radishes, and warm corn tortillas.

½ cup brewed coffee, hot
¼ cup raisins
⅓ cup chili powder
3 tablespoons all-purpose flour
1 teaspoon dried oregano
4 pounds boneless pork butt roast, pulled apart at seams, trimmed, and cut into 1½-inch pieces
 Salt and pepper
3 tablespoons vegetable oil
2 onions, chopped fine
6 garlic cloves, minced
1 tablespoon minced canned chipotle chile in adobo sauce
2 cups chicken broth
1 cup water
¼ cup minced fresh cilantro
1 teaspoon grated lime zest plus 1 tablespoon juice

1. Adjust oven rack to lower-middle position and heat oven to 325 degrees. Combine hot coffee and raisins in small bowl, cover, and let sit until raisins are plump, about 5 minutes. Combine chili powder, flour, and oregano in separate small bowl. Pat pork dry with paper towels and season with salt and pepper.

2. Heat 1 tablespoon oil in Dutch oven over medium-high heat until just smoking. Brown half of pork on all sides, 7 to 10 minutes; transfer to medium bowl. Repeat with 1 tablespoon oil and remaining pork.

3. Pour off all but 2 tablespoons fat from pot and reduce heat to medium. Add onions and cook until softened, about 5 minutes. Stir in garlic and chipotle and cook until fragrant, about 30 seconds. Stir in spice mixture and remaining 1 tablespoon oil and cook, stirring constantly, until fragrant, about 1 minute (do not let spices burn). Stir in broth, water, and raisin-coffee mixture, scraping up any browned bits.

4. Process sauce in blender until smooth, 1 to 2 minutes. Return sauce to now-empty pot. Stir in browned pork and any accumulated juices and bring to simmer. Cover, transfer pot to oven, and cook until pork is tender and sauce is thickened, about 2 hours, stirring halfway through cooking.

5. Remove pot from oven and stir in cilantro and lime zest and juice. Season with salt and pepper to taste. Serve.

Chili con Carne

Serves 6

✔ **WHY THIS RECIPE WORKS:** Classic Tex-Mex chili consists of hearty chunks of meat enveloped in a smooth, thick sauce with a consistency somewhere between soup and stew. We wanted to develop the ultimate version of this comforting dish. To develop layers of potent chile flavor, we used dried chiles rather than chile powder, which gave the dish a clean, multidimensional flavor. We chose a mix of ancho and New Mexican chiles for both earthy, fruity sweetness and crisp acidity. A few fresh jalapeños added bright flavor and bite. Beefy, well-marbled chuck eye worked perfectly for our chili. We cut the roast into easy-to-eat 1-inch pieces and browned the meat in rendered bacon fat, which added smoky, savory depth to the dish. From among the many different liquids called for in chili con carne recipes, we chose plain water—everything else diluted or competed with the flavor of the chiles. Although some recipes include neither tomatoes nor onions, we found that using both in small amounts added dimension. We thickened the chili by stirring in some masa harina, which also imparted a subtle corn flavor that complemented the other flavors nicely. You can substitute 3 tablespoons cornstarch mixed with 3 tablespoons water for the masa harina and water mixture in step 5. Serve with your favorite chili toppings.

- 3 **dried ancho chiles, stemmed, seeded, and torn into ½-inch pieces (¾ cup)**
- 3 **dried New Mexican chiles, stemmed, seeded, and torn into ½-inch pieces (¾ cup)**
- 2 **tablespoons cumin seeds**
- 2 **teaspoons dried oregano**
- 8 **cups water**
- 8 **slices bacon, cut into ¼-inch pieces**
- 4 **pounds boneless beef chuck-eye roast, pulled apart at seams, trimmed, and cut into 1-inch pieces**
  Salt and pepper
- 1 **onion, chopped fine**
- 4 **jalapeño chiles, stemmed, seeded, and minced**
- 5 **garlic cloves, minced**
- 1 **cup canned crushed tomatoes**
- 2 **tablespoons lime juice**
- ⅓ **cup masa harina**

1. Toast ancho and New Mexican chiles and cumin in Dutch oven over medium heat, stirring frequently, until fragrant, 2 to 6 minutes; transfer to spice grinder. Add oregano and grind to fine powder. Transfer spice mixture to bowl and stir in ½ cup water.

2. Cook bacon in now-empty pot over medium-low heat until crisp, about 10 minutes. Transfer bacon to paper towel–lined plate using slotted spoon. Pour off and reserve rendered fat in bowl.

3. Pat beef dry with paper towels and season with salt and pepper. Heat 1 tablespoon bacon fat in now-empty pot over medium-high until just smoking. Brown half of beef on all sides, 7 to 10 minutes; transfer to bowl. Repeat with 1 tablespoon bacon fat and remaining beef.

4. Heat 3 tablespoons bacon fat in now-empty pot over medium heat until shimmering. Add onion and cook until softened, about 5 minutes. Stir in jalapeños and garlic and cook until fragrant, about 1 minute. Stir in chile paste and cook until fragrant, about 2 minutes. Stir in 7 cups water, tomatoes, and lime juice and bring to simmer. Stir in crisp bacon and browned beef and any accumulated juices and simmer until meat is tender and juices are dark, rich, and starting to thicken, about 2 hours.

5. Mix masa harina and remaining ½ cup water in bowl to form paste. Increase heat to medium, stir in masa harina mixture, and simmer until thickened, 5 to 10 minutes. Season with salt and pepper to taste. Serve.

Black Bean Chili

Serves 6 to 8

✔ **WHY THIS RECIPE WORKS:** Hearty black bean chili unites a myriad of Mexican flavors in a bowl. But too often, black bean chili turns out dull and unremarkable. For a complexly flavored chili full of tender and well-seasoned beans, we started with dried beans. As with our Black Bean Soup (page 64), we found that soaking the beans overnight was unnecessary; some of the unsoaked beans burst during cooking, resulting in a thicker chili. Crushed tomatoes (added partway through cooking so that their acidity didn't toughen or discolor the beans) provided a bit of tartness. Some coarsely chopped mushrooms added meaty depth without giving themselves away, while garlic, chili powder, bay leaves, and cumin further rounded out the flavor of the chili. Minced chipotle added depth and smokiness, and a surprising ingredient—mustard seeds—created a new level of complexity. A spritz of lime and a sprinkling of minced cilantro finished our chili with fresh, bright notes. We strongly prefer the texture and flavor of mustard seeds and cumin seeds in this chili; however, ground spices can be substituted for the seeds by adding ½ teaspoon ground cumin and/or ½ teaspoon dry mustard to the pot with the chili powder in step 3. Serve with your favorite chili toppings.

1   **pound white mushrooms, trimmed and broken into rough pieces**
1   **tablespoon mustard seeds**
2   **teaspoons cumin seeds**
3   **tablespoons vegetable oil**
1   **onion, chopped**
9   **garlic cloves, minced**
1   **tablespoon minced canned chipotle chile in adobo sauce**
3   **tablespoons chili powder**
2½   **cups vegetable broth**
2½   **cups water, plus extra as needed**
1   **pound (2½ cups) dried black beans, picked over and rinsed**
1   **tablespoon packed light brown sugar**
2   **bay leaves**
⅛   **teaspoon baking soda**
1   **(28-ounce) can crushed tomatoes**
2   **red bell peppers, stemmed, seeded, and cut into ½-inch pieces**
½   **cup minced fresh cilantro**
    Salt and pepper
    Lime wedges

1. Adjust oven rack to lower-middle position and heat oven to 325 degrees. Pulse mushrooms in food processor until uniformly coarsely chopped, about 10 pulses; set aside.

2. Toast mustard seeds and cumin seeds in Dutch oven over medium heat, stirring constantly, until fragrant, about 1 minute. Stir in oil, onion, and processed mushrooms, cover, and cook until vegetables release liquid, about 5 minutes. Uncover and continue to cook until liquid has evaporated and vegetables are browned, 5 to 10 minutes.

3. Stir in garlic and chipotle and cook until fragrant, about 30 seconds. Stir in chili powder and cook, stirring constantly, until fragrant, about 1 minute (do not let mixture burn). Stir in broth, water, beans, sugar, bay leaves, and baking soda and bring to simmer, skimming foam from surface as needed. Cover, transfer pot to oven, and cook for 1 hour.

4. Stir in tomatoes and bell peppers, cover, and continue to cook in oven until beans are fully tender, about 1 hour longer. (If chili begins to stick to bottom of pot or looks too thick, stir in extra water as needed.)

5. Remove pot from oven and discard bay leaves. Stir in cilantro and season with salt and pepper to taste. Serve with lime wedges.

TAMALES WITH RED CHILE CHICKEN FILLING

Tacos, Tostadas, Tamales, and More

Corn Tortillas

Makes about 12 (6-inch) tortillas

✓ **WHY THIS RECIPE WORKS:** Fresh corn tortillas have a lightly sweet flavor and a soft, springy texture unmatched by store-bought kinds. We rested the dough for 5 minutes before pressing the tortillas to ensure that the masa was fully hydrated. Vegetable oil, although nontraditional, made the dough soft, pliable, and easy to work with. Be sure to use masa harina or Maseca Brand Instant Masa Corn Flour.

2   **cups (8 ounces) masa harina**
2   **teaspoons vegetable oil**
¼   **teaspoon salt**
1¼   **cups warm tap water, plus extra as needed**

1. Mix masa, 1 teaspoon oil, and salt together in medium bowl, then fold in water with rubber spatula. Using your hands, knead mixture in bowl, adding additional water, 1 tablespoon at a time, as needed, until dough is soft and tacky but not sticky, and has texture of Play-Doh. Cover dough with damp dish towel and let sit for 5 minutes.

2. Cut sides of 1-quart zipper-lock bag, leaving bottom seam intact. Line large plate with 2 damp dish towels. Divide dough into 12 equal pieces (1½ ounces each); keep covered. Working with 1 piece at a time, roll into ball, place on 1 side of zipper-lock bag, and fold other side over top. Press dough flat into 6½-inch-wide tortilla (about 1/16 inch thick) using tortilla press or pie plate; leave tortilla between plastic until skillet is hot.

3. Heat remaining 1 teaspoon oil in 8-inch non-stick skillet over medium-high heat until shimmering. Using paper towel, wipe out skillet, leaving thin film of oil on bottom. Remove plastic on top of tortilla, flip tortilla onto your palm, then remove plastic on bottom and lay tortilla in skillet. Cook tortilla, without moving it, until it moves freely when pan is shaken and has shrunken slightly in size, about 45 seconds.

4. Flip tortilla over and cook until edges curl and bottom is spotty brown, about 1 minute. Flip tortilla back over and continue to cook until first side is spotty brown and puffs up in center, 30 to 60 seconds. Lay toasted tortilla between damp dish towels. Repeat with remaining dough. (Tortillas can be refrigerated for up to 5 days.)

LEARN HOW **CORN TORTILLAS**

We like to use a tortilla press for perfectly even tortillas, but you can also press the dough with a pie plate.

1. KNEAD: Knead the dough until it is soft and tacky. Cover and set aside for 5 minutes.

2. ROLL: Divide the dough into 12 equal pieces (1½ ounces each). Working with 1 piece of dough at a time, roll into a ball.

3. PRESS: Place the ball in the center of the press in a split-open zipper-lock bag. Press gently and evenly into a 6½-inch tortilla.

Shredded Beef Tacos with Cabbage-Carrot Slaw

Serves 6

✔ **WHY THIS RECIPE WORKS:** *Carne deshebrada*, literally meaning "shredded beef," is a common offering at Mexican taco stands. It's made by braising a large cut of beef until ultratender and then shredding the meat and tossing it with a flavorful *rojo* sauce made with tomatoes and/or dried chiles. We started out by choosing the beefiest braising cut we could find: boneless short ribs. Although ribs are a bit nontraditional, their meaty flavor made them an excellent choice for this dish. To achieve flavorful browning without having to sear the short ribs, we raised the beef up out of the braising liquid by resting it on onion rounds. The ambient heat browned the short ribs just enough. Next, we created a braising liquid that would infuse the beef with flavor and later act as a base for our rojo sauce. Beer and cider vinegar provided depth and brightness, and tomato paste boosted savory flavor. Smoky-sweet ancho chiles gave the sauce a rounder flavor and a gentle, spicy kick. Cumin, cinnamon, cloves, oregano, and bay leaves added warmth and complexity. Once the beef had finished cooking, we pureed the braising liquid into a sauce with a smooth, luxurious consistency. A bright, tangy slaw provided a nice counterbalance to the rich meat. Use a full-bodied lager or ale such as Dos Equis or Sierra Nevada. If your Dutch oven does not have a tight-fitting lid, cover the pot tightly with a sheet of heavy-duty aluminum foil and then replace the lid. This filling also tastes great as a topping for Tostadas, Sopes, Gorditas, and Panuchos (pages 104–115) or as a filling for Tamales (page 116).

1½ cups beer
½ cup cider vinegar
4 dried ancho chiles, stemmed, seeded, and torn into ½-inch pieces (1 cup)
2 tablespoons tomato paste
6 garlic cloves, lightly crushed and peeled
3 bay leaves
2 teaspoons ground cumin
2 teaspoons dried oregano
½ teaspoon ground cloves
½ teaspoon ground cinnamon
Salt and pepper
1 large onion, sliced into ½-inch-thick rounds
3 pounds boneless beef short ribs, trimmed and cut into 2-inch cubes
18 (6-inch) corn tortillas, warmed
4 ounces queso fresco, crumbled (1 cup)
1 recipe Cabbage-Carrot Slaw (page 286)
Lime wedges

1. Adjust oven rack to lower-middle position and heat oven to 325 degrees. Combine beer, vinegar, anchos, tomato paste, garlic, bay leaves, cumin, oregano, cloves, cinnamon, 2 teaspoons salt, and ½ teaspoon pepper in Dutch oven. Arrange onion rounds in single layer on bottom of pot. Place beef on top of onion rounds in single layer. Cover and cook until meat is well browned and tender, 2½ to 3 hours.

2. Using slotted spoon, transfer beef to large bowl and cover. Strain liquid through fine-mesh strainer into 2-cup liquid measuring cup (do not wash pot). Discard onion rounds and bay leaves, then transfer remaining solids to blender. Let strained liquid settle for 5 minutes, then skim any fat off surface and add water as needed to equal 1 cup. Add liquid to blender with solids and process until smooth, about 2 minutes; transfer to now-empty pot.

3. Using 2 forks, shred beef into bite-size pieces. Bring sauce to simmer over medium heat. Stir in shredded beef and season with salt to taste. Serve with warm tortillas, queso fresco, slaw, and lime wedges.

Grilled Skirt Steak and Poblano Tacos

Serves 6

✓ **WHY THIS RECIPE WORKS:** In this popular northern Mexican taco filling, rich, smoky beef is perfectly complemented by sweet-hot poblano chiles and piquant onions. The combination is deliciously to the point, unencumbered by competing flavors, and also very simple to put together. We wanted an authentic version of these tacos that could be made on a home grill. First, we tackled the chiles. When roasted, peeled, seeded, and cut into strips, poblano chiles are called *rajas*, and they're used not only in tacos but also on tostadas or grilled seafood. We grilled the poblanos over a very hot fire; this left the skins charred and blistered while the flesh remained relatively unscathed. Putting the peppers in a covered bowl when they came off the grill made the bitter skins easy to peel off later. The onions needed only a quick stint over the fire to develop good grill marks. We found that marinating our skirt steak was unnecessary; instead, we covered the cooked steak with a flavorful puree of onion, lime juice, garlic, cumin, and salt while the steak rested. Finally, we sliced our skirt steak thin for a tender texture. If you can't find skirt steak, substitute flank steak, although the meat will be a bit more chewy. Serve with chopped cilantro and Mexican *crema* or sour cream.

4	**onions (3 sliced crosswise into ½-inch-thick rounds, 1 chopped coarse)**
6	**tablespoons lime juice (3 limes)**
3	**garlic cloves, minced**
½	**teaspoon ground cumin**
	Salt and pepper
1½	**pounds poblano chiles**
1	**tablespoon vegetable oil**
2	**pounds skirt steak, trimmed**
18	**(6-inch) corn tortillas**
	Lime wedges

1. Process chopped onion, lime juice, garlic, cumin, and 1 teaspoon salt in food processor until smooth. Brush onion rounds and poblanos with oil and season with salt and pepper. Pat steak dry and season with salt and pepper.

2A. FOR A CHARCOAL GRILL: Open bottom vent completely. Light large chimney starter filled with charcoal briquettes (6 quarts). When top coals are partially covered with ash, pour evenly over half of grill. Set cooking grate in place, cover, and open lid vent completely. Heat grill until hot, about 5 minutes.

2B. FOR A GAS GRILL: Turn all burners to high, cover, and heat grill until hot, about 15 minutes. Leave primary burner on high and turn other burner(s) off.

3. Clean and oil cooking grate. Place poblanos on hotter side of grill and onion rounds on cooler side of grill. Grill (covered if using gas), turning as needed, until poblanos are blistered and blackened and onions are softened and golden, 6 to 12 minutes. Transfer onions to platter and cover to keep warm. Transfer peppers to bowl, cover, and let steam while cooking steak and tortillas.

4. Place steak on hotter side of grill. Grill (covered if using gas), turning as needed, until well browned on both sides and meat registers 120 to 125 degrees (for medium-rare), 4 to 8 minutes. Transfer steak to 13 by 9-inch pan and poke all over with fork. Pour pureed onion mixture over top, cover, and let rest for 5 to 10 minutes.

5. Working in batches, grill tortillas, turning as needed, until warm and soft, about 30 seconds; wrap tightly in aluminum foil to keep soft.

6. Peel poblanos, then slice thin. Separate onions into rings and chop coarse, then toss with poblanos. Remove steak from marinade, slice into 4- to 6-inch lengths, then slice thin against grain. Serve with warm tortillas, poblano-onion mixture, and lime wedges.

Indoor Steak Tacos

Serves 4

✓ **WHY THIS RECIPE WORKS:** For an indoor steak taco recipe that would yield tender, juicy meat, we chose beefy flank steak. Pan searing gave us the browned exterior and crisp edges characteristic of grilled meat. A deeply flavorful oil-based herb paste gave our steak a flavor boost. Serve with chopped tomatoes, chopped onion, and diced avocado.

½ cup fresh cilantro leaves, plus extra
    for serving
3 scallions, chopped coarse
3 garlic cloves, chopped coarse
1 jalapeño chile, stemmed and chopped
    coarse
½ teaspoon ground cumin
6 tablespoons vegetable oil
1 tablespoon lime juice
1 (1½- to 1¾-pound) flank steak, trimmed and
    sliced with grain into 4 pieces
    Salt and pepper
½ teaspoon sugar
12 (6-inch) corn tortillas, warmed
    Lime wedges

1. Pulse cilantro, scallions, garlic, jalapeño, and cumin in food processor until finely chopped, 10 to 12 pulses. Add ¼ cup oil and process until mixture is smooth, about 15 seconds, scraping down bowl as needed. Transfer 2 tablespoons herb paste to medium bowl and stir in lime juice; set aside for serving.

2. Using dinner fork, poke each piece of steak 10 to 12 times on each side. Place steaks in large baking dish, rub thoroughly with 1½ teaspoons salt, then coat with remaining herb paste. Cover and refrigerate for 30 minutes to 1 hour.

3. Scrape herb paste off steaks and sprinkle with sugar and ½ teaspoon pepper. Heat remaining 2 tablespoons oil in 12-inch nonstick skillet over medium-high heat until just smoking. Cook steaks, turning as needed, until well browned on all sides and meat registers 120 to 125 degrees (for medium-rare), 4 to 6 minutes. Transfer steaks to cutting board and let rest for 5 minutes.

4. Slice steaks thin against grain, add to bowl with reserved herb paste, and toss to coat. Season with salt and pepper to taste. Serve with warm tortillas, extra cilantro, and lime wedges.

LEARN HOW **INDOOR STEAK TACOS**

For ultraflavorful pan-seared steak, we coat the meat with a potent herb paste before and after cooking.

1. SEASON: Slice flank steak with grain, pierce strips with a fork, then season and coat with herb paste.

2. COOK: Cook the steak in a hot 12-inch nonstick skillet using a generous 2 tablespoons of oil.

3. SLICE: Slice the steaks thin against the grain, then toss with additional herb paste and lime.

Classic Ground Beef Tacos

Serves 4

✔ **WHY THIS RECIPE WORKS:** This Tex-Mex classic layers spicy ground beef, shredded cheese, sweet chopped tomatoes, and cool iceberg lettuce in a crunchy corn taco shell. But stale-tasting supermarket seasoning packets and greasy store-bought shells leave a lot to be desired. We set out to develop a ground beef taco recipe with boldly spiced beef and fresh toppings. For the filling, we sautéed onions and garlic with a variety of spices that provided both savory and spicy notes. Brown sugar and cider vinegar rounded out the flavor of the filling. Using very lean ground beef prevented greasiness and adding tomato sauce and chicken broth to the beef ensured that the meat was tender and juicy. Tomato sauce is sold in cans in the same aisle that carries canned whole tomatoes. Do not use jarred pasta sauce in its place. Serve with shredded cheese, shredded lettuce, chopped tomatoes, diced avocado, chopped cilantro, and Mexican crema or sour cream.

1	tablespoon vegetable oil
1	onion, chopped fine
2	tablespoons chili powder
3	garlic cloves, minced
1	teaspoon ground cumin
1	teaspoon ground coriander
½	teaspoon dried oregano
¼	teaspoon cayenne pepper
	Salt
1	pound 90 percent lean ground beef
½	cup canned tomato sauce
½	cup chicken broth
2	teaspoons cider vinegar
1	teaspoon packed light brown sugar
8	taco shells, warmed

1. Heat oil in 10-inch skillet over medium heat until shimmering. Add onion and cook until softened, about 5 minutes. Stir in chili powder, garlic, cumin, coriander, oregano, cayenne, and 1 teaspoon salt and cook until fragrant, about 30 seconds.

2. Stir in ground beef and cook, breaking up meat with wooden spoon, until no longer pink, about 5 minutes. Stir in tomato sauce, broth, vinegar, and sugar and simmer until thickened, about 10 minutes. Season with salt to taste. Divide filling evenly among taco shells and serve.

Homemade Taco Shells

MAKES 8

For the best results, use the taco shells immediately.

¾	cup vegetable oil
8	corn tortillas

1. In 8-inch skillet, heat vegetable oil to 350 degrees. Using tongs, slip half of tortilla into hot oil and submerge using metal spatula. Fry until just set, but not brown, about 30 seconds.

2. Flip tortilla. Hold tortilla open about 2 inches while keeping bottom submerged in oil. Fry until golden brown, about 1½ minutes. Flip again and fry other side until golden brown.

3. Transfer shell, upside down, to paper towel–lined baking sheet to drain. Repeat with remaining tortillas, keeping oil between 350 and 375 degrees. Serve.

TEST KITCHEN TIP **SHAPING TACO SHELLS**

To shape tortilla shell, hold tortilla with tongs and dip half into hot oil, submerging with metal spatula. Fry until just set, flip; fry on both sides until golden.

Ground Pork Tacos with Almonds and Raisins

Serves 4

✔ **WHY THIS RECIPE WORKS:** Sometimes we crave something a bit different from familiar spiced ground beef taco fillings. We wanted to develop a ground meat filling with a bit more pizzazz and authentic Mexican flavor, so we turned to *picadillo Oaxaqueño*, a Mexican preparation of tender ground pork with onions, raisins, and warm spices like cinnamon and cloves. The combination of contrasting flavors and textures creates a savory-sweet filling for empanadas, chiles rellenos, or tacos. To create a deeply aromatic backbone for the pork, we started by softening the onion, then adding the garlic and spices so that their flavors would bloom. After sautéing the pork briefly, we added a little chicken broth and tomato sauce for depth, along with the raisins. But tasters found the filling a bit cloying: We needed to rein in the combined sweetness of the pork, raisins, tomato sauce, and warm spices. We tried cutting down on the tomato sauce, but tasters missed the rich tomato flavor; in the end, a bit of cider vinegar and some smoky chipotle brought the flavors into focus and balanced the sweetness just enough. We added toasted almonds just before serving, which preserved their crunch and provided nutty flavor and textural contrast to our rich pork. Depending on the fat level of the ground pork, you may need to drain off some excess grease before adding the tomato sauce and broth. We prefer Homemade Taco Shells (page 87), but you can use your favorite store-bought shells. Serve with shredded cheese, shredded lettuce, chopped tomatoes, chopped onion, diced avocado, chopped cilantro, and Mexican crema or sour cream.

1 tablespoon vegetable oil
1 small onion, chopped fine
2 garlic cloves, minced
½ teaspoon minced canned chipotle chile in adobo sauce
½ teaspoon ground cinnamon
⅛ teaspoon ground cloves
1 pound ground pork
1 cup chicken broth
½ cup canned tomato sauce
2 tablespoons chopped raisins
1 tablespoon cider vinegar
  Salt and pepper
¼ cup slivered almonds, toasted
8 taco shells, warmed

1. Heat oil in 12-inch nonstick skillet over medium heat until shimmering. Add onion and cook until softened, 5 to 7 minutes. Stir in garlic, chipotle, cinnamon, and cloves and cook until fragrant, about 30 seconds. Stir in pork and cook, breaking up meat with wooden spoon, until no longer pink, about 5 minutes.

2. Stir in broth, tomato sauce, raisins, vinegar, ½ teaspoon salt, and ½ teaspoon pepper and simmer until thickened, about 10 minutes. Stir in almonds and season with salt and pepper to taste. Divide filling evenly among taco shells and serve.

Carnitas

Serves 6 to 8

✓ **WHY THIS RECIPE WORKS:** Spanish for "little meats," *carnitas*—Mexico's version of pulled pork—offers fall-apart-tender hunks of pork with lightly crisped, caramelized exteriors. Traditionally, the flavor of the pork takes center stage, subtly accented by earthy oregano and sour orange. The chunks of meat are often deep-fried in lard or oil, but this method is impractical and messy at home. We were able to replicate deep-fried taste and texture by braising the pork in a small amount of liquid, then reducing the liquid into a syrupy glaze and incorporating it back into the meat. Broiling the glazed pork pieces on a rack not only crisped the exterior, but also allowed the excess fat to drip off, preventing a greasy final dish. For the finishing touch, we refined our cooking liquid's flavors with a mixture of lime and orange juices (which emulated the flavor of sour oranges), along with bay leaves, cumin, and oregano. Adding the spent orange halves to the braising liquid deepened the orange flavor and offered subtle floral notes. This pork also tastes great as a topping for Tostadas, Sopes, Gorditas, and Panuchos (pages 104–115) or as a filling for Tamales (page 116). Boneless pork butt roast is often labeled Boston butt in the supermarket. Serve with chopped onion, diced avocado, and thinly sliced radish.

- 1 (3½- to 4-pound) boneless pork butt roast, fat cap trimmed to ⅛ inch thick and cut into 2-inch chunks
- 2 cups water
- 1 onion, peeled and halved
- 2 tablespoons lime juice
- 1 teaspoon dried oregano
- 1 teaspoon ground cumin
- 2 bay leaves
  Salt and pepper
- ⅓ cup fresh orange juice, spent orange halves reserved
- 18–24 (6-inch) corn tortillas, warmed
  Fresh cilantro leaves
  Lime wedges

1. Adjust oven rack to lower-middle position and heat oven to 300 degrees. Combine pork, water, onion, lime juice, oregano, cumin, bay leaves, 1 teaspoon salt, and ½ teaspoon pepper in Dutch oven (liquid should just barely cover meat). Add orange juice and spent orange halves to pot. Bring mixture to simmer over medium-high heat, stirring occasionally. Cover pot, transfer to oven, and cook until meat is soft and falls apart when prodded with fork, about 2 hours, flipping pieces of meat once during cooking.

2. Remove pot from oven and turn oven to broil. Using slotted spoon, transfer pork to bowl; discard orange halves, onion, and bay leaves (do not skim fat from liquid). Being careful of hot pot handles, place pot over high heat and simmer braising liquid, stirring often, until thick and syrupy, 8 to 12 minutes; you should have about 1 cup reduced liquid.

3. Transfer pork to cutting board and pull each piece in half using 2 forks. Return pork to bowl, fold in reduced liquid, and season with salt and pepper to taste. Spread pork in even layer on wire rack set in rimmed baking sheet. Broil pork until well browned (but not charred) and edges are slightly crisp on both sides, 10 to 16 minutes, flipping meat halfway through broiling. Serve with warm tortillas, cilantro, and lime wedges.

LEARN HOW **CARNITAS**

Traditionally, pork carnitas are fried in gallons of lard or oil to achieve a crisp, beautifully caramelized crust. But at home, deep frying pork in batches can be messy and time-consuming. For equally crisp carnitas that can be made in a home kitchen, we reduce our braising liquid to a glaze, then broil the glazed pork pieces.

1. MAKE BRAISING LIQUID, ADD POR K, AND SIMMER: Combine the pork, water, spices, onion halves, and lime juice in a Dutch oven. Juice the orange halves, then add the juice and the spent orange halves to the Dutch oven. Using the spent oranges in the braising liquid imparts floral notes that complement the pork.

2. TRANSFER PORK TO OVEN: Cover the pot and transfer to a 300-degree oven. Cook for 2 hours, flipping the pork once during cooking, until the pork is completely tender. The moist, even heat of oven-braising melts away the fat and connective tissue in the pork, resulting in ultratender meat.

3. REMOVE PORK AND REDUCE BRAISING LIQUID: Remove the pork from the pot and transfer it to a bowl. Reduce the braising liquid over high heat until a spatula leaves a trail when pulled through it. The flavorful braising liquid makes a deeply complex, concentrated glaze for the pork.

4. PULL APART PORK PIECES: Using two forks, pull each piece of pork in half. These smaller pieces have lots of surface area that can brown and crisp under the broiler.

5. TOSS GLAZE WITH PORK: Fold the reduced braising liquid into the pork. The glaze creates deeper flavor and crisper edges on the pork, since the sugars in the glaze caramelize in the oven.

6. BROIL PORK: Spread the pork in an even layer on a wire rack set in a rimmed baking sheet. Broil on the lower-middle rack until the meat is browned and crisp. Raising the meat up on a wire rack encourages excess fat to drip down, preventing greasy pork.

Tacos al Pastor

Serves 6

✔ **WHY THIS RECIPE WORKS:** The traditional pork filling for *tacos al pastor,* or "shepherd-style" tacos, is made from thin slices of chile-marinated pork that are tightly packed onto a vertical spit and roasted. The concept of the vertical rotisserie was brought to Mexico by Arab immigrants in the 19th century (the process is similar to shawarma), but the flavors are thoroughly Mexican. The pork is often topped with a whole pineapple, the juices of which drip down the meat and encourage the pork to caramelize. When the exterior is browned and crisp, thin shavings of the roasted pork and pineapple are carved off into a warm tortilla and then topped with garnishes that contrast with the rich meat: minced raw onion, cilantro, and a squeeze of fresh lime. Of course, most home cooks don't own a vertical rotisserie, so we set out to translate this ultraflavorful taco filling for the American home kitchen. We started off with traditional pork shoulder; its rich marbling created good flavor and helped to keep the pork tender. To infuse the pork with our guajillo chile–tomato marinade, we braised ½-inch-thick slabs (the thinnest we could reasonably create with a chef's knife) in the marinade until they were tender and juicy. To replicate the crisp, browned exterior of authentic versions, we grilled the slabs over a hot fire. Basting the pork with the braising liquid, which was rich with the rendered pork drippings, made the meat ultratender. A few grilled pineapple rounds made a perfect traditional garnish. Boneless pork butt is often labeled Boston butt in the supermarket. This pork also tastes great as a topping for Tostadas, Sopes, Gorditas, and Panuchos (pages 104–115) or as a filling for Tamales (page 116). Serve with chopped onion, diced avocado, chopped cilantro, and thinly sliced radish.

12	dried guajillo chiles, stemmed, seeded and torn into ½-inch pieces (1½ cups)
1½	cups water
1¼	pounds plum tomatoes, cored and quartered
8	garlic cloves, peeled
4	bay leaves
	Salt and pepper
¾	teaspoon sugar
½	teaspoon ground cumin
⅛	teaspoon ground cloves
3	pounds boneless pork butt roast, fat cap trimmed to ¼ inch thick and sliced against grain into ½-inch-thick slabs
1	lime, cut into 8 wedges
½	pineapple, peeled, cored and cut into ½-inch-thick rings
	Vegetable oil
18	(6-inch) corn tortillas
½	cup chopped fresh cilantro

1. Toast guajillos in Dutch oven over medium heat, stirring frequently, until fragrant, 2 to 6 minutes. Stir in water, tomatoes, garlic, bay leaves, 2 teaspoons salt, ½ teaspoon pepper, sugar, cumin, and cloves. Increase heat to medium-high and bring to simmer. Cover, reduce heat to low, and simmer, stirring occasionally, until guajillos are softened and tomatoes mash easily, about 20 minutes.

2. Transfer mixture to blender and process until smooth, about 1 minute. Strain puree through fine-mesh strainer, pressing on solids to extract as much liquid as possible; discard solids and return puree to pot.

3. Add pork to pot, submerge in sauce, and bring to simmer over medium heat. Partially cover, reduce heat, and gently simmer until pork is tender but still holds together, 1½ to 1¾ hours, flipping and rearranging pork halfway through cooking. (Pork and sauce can be refrigerated for up to 2 days.)

4. Transfer pork to large plate, season both sides with salt, and cover tightly with aluminum foil. Whisk sauce to combine. Transfer ½ cup to bowl for grilling. Pour off all but ½ cup sauce left in pot (reserve excess sauce for another use). Squeeze 2 lime wedges into sauce in pot and add spent lime wedges; season with salt to taste. Brush pineapple with oil and season with salt.

5A. FOR A CHARCOAL GRILL: Open bottom vent completely. Light large chimney starter filled with charcoal briquettes (6 quarts). When top coals are partially covered with ash, pour evenly over grill. Set cooking grate in place, cover, and open lid vent completely. Heat grill until hot, about 5 minutes.

5B. FOR A GAS GRILL: Turn all burners to high, cover, and heat grill until hot, about 15 minutes. Turn all burners to medium.

6. Clean and oil cooking grate. Place pineapple on grill and cook, turning as needed, until softened and caramelized, 10 to 15 minutes; transfer to cutting board. Meanwhile, brush 1 side of pork with ¼ cup reserved sauce, then place on grill, sauce side down. Cook until well browned and crisp, 5 to 7 minutes. Repeat with second side using remaining ¼ cup reserved sauce; transfer to cutting board and tent with foil.

7. Working in batches, grill tortillas, turning as needed, until warm and soft, about 30 seconds; wrap tightly in foil to keep soft.

8. Chop pineapple and transfer to serving bowl. Using tongs to steady pork, slice each piece crosswise into ⅛-inch pieces. Bring sauce left in pot to simmer over medium heat. Off heat, add sliced pork and toss to coat with sauce. Serve with tortillas, cilantro, pineapple, and remaining 6 lime wedges.

LEARN HOW **TACOS AL PASTOR**

To imitate the tender pork and caramelized exterior of traditional vertical-roasted versions, we braise and grill thin slices of pork.

1. BRAISE: Add the pork to the pot; bring to a simmer. Partially cover, reduce the heat, and gently simmer until the pork is tender but still holds together. Braising infuses the pork with deep flavor.

2. GRILL: To get crisp, browned pork, brush one side of the pork with ¼ cup of the reserved sauce, then grill, sauce side down, until browned and crisp. Repeat on the second side.

3. COMBINE WITH SAUCE: Bring the sauce left in the pot to a simmer. Off the heat, add the grilled, sliced pork and toss to coat with the sauce.

Easy Chipotle Chicken Tacos

Serves 4

✔ **WHY THIS RECIPE WORKS:** Much of the appeal of traditional tacos is their essential simplicity. While we love braised, slow-cooked taco fillings, sometimes we want simple chicken tacos that we can make at home any night of the week. Boneless, skinless breasts were a convenient place to start, and poaching proved to be the easiest way to imbue them with flavor. To build our poaching liquid, we started by sautéing chipotle chile in adobo and garlic for a smoky, savory flavor base. Sautéing our aromatic ingredients in butter instead of oil added richness to the lean breast meat. We then added orange juice for citrusy freshness, cilantro for a pleasant herbal note, and Worcestershire for savory depth. Once the chicken was finished cooking, our poaching liquid pulled double duty: We reduced it to a sauce. A bit of mustard thickened the sauce and provided a sharp counterpoint to the sweet orange juice. Finally, we shredded and sauced the chicken; warm tortillas and a few basic toppings completed our tacos. Serve with shredded cheese, shredded lettuce, chopped tomatoes, diced avocado, and Mexican crema or sour cream.

3	tablespoons unsalted butter
4	garlic cloves, minced
2	teaspoons minced canned chipotle chile in adobo sauce
¾	cup chopped fresh cilantro
½	cup orange juice
1	tablespoon Worcestershire sauce
1½	pounds boneless, skinless chicken breasts, trimmed
1	teaspoon yellow mustard
	Salt and pepper
12	(6-inch) corn tortillas, warmed
	Lime wedges

1. Melt butter in 12-inch skillet over medium-high heat. Add garlic and chipotle and cook until fragrant, about 30 seconds. Stir in ½ cup cilantro, orange juice, and Worcestershire and bring to simmer. Nestle chicken into sauce. Cover, reduce heat to medium-low, and cook until chicken registers 160 degrees, 10 to 15 minutes, flipping chicken halfway through cooking. Transfer chicken to plate and cover.

2. Increase heat to medium-high and cook liquid left in skillet until reduced to ¼ cup, about 5 minutes. Off heat, whisk in mustard. Using 2 forks, shred chicken into bite-size pieces and return to skillet. Add remaining ¼ cup cilantro and toss until well combined. Season with salt and pepper to taste. Serve with warm tortillas and lime wedges.

TEST KITCHEN TIP **SHREDDING CHICKEN**

Using 2 forks, insert tines into meat and gently pull forks away from each other, breaking meat apart and into bite-size strands.

TEST KITCHEN TIP **WARMING TORTILLAS**

Stack tortillas on plate, cover with damp dish towel, and microwave for 60 to 90 seconds.

Grilled Chicken Tacos with Salsa Verde

Serves 4

✔ **WHY THIS RECIPE WORKS:** Simple grilled chicken, which cooks up quickly with a nice, smoky char, makes a perfect taco filling, especially when accompanied by a piquant green tomatillo salsa. Since it would be paired with other flavorful elements, we found that our chicken needed only a brief stint in a garlic-lime marinade before being grilled over a hot fire. A bit of salt and sugar in our marinade kept the chicken moist as it cooked and rounded out its flavor nicely. To complement the smoky, charred notes of the chicken, we decided to grill some of the salsa ingredients as well: sliced onion, a jalapeño chile, and half of the tomatillos cooked at the same rate as the chicken. We pulsed our grilled vegetables with additional raw tomatillos, which provided tart, citrusy notes, as well as fresh cilantro, lime juice, and garlic for freshness and bite. As a final touch, we grilled our tortillas briefly to warm and lightly char them. Serve with diced avocado and sliced radishes.

¼	cup vegetable oil
3	tablespoons lime juice (2 limes)
2	tablespoons water
	Sugar
	Salt and pepper
5	cloves garlic, minced
1½	pounds boneless, skinless chicken breasts, trimmed
1	onion, peeled and cut into ½-inch-thick rounds
1	jalapeño chile, stemmed, halved, and seeded
1	pound tomatillos, husks and stems removed, rinsed well and dried
12	(6-inch) corn tortillas
½	cup chopped fresh cilantro

1. Whisk 3 tablespoons oil, 1 tablespoon lime juice, water, 1 teaspoon sugar, 1½ teaspoons salt, ½ teaspoon pepper, and half of garlic together in medium bowl. Add chicken, cover, and refrigerate, turning occasionally, for 30 minutes. Brush onion, jalapeño, and half of tomatillos with remaining 1 tablespoon oil and season with salt. Halve remaining tomatillos; set aside.

2A. FOR A CHARCOAL GRILL: Open bottom vent completely. Light large chimney starter filled with charcoal briquettes (6 quarts). When top coals are partially covered with ash, pour evenly over grill. Set cooking grate in place, cover, and open lid vent completely. Heat grill until hot, about 5 minutes.

2B. FOR A GAS GRILL: Turn all burners to high, cover, and heat grill until hot, about 15 minutes. Leave all burners on high.

3. Clean and oil cooking grate. Place chicken and oiled vegetables on grill. Cook (covered if using gas), turning as needed, until chicken registers 160 degrees and vegetables are lightly charred and soft, 10 to 15 minutes. Transfer chicken and vegetables to cutting board and tent with aluminum foil.

4. Working in batches, grill tortillas, turning as needed, until warm and soft, about 30 seconds; wrap tightly in foil to keep soft.

5. Chop grilled vegetables coarse, then pulse with remaining tomatillos, cilantro, remaining garlic, remaining 2 tablespoons lime juice, ½ teaspoon salt, and pinch sugar in food processor until slightly chunky, 16 to 18 pulses. Slice chicken thin on bias and serve with tortillas and tomatillo salsa.

Baja Fish Tacos with Pickled Onion and Cabbage

Serves 6

✓ **WHY THIS RECIPE WORKS:** In Baja, battered and fried fish tacos are a common taco stand offering. We wanted a simple version with a perfect balance of flavors and textures: tender whitefish encased in a crisp coating and simply adorned with toppings like crunchy shredded cabbage and cooling crema. An ultrathin beer batter made with flour, cornstarch, and baking powder proved to be ideal for getting a light, crispy coating on the fish. Quick-pickled onions and jalapeños added tart spiciness, and tossing shredded cabbage with the pickling liquid added flavor without overcomplicating the dish. Light-bodied American lagers, such as Budweiser, work best here. Cut the fish on a slight bias if your fillets aren't quite 4 inches wide; you should end up with about 24 pieces of fish.

2   **pounds skinless whitefish fillets, such as cod, haddock, or halibut, cut crosswise into 4 by 1-inch strips**
    Salt and pepper
¾   **cup all-purpose flour**
¼   **cup cornstarch**
1   **teaspoon baking powder**
1   **cup beer**
1   **quart peanut or vegetable oil**
18   **(6-inch) corn tortillas, warmed**
1   **cup fresh cilantro leaves**
1   **cup Mexican crema**
1   **recipe Pickled Onion and Cabbage (recipe follows)**

1. Adjust oven rack to middle position and heat oven to 200 degrees. Set wire rack in rimmed baking sheet. Pat fish dry with paper towels and season with salt and pepper. Whisk flour, cornstarch, baking powder, and 1 teaspoon salt together in large bowl. Add beer and whisk until smooth. Add fish to batter and toss to coat evenly.

2. Add oil to large Dutch oven until it measures about ¾ inch deep and heat over medium-high heat to 350 degrees.

3. Remove 5 or 6 pieces of fish from batter, allowing excess to drip back into bowl, and add to hot oil, briefly dragging fish along surface of oil to prevent sticking. Adjust burner, if necessary, to maintain oil temperature between 325 and 350 degrees. Fry fish, stirring gently to prevent pieces from sticking together and turning as needed, until golden brown and crisp, about 8 minutes.

4. Transfer fish to prepared wire rack and place in oven to keep warm. Return oil to 350 degrees and repeat with remaining fish, working with 5 or 6 pieces at a time. Serve with warm tortillas, cilantro, crema, and Pickled Onion and Cabbage.

Pickled Onion and Cabbage
SERVES 6

1   **small red onion, halved and sliced thin**
2   **jalapeño chiles, stemmed and sliced into thin rings**
1   **cup white wine vinegar**
2   **tablespoons lime juice**
1   **tablespoon sugar**
    Salt and pepper
3   **cups shredded green cabbage**

Combine onion and jalapeños in medium bowl. Bring vinegar, lime juice, sugar, and 1 teaspoon salt to boil in small saucepan. Pour vinegar mixture over onion mixture and let sit for at least 30 minutes, or refrigerate for up to 2 days. Transfer ¼ cup pickling liquid to second medium bowl, add cabbage, ½ teaspoon salt, and ½ teaspoon pepper and toss to combine.

Grilled Shrimp Tacos with Jícama Slaw

Serves 6

✔ **WHY THIS RECIPE WORKS:** We wanted a fresh-tasting, easy-to-make taco featuring grilled Mexican-spiced shrimp. But delicate shrimp can turn from tender to rubbery in the blink of an eye—especially when grilled. Although their shells can shield them from the heat, any seasonings are stripped off along with the shells when it's time to eat. We decided to go with peeled shrimp, and coated them with an ultraflavorful spice rub. We crammed several extra-large shrimp together on each skewer, which protected them from overcooking. For a lively slaw to accompany our spicy shrimp, we started by thinly slicing delicately flavored and crunchy jícama, and tossed it with tangy orange juice, bold red onion, and bright cilantro leaves. You will need four 12-inch metal skewers for this recipe. To cut the jícama, use the shredding disk of a food processor, a V-slicer, or a sharp chef's knife. Serve with chopped onion, diced avocado, and thinly sliced radishes.

- 1 **pound jícama, peeled and cut into 3-inch-long matchsticks**
- 1 **teaspoon grated orange zest plus ⅓ cup juice**
- ¼ **cup thinly sliced red onion**
- 3 **tablespoons chopped fresh cilantro Salt**
- 3 **tablespoons vegetable oil**
- 1 **tablespoon minced fresh oregano or 1 teaspoon dried**
- 2 **teaspoons chipotle chile powder**
- 1 **teaspoon garlic powder**
- 2 **pounds extra-large shrimp (21 to 25 per pound), peeled, deveined, and tails removed**
- 18 **(6-inch) corn tortillas**
- 1 **cup Mexican crema Lime wedges**

1. Combine jícama, orange zest and juice, onion, cilantro, and ½ teaspoon salt in bowl, cover, and refrigerate until ready to serve.

2. Whisk oil, oregano, chile powder, garlic powder, and ½ teaspoon salt together in large bowl. Pat shrimp dry with paper towels, add to spice mixture, and toss to coat. Thread shrimp onto four 12-inch metal skewers, alternating direction of heads and tails.

3A. FOR A CHARCOAL GRILL: Open bottom vent completely. Light large chimney starter mounded with charcoal briquettes (7 quarts). When top coals are partially covered with ash, pour evenly over grill. Set cooking grate in place, cover, and open lid vent completely. Heat grill until hot, about 5 minutes.

3B. FOR A GAS GRILL: Turn all burners to high, cover, and heat grill until hot, about 15 minutes. Leave all burners on high.

4. Clean and oil cooking grate. Place shrimp on grill and cook (covered if using gas) until lightly charred on first side, about 4 minutes. Flip shrimp, pushing them together on skewer if they separate, and cook until opaque throughout, about 2 minutes. Transfer to platter and cover with aluminum foil.

5. Working in batches, grill tortillas, turning as needed, until warm and soft, about 30 seconds; wrap tightly in foil to keep soft.

6. Slide shrimp off skewers onto cutting board and cut into ½-inch pieces. Serve with tortillas, jícama slaw, crema, and lime wedges.

TEST KITCHEN TIP

SKEWERING SHRIMP FOR THE GRILL

Thread shrimp onto 4 skewers, alternating direction of heads and tails.

Grilled Fish Tacos
Serves 6

☑ **WHY THIS RECIPE WORKS:** In the Yucatán Peninsula, far from the battered-and-fried-fish taco stands of Baja, another style of fish taco is popular: grilled fish tacos. Traditionally, a whole fish is split in half lengthwise, bathed in a chile-citrus marinade, and grilled. The flavor-packed fish is eaten with tortillas and some simple sides. We wanted grilled fish tacos featuring a similarly bold flavor profile, but a simpler approach—no dealing with whole, skin-on fish. Although traditional recipes use whole snapper or grouper, we found that swordfish was easier to find, stood up well to flipping on the grill, and steaks that were 1 inch thick spent enough time on the grill to pick up plenty of flavorful char before the interior cooked through. Cutting the fish into 1-inch-wide strips meant that the fish could go from grill to taco with minimal additional prep. We created a flavorful paste from ancho and chipotle chile powders, oregano, and ground coriander, which we bloomed in oil to bring out their flavors. Tomato paste provided a savory-sweet punch. To replicate the flavor of traditional sour oranges, we used a combination of lime and orange juices. A fresh pineapple salsa was the perfect accompaniment to our spicy, earthy fish. Grouper, mahi mahi, and snapper fillets are all suitable substitutes for the swordfish. To ensure the best results, buy 1-inch-thick fillets. The recipe for the pineapple salsa makes more than is needed for the tacos; leftovers can be refrigerated for up to 2 days. Serve with shredded lettuce, diced avocado, and lime wedges.

3	tablespoons vegetable oil
1	tablespoon ancho chile powder
2	teaspoons chipotle chile powder
2	garlic cloves, minced
1	teaspoon dried oregano
1	teaspoon ground coriander
	Salt
2	tablespoons tomato paste
½	cup orange juice
6	tablespoons lime juice (3 limes)
2	pounds skinless swordfish steaks, 1 inch thick, cut lengthwise into 1-inch thick strips
1	pineapple, peeled, quartered lengthwise, cored, and each quarter halved lengthwise
1	jalapeño chile
18	(6-inch) corn tortillas
1	red bell pepper, stemmed, seeded, and cut into ¼-inch pieces
2	tablespoons minced fresh cilantro, plus extra for serving

1. Heat 2 tablespoons oil, ancho chile powder, and chipotle chile powder in 8-inch skillet over medium heat, stirring constantly, until fragrant and some bubbles form, 2 to 3 minutes. Add garlic, oregano, coriander, and 1 teaspoon salt and continue to cook until fragrant, about 30 seconds. Add tomato paste and, using spatula, mash tomato paste with spice mixture until combined, about 20 seconds. Stir in orange juice and 2 tablespoons lime juice. Cook, stirring constantly, until thoroughly mixed and reduced slightly, about 2 minutes. Transfer chile mixture to large bowl and let cool for 15 minutes.

2. Add swordfish to chile mixture and stir gently to coat. Cover and refrigerate for at least 30 minutes or up to 2 hours. Brush pineapple and jalapeño with remaining 1 tablespoon oil.

3A. FOR A CHARCOAL GRILL: Open bottom vent completely. Light large chimney starter mounded with charcoal briquettes (7 quarts). When top coals are partially covered with ash, pour evenly over grill. Set cooking grate in place, cover, and open lid vent completely. Heat grill until hot, about 5 minutes.

3B. FOR A GAS GRILL: Turn all burners to high, cover, and heat grill until hot, about 15 minutes. Turn all burners to medium-high.

4. Clean and oil cooking grate. Place fish, pineapple, and jalapeño on grill. Cover and cook until fish, pineapple, and jalapeño have begun to brown, 3 to 5 minutes. Using thin spatula, turn fish, pineapple, and jalapeño. Cover and cook until pineapple and jalapeño are well browned and swordfish registers 140 degrees, 3 to 5 minutes; transfer to platter and cover with aluminum foil.

5. Working in batches, grill tortillas, turning as needed, until warm and soft, about 30 seconds; wrap tightly in foil to keep soft.

6. Chop pineapple and jalapeño fine and combine with bell pepper, cilantro, and remaining 4 tablespoons lime juice in bowl. Season with salt to taste. Using 2 forks, pull fish apart into large flakes and serve with pineapple salsa and tortillas.

LEARN HOW **GRILLED FISH TACOS**

Marinating our fish in a chile-citrus mixture and grilling both the fish and the salsa ingredients give our tacos greath depth of flavor.

1. BLOOM AROMATICS FOR MARINADE: Heat the chile powders in oil until fragrant. Add garlic, oregano, and coriander, then mash in tomato paste with a spatula.

2. MAKE CHILE MARINADE: After cooking the spices and tomato paste, stir in lime and orange juices and reduce slightly.

3. MARINATE FISH: Toss the swordfish with the cooled chile marinade and refrigerate for at least 30 minutes or up to 2 hours.

4. GRILL FISH, PINEAPPLE, AND JALAPEÑO: Place the fish, pineapple, and jalapeño on the grill and cook until they are well-browned on both sides.

5. GRILL TORTILLAS: Working in batches, grill the tortillas until they're warm and soft; wrap them tightly in foil to keep them soft.

6. MAKE SALSA: Finely chop the pineapple and jalapeño; combine with the bell pepper, cilantro, and lime juice. Season with salt to taste.

Tostadas

Makes 12 tostadas; serves 4 to 6

✔ **WHY THIS RECIPE WORKS:** Tostadas are flat, crisped tortillas that serve as a crunchy base for rich, flavorful toppings. Much like tacos, tostadas are eaten as snacks in Mexico. Homemade tostada shells are far better than store-bought, and they're easy to make. We poked a few holes in each tortilla with a fork so that they wouldn't puff up when we fried them. We liked the crunch that the larger crystals of kosher salt added. Look for fresh, locally made tortillas (choose the thinnest brand your market sells), or make your own (see page 80). We prefer the flavor of peanut oil when deep-frying, but vegetable or corn oil will also work well.

12   **(6-inch) corn tortillas**
¾   **cup peanut oil**
     Kosher salt
1   **recipe topping (pages 106–107), warmed**

1. Using fork, poke center of each tortilla 3 or 4 times (to prevent puffing and allow for even cooking). Heat oil in 8-inch skillet over medium heat to 350 degrees. Line baking sheet with several layers of paper towels.

2. Working with 1 tortilla at a time, add to hot oil and place metal potato masher on top to keep tortilla flat and submerged in oil. Fry until crisp and lightly browned, 45 to 60 seconds (no flipping is necessary). Transfer fried tortilla to prepared baking sheet. Repeat with remaining tortillas. Sprinkle with salt. (Tostadas can be stored at room temperature for up to 1 day.)

3. Spoon filling onto center of each tostada and serve.

Baked Tostadas

Spray tortillas thoroughly with vegetable oil spray and spread out over 2 rimmed baking sheets. Bake on upper-middle and lower-middle racks in 450-degree oven until lightly browned and crisp, about 10 minutes, switching and rotating sheets halfway through baking. Sprinkle lightly with salt.

LEARN HOW **FRIED TOSTADAS**

Frying tostadas makes them extraordinarily crisp and crunchy.

1. POKE TOSTADAS: Using a fork, poke the center of each tortilla 3 or 4 times to prevent puffing.

2. FRY TOSTADAS: Add a tortilla to the hot oil and submerge with a metal potato masher. Fry until crisp and browned.

3. SPRINKLE WITH SALT: After all the tortillas have been fried, sprinkle them lightly with salt.

TOPPINGS AND FILLINGS FOR TOSTADAS, SOPES, GORDITAS, AND PANUCHOS

Whether being used to fill a taco, top a panucho, or stuff a gordita, savory fillings or toppings complete many a Mexican dish. Although the combinations are endlessly variable, these four are among our favorites. Simple yet full of flavor, each of these versatile recipes will make enough for 12 Tostadas, Sopes, Gorditas, or Panuchos (pages 104–115).

Spicy Zucchini with Scallions and Cotija Cheese

1	tablespoon vegetable oil
1	small onion, chopped fine
1	serrano chile, stemmed, seeded, and minced
2	tablespoons tomato paste
3	garlic cloves, minced
½	teaspoon dried oregano
1	cup vegetable broth
	Salt and pepper
1	pound zucchini, cut into ½-inch pieces
1	tablespoon chopped fresh cilantro
2	scallions, sliced thin
4	ounces Cotija cheese, crumbled (1 cup)

1. Heat oil in 12-inch nonstick skillet over medium heat until shimmering. Add onion and serrano and cook until lightly browned, about 8 minutes. Stir in tomato paste, garlic, and oregano and cook until fragrant, about 1 minute. Stir in broth, 1 teaspoon salt, and ½ teaspoon pepper and simmer until slightly thickened, about 6 minutes.

2. Stir in zucchini, cover, and cook until zucchini is slightly softened, 5 to 7 minutes. Uncover, increase heat to medium-high, and cook, stirring often, until sauce has thickened and coats zucchini, about 4 minutes. Off heat, stir in cilantro and season with salt and pepper to taste. Garnish with scallions and Cotija.

Chicken with Pickled Onion and Cabbage

2	tablespoons vegetable oil
1	small onion, chopped fine
1	tablespoon ancho chile powder
2	garlic cloves, minced
½	teaspoon dried oregano
½	teaspoon grated lime zest plus 1 tablespoon juice
	Salt and pepper
½	cup chicken broth
1	pound boneless, skinless chicken breasts, trimmed
1	tablespoon chopped fresh cilantro
1	avocado, halved, pitted, and sliced thin
1	recipe Pickled Onion and Cabbage (page 99)
2	ounces queso fresco, crumbled (½ cup)

1. Heat oil in medium saucepan over medium heat until shimmering. Add onion and cook until softened, about 4 minutes. Stir in chile powder, garlic, oregano, lime zest, and pinch salt and cook for 30 seconds. Stir in broth and bring to simmer. Nestle chicken into sauce. Cover, reduce heat to medium-low, and cook until chicken registers 160 degrees, 10 to 15 minutes, flipping halfway through cooking.

2. Transfer chicken to carving board and let cool slightly. Using 2 forks, shred chicken into small pieces. Return sauce to high heat and simmer until thickened, about 5 minutes. Off heat, stir in shredded chicken, lime juice, and cilantro and season with salt and pepper to taste. Garnish with avocado, Pickled Onion and Cabbage, and queso fresco.

Tomatillo Chicken with Radishes and Queso Fresco

1	pound fresh tomatillos, husks and stems removed, rinsed well and dried
½	small onion, chopped
1	jalapeño chile, stemmed, halved, and seeded
1	garlic clove, peeled
1	teaspoon vegetable oil
¾	cup fresh cilantro leaves plus ¼ cup chopped
¼	cup chicken broth
1	tablespoon lime juice
	Salt and pepper
1	pound boneless, skinless chicken breasts, trimmed
4	radishes, sliced thin
4	ounces queso fresco, crumbled (1 cup)

1. Adjust oven rack 6 inches from broiler element and heat broiler. Line rimmed baking sheet with aluminum foil. Toss tomatillos, onion, jalapeño, and garlic with oil and spread over prepared sheet. Broil, shaking sheet occasionally, until vegetables are well charred, 10 to 12 minutes.

2. Transfer broiled vegetables to food processor and let cool slightly. Add cilantro, broth, lime juice, and ¼ teaspoon salt and pulse until coarsely chopped, about 7 pulses. Transfer to 10-inch nonstick skillet, season with salt to taste, and bring to simmer.

3. Nestle chicken into sauce. Cover, reduce heat to medium-low, and cook until chicken registers 160 degrees, 10 to 15 minutes, flipping halfway through cooking. Transfer chicken to carving board and let cool slightly. Using 2 forks, shred chicken into small pieces. Toss chicken with sauce left in pan and season with salt and pepper to taste. Garnish with radishes, queso fresco, and cilantro.

Pork Tinga with Avocado and Queso Fresco

2	pounds boneless pork butt roast, trimmed and cut into 1-inch pieces
2	onions (1 quartered, 1 chopped fine)
5	garlic cloves (3 peeled and smashed, 2 minced)
4	sprigs fresh thyme
	Salt
2	tablespoons olive oil
½	teaspoon dried oregano
1	(15-ounce) can tomato sauce
1	tablespoon minced canned chipotle chile in adobo sauce
2	bay leaves
1	avocado, halved, pitted, and diced
2	ounces queso fresco, crumbled (½ cup)
¼	cup fresh cilantro leaves
	Lime wedges

1. Bring pork, quartered onion, smashed garlic, thyme sprigs, 1 teaspoon salt, and 6 cups water to simmer in large saucepan over medium-high heat, skimming off any foam that rises to surface. Reduce heat to medium-low, partially cover, and cook until pork is tender, 1¼ to 1½ hours.

2. Drain pork, reserving 1 cup cooking liquid. Discard onion, garlic, and thyme. Return pork to now-empty saucepan and mash into rough ½-inch pieces using potato masher. (Pork can be refrigerated for up to 2 days.)

3. Heat oil in 12-inch nonstick skillet over medium-high heat until shimmering. Add oregano, shredded pork, and chopped onion and cook, stirring often, until pork is well browned and crisp, 7 to 10 minutes. Stir in minced garlic and cook until fragrant, about 30 seconds. Stir in tomato sauce, chipotle, bay leaves, and reserved pork cooking liquid and simmer until almost all liquid has evaporated, 5 to 7 minutes. Discard bay leaves and season with salt to taste. Garnish with avocado, queso fresco, cilantro, and lime wedges.

Sopes

Makes 12 sopes; serves 4 to 6

✔ **WHY THIS RECIPE WORKS:** *Sopes* are small, savory tarts, traditionally served for dinner with endlessly variable fillings. The sopes shells are made with the same ingredients used to make tortillas, although they are thicker and have a rimmed edge to hold the fillings. The key to this recipe was to create a dough that was easy to shape, fry, and fill. For the base of the dough, we turned to masa harina. For the water, we found that slightly less than a 1:1 ratio of water to masa harina gave us the perfect texture: malleable enough to handle, but not over-hydrated and sticky. Traditionally, the dough is flattened like a tortilla and cooked on an ungreased cast-iron pan called a *comal*. The edges are then pinched up and, finally, the sopes are shallow-fried. Handling hot dough was a nonstarter for us; we wanted to find an easier and less painful way. We started by making flat, thick tortillas; although some recipes used a tortilla press to flatten the dough, we preferred the equally common method of pressing the dough with a pie plate. This allowed us to see our progress through the plate's clear bottom, and also made it less likely that we would press the dough too thin. We then pinched the raw dough to create rimmed edges. Putting the raw shells directly in the frying oil produced exceedingly greasy results with either a doughy or overly crisp texture. Our simple solution was to parcook the shells in a dry skillet before frying. This gave us the crispy outside and tender inside we were looking for. Be sure to use masa harina or Maseca Brand Instant Masa Corn Flour. We like to use a straight-sided sauté pan here because it makes frying the sopes in step 5 a little easier; however, a 12-inch skillet can be substituted. Any type of refried beans will work well here; if you want to make your own, see the recipes on page 293.

2	cups (8 ounces) masa harina
1	teaspoon salt
1¾	cups hot tap water
2	cups vegetable oil
1	cup refried beans
1	recipe filling (pages 106–107), warmed

1. Mix masa harina and salt in medium bowl, then fold in water with rubber spatula. Using your hands, knead mixture in bowl until soft dough forms, 1 to 2 minutes. Cover dough with damp dish towel and let sit for 5 minutes.

2. Line baking sheet with parchment paper. Cut sides of 1-quart zipper-lock bag, leaving bottom seam intact. Knead dough briefly, then divide into 12 equal pieces, roll into balls, and place on prepared sheet. Cover dough with damp dish towel.

3. Working with 1 piece dough at a time, place on 1 side of zipper-lock bag and fold other side over top. Press dough flat into 3½-inch-wide disk using pie plate. Remove plastic from top and pinch dough around edges as needed to create ¾-inch-tall sides. Remove plastic from bottom of sope, return sope to baking sheet, and cover with damp dish towel.

4. Adjust oven rack to middle position and heat oven to 200 degrees. Heat 11-inch straight-sided sauté pan over medium heat until hot, 2 to 3 minutes. Carefully place 6 sopes in hot, dry pan. Using paper towels, press lightly in center of each sope to ensure contact with pan. Cook until bottoms begin to brown, 4 to 5 minutes; return to baking sheet (do not cover). Repeat with remaining sopes. (Sopes can be wrapped tightly in plastic wrap and frozen for up to 3 months; thaw completely before continuing.)

5. Line baking sheet with paper towels. Carefully add oil to now-empty pan and heat over medium-high heat to 375 degrees. Add 6 sopes, browned side down, and fry until bottom is crisp and golden, 2 to 3 minutes, adjusting heat as needed to maintain oil temperature of 325 to 350 degrees. Gently flip sopes and fry until sides are crisp and golden (center of sopes will not brown), 2 to 3 minutes.

6. Transfer sopes upright to prepared sheet and dab with paper towels to remove excess oil; keep warm in oven. Repeat with remaining sopes. Spread refried beans evenly into center of sopes, then top with filling and serve.

LEARN HOW **SOPES**
The rimmed edges on these small, savory tarts hold in the fillings.

1. MAKE DOUGH: Mix the masa harina and salt in a bowl, then fold in the water. Knead the mixture until a soft dough forms, 1 to 2 minutes. Cover the dough with a damp dish towel and let it sit for 5 minutes.

2. PORTION DOUGH: Knead the dough briefly, then divide it into 12 equal pieces using a chef's knife. Roll the dough into balls and cover them with a damp dish towel to prevent them from drying out.

3. FLATTEN DOUGH INTO DISKS: Working with one piece of dough at a time, press flat into a 3½-inch-wide disk between a split-open zipper-lock bag using a pie plate.

4. PINCH TO CREATE RIMMED EDGE: Remove the plastic and pinch the dough around the edges as needed to create ¾-inch-tall sides; place the sope on the baking sheet and cover with a damp dish towel.

5. BROWN SOPES: Working in batches, cook the sopes in a dry sauté pan over medium heat, pressing the centers lightly with paper towels, until the bottoms begin to brown, 4 to 5 minutes. Return sopes to the baking sheet.

6. FRY SOPES: Heat oil in the now-empty pan. Working in batches, fry the sopes in oil until they are golden and crisp on both sides, 4 to 6 minutes, flipping them over halfway through cooking.

Gorditas

Makes 12 gorditas; serves 4 to 6

✓ **WHY THIS RECIPE WORKS:** A *gordita*, literally meaning "little fat one" in Spanish, is a traditional Mexican dish that is often eaten as a midday snack. The puffy shells are opened like pockets and can be stuffed with a wide assortment of cheese, meat, vegetables, or other fillings. Getting the cooking method right was essential to achieving the pocket that defines gorditas. Typically, the thick tortilla-like dough gets cooked twice: First, the flat tortillas are browned to develop flavor and achieve a crust on the exterior. Then, the tortillas are deep-fried. The moisture in the dough turns to steam, which expands and puffs the tortilla, creating a hollow pocket inside the gordita. The gorditas are then opened up and stuffed. We started by making a thick corn tortilla using masa harina. Using just the right amount of water ensured a well-hydrated dough that wasn't too dry and crumbly or too moist and sticky. After dividing the dough and pressing it into tortillas, we found that it was essential to smooth out the edges of the dough to eliminate any small cracks that had developed during flattening. This ensured that air got trapped in the tortillas during the frying step, which meant that they could puff properly. We then turned our attention to cooking the tortillas. For the initial browning step, using a hot pan was important; the heat created a golden crust on the exterior before the interior had a chance to dry out. Next, we deep-fried the browned tortillas so that they puffed up nicely. The soft, almost creamy centers were perfectly complemented by the crisp, crunchy exteriors; a rich, flavorful filling completed our gorditas. When smoothing out the edges of the flattened tortillas, make sure you press just enough to eliminate cracks, but not hard enough to form a rim. Be sure to use masa harina or Maseca Brand Instant Masa Corn Flour. We like to use a straight-sided sauté pan here because it makes frying the gorditas in step 5 a little easier; however, a 12-inch skillet can be substituted.

2 cups (8 ounces) masa harina
1 teaspoon salt
1¾ cups hot tap water
2 cups vegetable oil
1 recipe filling (pages 106–107), warmed

1. Mix masa harina and salt in medium bowl, then fold in water with rubber spatula. Using your hands, knead mixture in bowl until soft dough forms, 1 to 2 minutes. Cover dough with damp dish towel and let sit for 5 minutes.

2. Cut twenty-four 8-inch squares of parchment paper. Knead dough briefly, then divide into 12 equal pieces, roll into balls, and place on baking sheet. Cover dough with damp dish towel.

3. Working with 1 piece dough at a time, press flat into 3½-inch-wide disk between 2 pieces parchment using pie plate. Remove top piece parchment, gently push in edges to make slightly thicker and smooth out any cracks, then flatten slightly to level; edges should be smooth, flat, and slightly thicker than center. Transfer to plate, leaving bottom piece parchment in place, and cover with damp dish towel; tortillas can be stacked.

4. Heat 11-inch straight-sided sauté pan over medium heat until hot, 2 to 3 minutes. Place 1 tortilla parchment side up in your palm, remove parchment, then gently lay tortilla in hot, dry pan; repeat with 2 more tortillas. Cook until lightly golden on both sides, 4 to 6 minutes, flipping halfway through cooking; transfer to baking sheet. Repeat with remaining tortillas, lowering heat as needed to prevent scorching. (Gorditas can be stacked between parchment paper, wrapped in plastic wrap, and refrigerated for up to 1 day or frozen for up to 3 months; thaw completely before continuing.)

5. Line second baking sheet with several layers of paper towels. Carefully add oil to now-empty pan and heat over medium-high heat to 375 degrees. Working in batches, fry tortillas, flipping often, until they puff, 2 to 3 minutes. Transfer to prepared baking sheet and let cool slightly. Using paring knife, cut puffed tortillas open halfway around edge. Stuff each tortilla with filling and serve.

LEARN HOW **GORDITAS**

These puffy, filled pockets are browned and then fried; the right shaping technique ensures that they will puff perfectly every time.

1. PORTION DOUGH: Knead the dough briefly, then divide it into 12 equal pieces using a chef's knife. Roll the dough into balls, then cover them with a damp dish towel to prevent them from drying out.

2. FLATTEN DOUGH INTO DISKS: Working with one piece of dough at a time, press flat into a 3½-inch-wide disk between pieces of parchment paper using a pie plate.

3. SMOOTH OUT EDGES: Remove the top piece of parchment. Gently push in the edges, smooth out any cracks, then flatten slightly to level. The edges should be smooth and slightly thicker than the center.

4. BROWN GORDITAS: Working in batches, cook the gorditas in a dry sauté pan over medium heat until golden on both sides, 4 to 6 minutes. Set gorditas aside and heat oil in now-empty pan.

5. FRY GORDITAS: Working in batches, fry the gorditas, flipping often, until they puff, about 2 minutes; transfer to a paper towel–lined baking sheet to drain.

6. CUT OPEN AND FILL: Using a paring knife, cut the puffed gorditas open halfway around the edge. Stuff each gordita with filling.

Panuchos

Makes 12 panuchos; serves 4 to 6

✔ **WHY THIS RECIPE WORKS:** A twist on the classic Mexican tostada, *panuchos* are a specialty of the Yucatán. The crispy yet tender panucho shells are essentially corn tortillas that are puffed, filled with creamy refried beans, and then flattened before being cooked in oil until perfectly golden and crisp. The beans keep the thin top layer tender as the bottom crisps. Like tostadas, they are served topped with flavorful combinations of meat, cheese, and vegetables. Although the most traditional topping is shredded chicken and tangy pickled onions (see Chicken with Pickled Onion and Cabbage, page 106), we like to pair them with a wide variety of toppings, from Pork Tinga with Avocado and Queso Fresco (page 107) to Spicy Zucchini with Scallions and Cotija Cheese (page 106). We used widely available masa harina for the dough. Allowing the dough to rest gave it time to hydrate so that the tortillas could be formed with ease. A pie plate worked best to flatten the tortillas, and pressing them between squares of parchment paper kept them from sticking to each other and streamlined the process. We discovered two tricks to getting the tortillas to puff during their initial cooking. First, it was crucial to smooth out and seal the edges of the tortillas after pressing them, since this enabled steam to build inside the tortilla during cooking. Second, we found it necessary to brown both sides first, then flip the tortillas again and press firmly around the centers with a wad of paper towels, which encouraged the tortillas to puff properly. Once they had puffed and slightly cooled, we simply cut a slit in the sides and spooned in the refried beans. We then pressed them to distribute the beans and shallow-fried the panuchos in the skillet to create a golden exterior with a crisp texture. Be sure to use masa harina or Maseca Brand Instant Masa Corn Flour. Any type of refried beans will work well here; if you want to make your own, see the recipes on page 293.

2 cups (8 ounces) masa harina
  Salt
1¾ cups hot tap water
1 teaspoon plus ¼ cup vegetable oil, plus extra as needed
1 cup refried beans
1 recipe topping (pages 106–107), warmed

1. Mix masa harina and 1 teaspoon salt in medium bowl, then fold in water with rubber spatula. Using your hands, knead mixture in bowl until soft dough forms, 1 to 2 minutes. Cover dough with damp dish towel and let sit for 5 minutes.

2. Cut twenty-four 8-inch squares of parchment paper. Knead dough briefly then divide into 12 equal pieces, roll into balls, and place on baking sheet. Cover dough with damp dish towel.

3. Working with 1 ball at a time, press dough flat into 4½-inch-wide disk between 2 pieces parchment using pie plate. Remove top piece parchment and gently smooth out any cracks. Transfer to plate, leaving bottom piece parchment in place, and cover with damp dish towel; tortillas can be stacked.

4. Line baking sheet with paper towels. Heat 1 teaspoon oil in 12-inch nonstick skillet over medium-high heat until just shimmering. Place 1 tortilla parchment side up in your palm, remove parchment, then gently lay tortilla in hot pan; repeat with 2 more tortillas. Cook until lightly golden on both sides, about 6 minutes, flipping halfway through cooking.

5. Flip again and press firmly around center of each tortilla with wad of paper towels until puffed; transfer to prepared sheet. Repeat with remaining tortillas, adding 1 teaspoon oil to pan between batches and lowering heat as needed to prevent scorching.

6. Using paring knife, cut 2-inch opening around edge of tortillas. Spoon 1 generous tablespoon beans inside each tortilla then gently press on tortilla to spread out beans. (Panuchos can be stacked between parchment paper, wrapped in plastic wrap, and refrigerated for up to 1 day or frozen for up to 3 months; thaw completely before continuing.)

7. Heat remaining ¼ cup oil in now-empty skillet over medium-high heat until shimmering. Working in batches, fry panuchos until golden and crisp on each side, 5 to 7 minutes, flipping tortillas and adding extra oil to pan between batches as needed. Return to baking sheet and season lightly with salt. Spoon topping onto center of each panucho and serve.

LEARN HOW **PANUCHOS**

These flat, bean-filled tostadas get cooked twice: once to puff them enough to cut open and fill, and again to brown and crisp the flattened panuchos.

1. PORTION DOUGH: Knead the dough briefly, then divide into 12 equal pieces using a chef's knife. Roll the dough into balls, place on a baking sheet, and cover with a damp dish towel.

2. PRESS AND SEAL DOUGH: After pressing the dough into 4½-inch disks between parchment paper, remove the top piece of parchment; gently smooth out any cracks and seal the edges.

3. BROWN AND PUFF: After browning the panuchos lightly on both sides, flip the panuchos again and press firmly around the centers with paper towels until they puff.

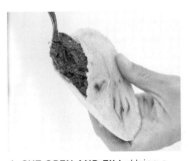

4. CUT OPEN AND FILL: Using a paring knife, cut a 2-inch opening at the edge of each panucho. Spoon refried beans inside the panucho, then gently press to spread out the beans.

5. PAN-FRY PANUCHOS: Working in batches, fry the filled panuchos with ¼ cup oil in a skillet over medium-high heat until they are golden on both sides.

6. TOP AND SERVE: Transfer the panuchos to a paper towel–lined baking sheet and season with salt. Spoon the topping onto the center of each panucho and serve.

Tamales

Makes 18 tamales; serves 6 to 8

✔ **WHY THIS RECIPE WORKS:** Tamales are small, moist corn cakes that can be stuffed with a variety of fillings—usually shredded chicken, pork, or beef, or a combination of cheese and chiles. The filled corn cakes are wrapped in corn husks and steamed. On the Mexican table, they can either be served as breakfast or as the main course at dinner, served alongside beans and other hearty dishes like roasted meat or poultry. Often served during the holidays, tamales are time-consuming to prepare, with families gathering together in the kitchen to pitch in. We wanted to simplify the process while staying true to the tamales' subtle but hearty flavor and light texture.

We started with the corn dough that comprises the bulk of the tamale. Although masa dough (made from corn kernels that have been cooked with slaked lime, ground to a flour, and mixed with water) is traditional, it can be difficult to find in many parts of the United States. Instead, we turned to widely available masa harina, but found that when used alone, it was too fine-textured and the corn flavor was bland. We tried adding both cornmeal and grits to supplement flavor and texture. Although cornmeal had great corn flavor, the texture of the tamales made with it reminded tasters of corn muffins. Grits, on the other hand, had a more granular texture similar to authentic tamales and didn't sacrifice any of the flavor. Fresh corn is a common addition in many tamale recipes, and we thought it would reinforce the corn flavor and provide textural contrast. We experimented with varying amounts and landed on 1 cup. We also tested tamales made with frozen corn; tasters couldn't distinguish the difference between frozen and fresh kernels, so we opted to call for frozen since they are available year-round and are easy to prepare (no cutting kernels off of cobs).

For the fat in the dough, we tried several options: vegetable shortening, vegetable oil, butter, and lard. In the end, the vegetable shortening and vegetable oil gave the tamales an unpleasant, artificial flavor. We preferred the traditional combination of lard supplemented with butter for richness and flavor. To prevent the dough from cooking up with a hard, dense texture, we added baking powder and used a food-processor mixing method to incorporate some air into the dough.

Traditional Mexican tamales are usually wrapped in dried and soaked corn husks, although in some regions, banana leaves are the common choice. We chose to work with widely available corn husks, and soaked a few extras to make up for any that were cracked or too small. When it came time to fold the tamales, most of the recipes we found required tying each one closed, a process we found we could do without by simply folding the tamales and placing them with the seam sides facing the edges of the steamer basket.

With our dough and cooking method settled, we turned our attention to creating flavorful fillings for our tamales: a rich red chile chicken filling and a smoky-spicy chipotle beef filling. Quick and simple moles, chile-based sauces found throughout Mexico, served as savory poaching liquids as well as flavorful sauces. For the chicken filling, hearty chicken thighs worked best for the long cooking time. A combination of ancho and New Mexican chiles resulted in a sauce with subtle spice and sweetness. As for the beef filling, blade steaks turned meltingly tender with the extended cooking, and tasters liked smoky, spicy flavor of chipotle chiles, which enhanced the beef's already rich flavor and gave the sauce some punch. Once cooked, the tamales peeled easily away from the husks, revealing warm, moist corn cakes with rich, flavorful fillings.

TAMALE FILLINGS

Each filling makes enough for 18 tamales.

Chipotle Beef Filling

4	dried ancho chiles, stemmed, seeded, and torn into ½-inch pieces (1 cup)
3	tablespoons vegetable oil
1	large onion, chopped
6	garlic cloves, minced
1½	tablespoons minced canned chipotle chile in adobo sauce
1	teaspoon dried oregano
1	teaspoon sugar, plus extra as needed
¾	teaspoon ground cumin
½	teaspoon ground cinnamon
⅛	teaspoon ground cloves
	Salt and pepper
3	cups beef broth
1¾	pounds top blade steaks, trimmed
1½	tablespoons red wine vinegar

1. Toast anchos in 12-inch skillet over medium heat, stirring frequently, until fragrant, 2 to 6 minutes; transfer to bowl.

2. Heat oil in now-empty skillet over medium heat until shimmering. Add onion and cook until softened, 5 to 7 minutes. Stir in garlic, chipotle, oregano, sugar, cumin, cinnamon, cloves, 1 teaspoon salt, and toasted chiles and cook for 30 seconds. Stir in broth and simmer until slightly reduced, about 10 minutes. Transfer mixture to blender and process until smooth, about 20 seconds; return to skillet.

3. Season beef with salt and pepper, nestle into skillet, and bring to simmer over medium heat. Cover, reduce heat to low, and cook until beef is very tender, about 1½ hours.

4. Transfer beef to carving board and let cool slightly. Using 2 forks, shred beef into small pieces. Stir vinegar into sauce and season with salt, pepper, and sugar to taste. Toss shredded beef with 1 cup sauce. Reheat remaining sauce and serve with tamales.

Red Chile Chicken Filling

4	dried ancho chiles, stemmed, seeded, and torn into ½-inch pieces (1 cup)
4	dried New Mexican chiles, stemmed, seeded, and torn into ½-inch pieces (1 cup)
3	tablespoons vegetable oil
1	large onion, chopped
6	garlic cloves, minced
¾	teaspoon ground cumin
¾	teaspoon dried oregano
	Salt and pepper
3	cups chicken broth
1¼	pounds boneless, skinless chicken thighs, trimmed
1½	tablespoons cider vinegar
	Sugar

1. Toast anchos and New Mexican chiles in 12-inch skillet over medium heat, stirring frequently, until fragrant, 2 to 6 minutes; transfer to bowl.

2. Heat oil in now-empty skillet over medium heat until shimmering. Add onion and cook until softened, 5 to 7 minutes. Stir in garlic, cumin, oregano, ½ teaspoon salt, and toasted chiles and cook for 30 seconds. Stir in broth and simmer until slightly reduced, about 10 minutes. Transfer mixture to blender and process until smooth, about 20 seconds; return to skillet.

3. Season chicken with salt and pepper, nestle into skillet, and bring to simmer over medium heat. Cover, reduce heat to low, and cook until chicken registers 160 degrees, 20 to 25 minutes.

4. Transfer chicken to carving board and let cool slightly. Using 2 forks, shred chicken into small pieces. Stir vinegar into sauce and season with salt, pepper, and sugar to taste. Toss shredded chicken with 1 cup sauce. Reheat remaining sauce and serve with tamales.

Tamales

Makes 18

If you're short on time, you can make a simple tamale filling by combining 12 ounces of shredded Monterey Jack and 3 tablespoons of minced pickled jalapeños; serve jalapeño-cheese tamales with Tomatillo Salsa (page 20). We found it easiest to use large corn husks that measure about 8 inches long by 6 inches wide; if the husks are small, you may need to use two per tamale and shingle them as needed to hold all of the filling. You can substitute butter for the lard if deired, but the tamales will have a distinctive buttery flavor. Steamed tamales can be cooled completely, wrapped individually in plastic wrap, and frozen for up to 3 months. To reheat six or fewer tamales, place them on a large plate with 1 tablespoon water, cover with damp paper towels, then wrap with plastic wrap; microwave at 50 percent power until the tamales are hot throughout, about 4 minutes. If reheating a large batch of tamales, re-steam them as directed in step 4 until hot throughout, 15 to 20 minutes. Be sure to use quick, not instant, grits in this recipe. For an accurate measurement of boiling water, bring a full kettle of water to a boil and then measure out the desired amount. See the photo on page 78.

1	**cup plus 2 tablespoons quick grits**
1½	**cups boiling water**
1	**cup (4 ounces) plus 2 tablespoons masa harina**
20	**large dried corn husks**
1½	**cups frozen corn, thawed**
6	**tablespoons unsalted butter, cut into ½-inch cubes and softened**
6	**tablespoons lard, softened**
1	**tablespoon sugar**
2¼	**teaspoons baking powder**
¾	**teaspoon salt**
1	**recipe filling (page 117)**

1. Place grits in medium bowl, whisk in boiling water, and let stand until water is mostly absorbed, about 10 minutes. Stir in masa harina, cover, and let cool to room temperature, about 20 minutes. Meanwhile, place husks in large bowl, cover with hot water, and let soak until pliable, about 30 minutes.

2. Process masa dough, corn, butter, lard, sugar, baking powder, and salt together in food processor until mixture is light, sticky, and very smooth, about 1 minute, scraping down sides as necessary. Remove husks from water and pat dry with dish towel.

3. Working with 1 husk at a time, lay on counter, cupped side up, with long side facing you and wide end on right side. Spread ¼ cup tamale dough into 4-inch square over bottom right-hand corner, pushing it flush to bottom edge but leaving ¼-inch border at wide edge. Mound 2 scant tablespoons filling in line across center of dough, parallel to bottom edge. Roll husk away from you and over filling, so that dough surrounds filling and forms cylinder. Fold up tapered end, leaving top open, and transfer seam side down to platter.

4. Fit large pot or Dutch oven with steamer basket, removing feet from steamer basket if pot is short. Fill pot with water until it just touches bottom of basket and bring to boil. Gently lay tamales in basket with open ends facing up and seam sides facing out. Cover and steam, checking water level often and adding additional water as needed, until tamales easily come free from husks, about 1 hour. Transfer tamales to large platter. Reheat remaining sauce from filling in covered bowl in microwave, about 30 seconds, and serve with tamales.

LEARN HOW **TAMALES**

Traditional tamales are a labor of love, from boiling and grinding masa for dough, to tying each individual tamale closed for steaming. Our recipe makes the process easier and faster while still capturing the essential elements of tamales—soft, lightly sweet corn cakes and rich, flavorful fillings.

1. MAKE DOUGH: Whisk boiling water into the grits and let stand until the water is absorbed. Stir in the masa harina to form a dough. Cover; let cool to room temperature. Process the masa harina mixture with the corn and remaining dough ingredients until very smooth. Using real corn gives the dough a boost of corn flavor.

2. SOAK CORN HUSKS: Place the dried corn husks in a large bowl and cover with hot water. Soaking the husks rids them of any dirt and makes them pliable enough to roll around the tamale filling.

3. SPREAD DOUGH INTO CORN HUSKS: Lay one corn husk on the counter, with the long side parallel to the edge of the counter. Spoon ¼ cup of dough onto the bottom right-hand corner of the husk. Spread into a 4-inch square, flush with the bottom edge. This ensures that the filling will be completely surrounded by dough.

4. ADD FILLING: Place a scant 2 tablespoons of filling down the center of the dough, parallel to the long side of the husk. Roll the husk away from you so that the dough surrounds the filling. It is important to roll the tamales tightly so they don't leak while cooking.

5. FOLD TAMALES: Fold the tapered end of the tamale up, leaving the top open, and transfer to a platter, seam side down. Keeping the tamales seam side down means you can skip the tedious task of tying each one closed.

6. STEAM TAMALES: Place the tamales in the steamer basket, with the seams facing the edge of the pot and the open ends facing up. Cover and steam for about 1 hour. Placing the seams against the sides of the Dutch oven keeps the tamales sealed.

CHICKEN CHIMICHANGAS

Burritos, Chimichangas, and Quesadillas

Flour Tortillas

Makes 12 (8-inch) tortillas

✓ **WHY THIS RECIPE WORKS:** Supple and flavorful, homemade flour tortillas far surpass store-bought versions. Although we tried using a tortilla press to make even disks, a rolling pin worked better for this elastic dough. To make the process easier, we let the dough rest in the refrigerator, which firmed up the shortening so that the dough wasn't too sticky to roll. This recipe can be doubled.

2¾ cups (13¾ ounces) all-purpose flour
1½ teaspoons salt
6   tablespoons vegetable shortening,
    cut into 6 pieces
¾   cup plus 2 tablespoons water, heated to
    110 degrees
1   teaspoon vegetable oil

1. Combine flour and salt in large bowl. Using your hands, rub shortening into flour until mixture resembles coarse meal. Stir in water with wooden spoon until incorporated and dough forms. Turn dough out onto counter and knead briefly to form smooth, cohesive ball. Divide dough into 12 pieces (2½ tablespoons each), roll into balls, and transfer to plate. Cover with plastic wrap and refrigerate until dough is firm, at least 30 minutes or up to 3 days.

2. Working with 1 piece dough at a time and two 12-inch squares greased parchment paper, roll dough into 8-inch tortilla with rolling pin. Remove top piece of parchment and gently reshape edges as needed.

3. Heat oil in 12-inch nonstick skillet over medium-high heat until shimmering. Using paper towel, wipe out skillet, leaving thin film of oil on bottom. Flip tortilla onto your palm, remove parchment on bottom, and lay tortilla in skillet. Cook tortilla until surface begins to bubble and it moves freely when pan is shaken, about 1 minute.

4. Flip tortilla over and cook until puffed and bottom is spotty brown, about 1 minute. Transfer to plate and cover with dish towel. Repeat with remaining tortillas. Serve. (Tortillas can be layered between clean parchment paper, wrapped in plastic wrap, and refrigerated for up to 3 days.)

10-Inch Flour Tortillas

Double recipe, divide dough evenly into 10 pieces, and roll each into 10-inch round; cook as directed.

TEST KITCHEN TIP SHAPING FLOUR TORTILLAS

1. Divide dough into 12 pieces. Roll pieces into balls; cover with plastic and refrigerate for 30 minutes.

2. Using rolling pin, roll dough balls between sheets of greased parchment into 8-inch tortillas.

3. Remove top piece parchment. Flip tortilla onto your palm, remove parchment, and lay tortilla in pan.

Baked Beef and Bean Burritos

Serves 6

✔ **WHY THIS RECIPE WORKS:** Supersized Tex-Mex burritos are mainstays in restaurants across the United States, and it's hard to deny their appeal: They're full of flavor and fun to eat. But making them at home can be surprisingly tricky—making the filling and assembling the burritos can be time-consuming, and the flour tortillas get soggy and gummy, or worse, can fall apart altogether. We wanted a streamlined recipe that we could make anytime. First, we traded long-braised meat for ground beef, which cooked quickly and lent itself nicely to flavorful seasonings. Creamy pinto beans complemented the beef well. Browning our aromatics and spices bloomed their flavors, and adding tomato paste gave the mixture a concentrated savory flavor. To keep the filling from falling out of the wrapped burritos, we mashed a portion of the beans into a paste to bind everything together. For even more flavor and a bit of pizzazz, we sprinkled on extra cheese and broiled the assembled burritos. The crisped tortillas provided a crunchy contrast to the rich burrito filling.

1¾   **cups chicken broth**
¾   **cup long-grain white rice, rinsed**
3   **garlic cloves, minced**
   Salt
¼   **cup minced fresh cilantro**
1   **tablespoon vegetable oil**
1   **onion, chopped fine**
3   **tablespoons tomato paste**
3   **garlic cloves, minced**
1   **tablespoon ground cumin**
1   **teaspoon dried oregano**
1   **teaspoon chipotle chile powder**
12   **ounces 90 percent lean ground beef**
1   **(15-ounce) can pinto beans, rinsed**
1   **tablespoon lime juice**
6   **(10-inch) flour tortillas**

10   **ounces sharp cheddar cheese, shredded (2½ cups)**
6   **tablespoons sour cream**

1. Bring 1¼ cups broth, rice, garlic, and ½ teaspoon salt to boil in small saucepan over medium-high heat. Cover, reduce heat to low, and cook until rice is tender and broth is absorbed, about 20 minutes. Remove rice from heat and let sit, covered, for 10 minutes. Add cilantro and fluff with fork to incorporate; cover to keep warm.

2. Meanwhile, heat oil in 12-inch nonstick skillet over medium heat until shimmering. Add onion and cook until softened, about 5 minutes. Stir in tomato paste, garlic, cumin, oregano, and chile powder and cook until fragrant, about 1 minute. Add beef, breaking up pieces with wooden spoon, and cook until no longer pink, 8 to 10 minutes.

3. Using potato masher, coarsely mash half of beans with remaining ½ cup broth in bowl, then stir into skillet. Cook, stirring constantly, until nearly all liquid has evaporated, about 3 minutes. Off heat, stir in remaining whole beans, lime juice, and ¾ teaspoon salt; cover to keep warm.

4. Adjust oven rack 6 inches from broiler element and heat broiler. Line baking sheet with aluminum foil. Wrap tortillas in damp dish towel and microwave until warm and pliable, about 1 minute. Lay warm tortillas on counter. Mound warm rice, beef mixture, and 1½ cups cheddar across center of tortillas, close to bottom edge, then top with sour cream. Working with 1 tortilla at a time, fold sides then bottom of tortilla over filling, pulling back on it firmly to tighten it around filling, then continue to roll tightly into burrito.

5. Place burritos, seam side down, on prepared sheet and sprinkle remaining 1 cup cheddar over top. Broil until cheese is melted and starting to brown, 3 to 5 minutes. Serve.

Ancho-Orange Pork Burritos

Serves 8

✔ **WHY THIS RECIPE WORKS:** In the Mexican state of Sinaloa, mildly spiced, orange-infused pork known as *chilorio* is one of the region's most popular dishes. It's so popular, in fact, that markets sell the pork ready-made. In traditional versions, the pork is slow-simmered until fall-apart tender, pulled into bite-size pieces and fried, and then cooked again in a chile sauce. We wanted to make this ultraflavorful pork into a unique burrito filling. To achieve moist, tender, and richly flavored pork, we cooked boneless pork butt slowly and gently in the oven in a sauce base of orange juice, vinegar, chipotle chile in adobo, and dried ancho chiles. To impart even more flavor, we also added garlic, bay leaves, oregano, and cumin to the braising liquid. After a couple of hours of braising, the pork was meltingly tender and shreddable. While the pork cooled, we defatted the flavorful liquid left behind in the pot, then pureed it until smooth and tossed it with the shredded pork. Since we wanted the pork to be the star, we used just rice, no cheese or beans, when assembling these rich and satisfying burritos. If you are short on braising liquid for the sauce in step 2, you can make up the difference with chicken broth or water.

¾ cup orange juice (2 oranges)
½ cup distilled white vinegar
4 dried ancho chiles, stemmed, seeded, and torn into ½-inch pieces (1 cup)
2 tablespoons tomato paste
2 tablespoon minced canned chipotle chile in adobo sauce
5 garlic cloves, lightly crushed and peeled
2 bay leaves
2 teaspoons ground cumin
2 teaspoons dried oregano
Salt and pepper
4 pounds boneless pork butt roast, trimmed and cut into 2-inch pieces

2 cups water
1½ cups long-grain white rice, rinsed
¼ cup minced fresh cilantro
2 scallions, sliced thin
8 (10-inch) flour tortillas

1. Adjust oven rack to lower-middle position and heat oven to 300 degrees. Whisk orange juice, vinegar, anchos, tomato paste, chipotle, garlic, bay leaves, cumin, oregano and 1 teaspoon salt together in Dutch oven. Season pork with salt and pepper, stir into pot, and arrange in single layer. Cover and cook in oven until pork is very tender, about 2 hours.

2. Transfer pork to large bowl using slotted spoon and let cool slightly. Using 2 forks, shred pork into bite-size pieces. Strain braising liquid into fat separator, reserving solids, and let settle for 5 minutes. Discard bay leaves and transfer solids to blender. Add 1½ cups defatted liquid to blender and process until smooth, about 1 minute. Combine sauce and pork in now-empty Dutch oven; before making burritos, reheat mixture over medium heat until hot. (Pork can refrigerated for up to 3 days or frozen for up to 1 month.)

3. Meanwhile, bring water, rice, and 1 teaspoon salt to boil in medium saucepan over medium-high heat. Cover, reduce heat to low, and cook until rice is tender and water is absorbed, about 20 minutes. Remove rice from heat and let sit, covered, for 10 minutes. Add cilantro and scallions and fluff with fork to incorporate; cover to keep warm.

4. Wrap tortillas in damp dish towel and microwave until warm and pliable, about 1 minute. Lay warm tortillas on counter. Mound warm rice and pork across center of tortillas, close to bottom edge. Working with 1 tortilla at a time, fold sides then bottom of tortilla over filling, pulling back on it firmly to tighten it around filling, then continue to roll tightly into burrito. Serve.

Chicken Burritos Mojados

Serves 6

✓ **WHY THIS RECIPE WORKS:** Often found on taqueria menus, festive *burritos mojados* are draped with three distinct sauces—red chile sauce, white Mexican *crema*, and green tomatillo sauce—representing the colors of the Mexican flag. To re-create this dish at home without spending hours making multiple sauces, we used premade tomatillo salsa and boosted its flavor with fresh cilantro. Cooking the chicken and the red chile sauce together further streamlined the recipe. Although store-bought salsa saves time here, you can also make your own (see page 20). If the tomatillo salsa is very thick or chunky, loosen it with several tablespoons of water and puree it quickly in the blender before heating in step 5.

2¼ cups chicken broth
¾ cup long-grain white rice, rinsed
1 (15-ounce) can pinto beans, rinsed
3½ tablespoons chili powder
   Salt and pepper
2 scallions, sliced thin
2 tablespoons vegetable oil
3 garlic cloves, minced
2 (8-ounce) cans tomato sauce
1½ pounds boneless, skinless chicken breasts, trimmed
6 tablespoons minced fresh cilantro
6 (10-inch) flour tortillas
2 avocados, halved, pitted, and cut into ½-inch pieces
8 ounces Monterey Jack cheese, shredded (2 cups)
1½ cups tomatillo salsa
   Water, as needed
½ cup Mexican crema

1. Bring 1¼ cups broth, rice, beans, 1½ teaspoons chili powder, and ½ teaspoon salt to boil in medium saucepan oven over medium-high heat. Cover, reduce heat to low, and cook until rice is tender and broth is absorbed, about 20 minutes. Remove rice from heat and let sit, covered, for 10 minutes. Add scallions and fluff with fork to incorporate; cover to keep warm.

2. Meanwhile, cook oil, garlic, and remaining 3 tablespoons chili powder in large saucepan over medium-high heat until fragrant, 1 to 2 minutes. Stir in tomato sauce and remaining 1 cup broth and bring to simmer. Nestle chicken into sauce. Cover, reduce heat to medium-low, and cook until chicken registers 160 degrees, 10 to 15 minutes, flipping halfway through cooking.

3. Transfer chicken to cutting board and let cool slightly. Using 2 forks, shred chicken into bite-size pieces. Toss chicken with ¼ cup sauce and 2 tablespoons cilantro in bowl. Set remaining sauce aside.

4. Adjust oven rack to middle position and heat oven to 450 degrees. Line baking sheet with aluminum foil. Wrap tortillas in damp dish towel and microwave until warm and pliable, about 1 minute. Lay warm tortillas on counter. Mound rice in center of tortillas, close to bottom edge, then top with chicken, avocado, and Monterey Jack. Working with 1 tortilla at a time, fold sides then bottom of tortilla over filling, pulling back on it firmly to tighten it around filling, then continue to roll tightly into burrito. (Burritos can be held at room temperature for up to 1 hour before baking.) Place burritos seam side down on prepared sheet, cover tightly with foil, and bake until hot throughout, 20 to 30 minutes.

5. Before serving, whisk salsa and 2 tablespoons cilantro together in bowl, cover, and microwave until hot, about 1 minute. Reheat red sauce in saucepan over medium heat until hot, about 3 minutes, adding water as needed to loosen consistency

6. Arrange burritos on individual plates. Pour tomatillo sauce over half of each burrito and pour red sauce over other half of burrito. Drizzle with crema, sprinkle with remaining 2 tablespoons cilantro, and serve.

Swiss Chard and Pinto Bean Burritos

Serves 6

✔ **WHY THIS RECIPE WORKS:** We wanted a burrito that balanced the usual beans and cheese with fresh, hearty vegetables. To that end, we sautéed a pound of Swiss chard in aromatics and simmered it until tender. We mashed some of the beans into a paste with some vegetable broth and left the rest whole to create a more cohesive filling. We relied on tomato paste, spices, and lime juice to bump up the flavor. White rice, cooked in broth for more flavor and sprinkled with cilantro, and Monterey Jack cheese round out the filling. Given that the vegetable filling had a relatively soft texture, we decided to run the assembled burritos under the broiler briefly to crisp up the tortillas before serving. For a final flavor boost, we sprinkled some more cheese over the top before broiling.

2¼	cups vegetable broth
¾	cup long-grain white rice, rinsed
6	garlic cloves, minced
	Salt
¼	cup minced fresh cilantro
1	tablespoon vegetable oil
1	onion, chopped fine
3	tablespoons tomato paste
1	teaspoon minced canned chipotle chile in adobo sauce
1	tablespoon ground cumin
1	teaspoon dried oregano
1	pound Swiss chard, stemmed, leaves sliced into 1-inch-wide strips
1	(15-ounce) can pinto beans, rinsed
1	tablespoon lime juice
6	(10-inch) flour tortillas
10	ounces Monterey jack, shredded (2½ cups)

1. Bring 1¼ cups broth, rice, half of garlic, and ½ teaspoon salt to boil in small saucepan over medium-high heat. Cover, reduce heat to low, and cook until rice is tender and broth is absorbed, about 20 minutes. Remove rice from heat and let sit, covered, for 10 minutes. Add cilantro and fluff with fork to incorporate; cover to keep warm.

2. Meanwhile, heat oil in Dutch oven over medium heat until shimmering. Add onion and cook until just beginning to brown, about 5 minutes. Stir in tomato paste, chipotle, cumin, oregano, remaining garlic, and ½ teaspoon salt and cook until fragrant, about 1 minute. Add chard and ½ cup broth, cover, and simmer until chard is tender, about 15 minutes.

3. Using potato masher, coarsely mash half of beans with remaining ½ cup broth in bowl, then stir into pot. Cook, stirring constantly, until liquid is nearly evaporated, about 3 minutes. Off heat, stir in lime juice and remaining whole beans; cover to keep warm.

4. Adjust oven rack 6 inches from broiler element and heat broiler. Line baking sheet with aluminum foil. Wrap tortillas in damp dish towel and microwave until warm and pliable, about 1 minute. Lay warm tortillas on counter. Mound warm rice, chard-bean mixture, and 1½ cups Monterey Jack across center of tortillas, close to bottom edge. Working with 1 tortilla at a time, fold sides then bottom of tortilla over filling, pulling back on it firmly to tighten it around filling, then continue to roll tightly into burrito.

5. Place burritos, seam side down, on prepared sheet and sprinkle remaining 1 cup Monterey Jack over top. Broil until cheese is melted and starting to brown, 3 to 5 minutes. Serve.

Chorizo and Black Bean Chimichangas

Serves 4

✔ **WHY THIS RECIPE WORKS:** Like burritos, chimichangas begin with flour tortillas rolled around a generous amount of filling. But unlike burritos, chimichangas are deep-fried until crisp and bronzed on the outside. For a flavorful chimichanga filling that would stand up to the crunchy fried tortilla, we started with Mexican chorizo. To impart extra layers of flavor to the rich sausage, we sautéed it with plenty of aromatics. Black beans rounded out our filling; we mashed half and left the rest whole for textural contrast. A bit of cheddar cheese and rice, freshened up with cilantro and scallion, completed our filling. To prevent the filling from leaking out during frying, we placed it in the center of each tortilla and then brushed the tortilla's circumference with a flour-and-water paste. The paste acted as glue, securely sealing the chimichanga. We then folded the chimichangas, brushing the ends with additional flour paste, and started frying them seam side down, which encouraged a strong seal. See Learn How on page 132.

1½	cups plus 2 tablespoons water
½	cup long-grain white rice, rinsed
	Salt
2	tablespoons minced fresh cilantro
1	scallion, sliced thin
1	tablespoon plus 3 cups vegetable oil
1	onion, chopped fine
1	tablespoon minced canned chipotle chile in adobo sauce
2	garlic cloves, minced
1	teaspoon chili powder
½	teaspoon ground cumin
12	ounces Mexican-style chorizo sausage, casings removed
1	(15-ounce) can black beans, rinsed
2	tablespoons all-purpose flour
4	(10-inch) flour tortillas
4	ounces sharp cheddar cheese, shredded (1 cup)

1. Bring 1 cup water, rice, and ½ teaspoon salt to boil in small saucepan over medium-high heat. Reduce heat to low, cover, and cook until rice is tender and water is absorbed, about 20 minutes. Remove rice from heat and let sit, covered, for 10 minutes. Add cilantro and scallion and fluff with fork to incorporate; cover to keep warm.

2. Meanwhile, heat 1 tablespoon oil in 12-inch nonstick skillet oven over medium heat until shimmering. Add onion and cook until softened, about 5 minutes. Stir in chipotle, garlic, chili powder, and cumin and cook until fragrant, about 30 seconds. Add chorizo and cook, breaking up pieces with wooden spoon, until no longer pink, about 5 minutes. Coarsely mash half of beans with ½ cup water in bowl using potato masher, then add to skillet with remaining beans. Simmer until beans are warmed through, about 5 minutes; remove from heat.

3. Whisk flour and remaining 2 tablespoons water together in bowl. Wrap tortillas in damp dish towel and microwave until warm and pliable, about 1 minute. Lay warm tortillas on counter. Mound rice, chorizo-bean mixture, and cheddar across center of tortillas. Working with 1 tortilla at a time, brush edges of tortilla with flour paste, then wrap top and bottom of tortilla tightly over filling and press firmly to seal. Brush ends of tortilla thoroughly with paste, fold into center, and press firmly to seal.

4. Adjust oven rack to middle position and heat oven to 200 degrees. Line plate with several layers of paper towels. Set wire rack in rimmed baking sheet. Heat remaining 3 cups oil in Dutch oven over medium-high heat to 325 degrees. Place 2 chimichangas, seam side down, in oil. Fry, turning as needed, until well browned on both sides, about 4 minutes, adjusting burner as necessary to maintain oil temperature between 300 and 325 degrees. Let drain briefly on paper towels, then transfer to wire rack and keep warm in oven while frying remaining 2 chimichangas. Serve.

LEARN HOW **CHIMICHANGAS**

Chimichangas, the deep-fried cousins of burritos, are a Mexican restaurant favorite. But too often, making them at home results in leaky, greasy fillings. To ensure that our filling stayed inside the chimichangas (and away from the frying oil), we developed a foolproof rolling and sealing technique.

1. MAKE FLAVORFUL RICE: Cook the rice on the stovetop until the rice is tender. Let the cooked rice sit, covered, for 10 minutes, then fold in the flavorings. Plain rice tastes bland in the chimichangas; adding subtle flavorings like fresh herbs keeps the fillings lively and vibrant.

2. MAKE FILLING: Make the filling according to the recipe. Coarsely mash half of the beans and add to the filling mixture. Mashing just some of the beans ensures that the filling holds together but doesn't become pasty.

3. WARM TORTILLAS: Wrap the flour tortillas in a damp dish towel and microwave until warm and pliable, about 1 minute. Microwaving the tortillas before filling them ensures that they are soft enough to roll without cracking.

4. FILL TORTILLAS AND BRUSH WITH FLOUR PASTE: Mound the rice, filling, and cheese across the center of each tortilla. Brush the edges of the tortillas with flour paste. The flour paste helps glue the chimichangas closed.

5. ROLL AND CLOSE: Wrap the top and bottom of each tortilla tightly over the filling and press firmly to seal. Brush the ends of the tortillas thoroughly with paste, fold into the center, and press firmly to seal. Brushing the ends with extra flour paste is essential to keep the filling from leaking out the ends.

6. FRY CHIMICHANGAS: Add the chimichangas to the hot oil, seam side down. Fry, turning as needed, until well browned on all sides, about 4 minutes. Starting the chimichangas seam side down ensures a firm seal.

Chicken Chimichangas

Serves 4

✔ **WHY THIS RECIPE WORKS:** To create great chicken chimichangas, we cooked the chicken right in a flavorful chile sauce. This kept the chicken moist and tender and ensured that it was packed with plenty of chile flavor. A bit of flour and some mashed pinto beans thickened the sauce and filling nicely. Cheddar cheese provided a complementary tang. We assembled and fried the chimichangas using the same method we used for our Chorizo and Black Bean Chimichangas (page 130). Serve with salsa. See the photo on page 120.

1	cup plus 2 tablespoons water
½	cup long-grain white rice, rinsed
	Salt and pepper
2	tablespoons minced fresh cilantro
1	scallion, sliced thin
1	tablespoon plus 3 cups vegetable oil
1	onion, chopped fine
2	tablespoons ancho chile powder
1	tablespoon minced canned chipotle chile in adobo sauce
2	garlic cloves, minced
½	teaspoon ground cumin
1	cup chicken broth
1	pound boneless, skinless chicken breasts, trimmed
1	(15-ounce) can pinto beans, rinsed
2	tablespoons all-purpose flour
4	(10-inch) flour tortillas
4	ounces sharp cheddar cheese, shredded (1 cup)

1. Bring 1 cup water, rice, and ¼ teaspoon salt to boil in small saucepan over medium-high heat. Reduce heat to low, cover, and cook until rice is tender and water is absorbed, about 20 minutes. Remove rice from heat and let sit, covered, for 10 minutes. Add cilantro and scallion and fluff with fork to incorporate; cover to keep warm.

2. Meanwhile, heat 1 tablespoon oil in 12-inch nonstick skillet over medium heat until shimmering. Add onion and cook until softened, about 5 minutes. Stir in chile powder, chipotle, garlic, and cumin and cook until fragrant, about 1 minute. Stir in broth and bring to simmer. Nestle chicken into sauce. Cover, reduce heat to medium-low, and cook until chicken registers 160 degrees, 10 to 15 minutes, flipping halfway through cooking.

3. Transfer chicken to cutting board, let cool slightly, then cut crosswise into very thin pieces. Continue to simmer sauce until thickened and measures ½ cup, about 10 minutes; remove from heat. Coarsely mash half of beans in bowl using potato masher, then add to sauce with remaining beans and sliced chicken.

4. Whisk flour and remaining 2 tablespoons water together in bowl. Wrap tortillas in damp dish towel and microwave until warm and pliable, about 1 minute. Lay warm tortillas on counter. Mound rice, chicken-bean mixture, and cheddar across center of tortillas. Working with 1 tortilla at a time, brush edges of tortilla with flour paste, then wrap top and bottom of tortilla tightly over filling and press firmly to seal. Brush ends of tortilla thoroughly with paste, fold into center, and press firmly to seal.

5. Adjust oven rack to middle position and heat oven to 200 degrees. Line plate with several layers of paper towels. Set wire rack in rimmed baking sheet. Heat remaining 3 cups oil in Dutch oven over medium-high heat to 325 degrees. Place 2 chimichangas, seam side down, in oil. Fry, turning as needed, until well browned on both sides, about 4 minutes, adjusting burner as necessary to maintain oil temperature between 300 and 325 degrees. Let drain briefly on paper towels, then transfer to wire rack and keep warm in oven while frying remaining 2 chimichangas. Serve.

Spicy Chicken Flautas

Serve 4 to 6

✔ **WHY THIS RECIPE WORKS:** Take a soft flour tortilla, roll it around a small amount of flavorful filling and fry it until satisfyingly crisp and golden brown, and you have a *flauta*. Spanish for "flute", these crunchy, fun-to-eat rolls are similar to taquitos, but while taquitos are small and use corn tortillas, flautas are much larger and are made from flour tortillas. To make a rich chicken filling, we built a spicy tomato sauce by sautéing onion, jalapeño, garlic, oregano, chili powder and cayenne to bloom their flavors. After adding a can of tomato sauce, we simply nestled the chicken in the skillet, covered it, and let the chicken cook through. As the chicken cooked, it absorbed the sauce's spicy flavor; once it was cooked through, we shredded the chicken into bite-size pieces, added it back to the sauce, and stirred in cilantro and lime juice for bright flavor. To make the flautas, we decided to use 8-inch flour tortillas, which were large enough to hold a pleasing amount of filling but small enough to allow us to fry all the flautas in just two batches. But when we rolled the flautas, we found that the tortillas were too long, leaving large flaps of excess tortilla. These flaps didn't get as crisp when fried and didn't allow the filling to shine. We solved this problem by cutting off one-third of the tortilla before we added the filling. To keep the flautas from opening up during frying, we "glued" the flaps down using a paste made from equal parts flour and water, and then fried them seam side down. Using merely a cup of oil, we were able to turn out flautas with ultracrisp, golden-brown exteriors in just a few minutes. The leftover trimmed pieces of tortilla can be used to make Homemade Baked Tortilla Chips (page 21).

1	tablespoon plus 1 cup vegetable oil
1	onion, chopped fine
2	jalapeño chiles, stemmed, seeded, and minced
1	tablespoon chili powder
2	garlic cloves, minced
¼	teaspoon dried oregano
⅛	teaspoon cayenne pepper
1	(8-ounce) can tomato sauce
2	pounds boneless, skinless chicken breasts, trimmed
	Salt and pepper
2	tablespoons minced fresh cilantro
2	tablespoons lime juice
2	tablespoons all-purpose flour
2	tablespoons water
12	(8-inch) flour tortillas
1	recipe Avocado Sauce (recipe follows)

1. Heat 1 tablespoon oil in 12-inch nonstick skillet over medium heat until shimmering. Add onion and cook until softened, about 5 minutes. Stir in jalapeños, chili powder, garlic, oregano, and cayenne and cook until fragrant, about 30 seconds. Stir in tomato sauce and bring to simmer.

2. Season chicken with salt and pepper and nestle into sauce. Cover, reduce heat to medium-low, and cook until chicken registers 160 degrees, 10 to 15 minutes, flipping halfway through cooking. Transfer chicken to cutting board and let cool slightly. Using 2 forks, shred chicken fine. Stir shredded chicken, cilantro, and lime juice into sauce.

3. Line rimmed baking sheet with parchment paper. Whisk flour and water together in bowl. Cut off bottom third of each tortilla (discard or reserve for another use). Wrap tortillas in damp dish towel and microwave until warm and pliable, about 1 minute.

4. Lay 6 warm tortillas on counter with trimmed edge facing you. Mound half of chicken filling alongside trimmed edges. Roll trimmed edge of 1 tortilla up over filling, then pull back on tortilla to tighten it around filling. Working with 1 tortilla at a time, brush remaining exposed tortilla with flour paste, then roll it up tightly around filling. Press on edges firmly to seal; transfer to prepared baking sheet. Repeat with remaining 6 tortillas and remaining filling. (Flautas can be covered with damp towel, wrapped tightly in plastic wrap, and refrigerated for up to 24 hours.)

5. Adjust oven rack to middle position and heat oven to 200 degrees. Line plate with several layers of paper towels. Set wire rack in second rimmed baking sheet. Heat remaining 1 cup oil in clean 12-inch nonstick skillet over medium-high heat until 325 degrees. Place 6 flautas, seam side down, in oil. Fry, turning as needed, until golden brown on all sides, 3 to 5 minutes, adjusting burner as necessary to maintain oil temperature between 300 and 325 degrees. Let drain briefly on paper towels, then transfer to wire rack and keep warm in oven while frying remaining 6 flautas. Serve with Avocado Sauce.

Avocado Sauce

MAKES 2½ CUPS

Be sure to use very ripe avocados when making this sauce.

2	avocados, halved, pitted, and chopped coarse
½	cup sour cream
¼	cup water
3	tablespoons lime juice (2 limes)
2	tablespoons minced fresh cilantro
	Salt and pepper

Mash all ingredients together in bowl with potato masher (or fork) until smooth. Season with salt and pepper to taste. Serve.

TEST KITCHEN TIP ASSEMBLING FLAUTAS

1. Cut off bottom third of each tortilla (discard or reserve for another use, such as homemade tortilla chips on page 21).

2. Mound chicken filling about ¼ inch from trimmed edge of tortilla. Roll trimmed edge up over filling, then pull back on tortilla to tighten it around filling.

3. Brush remaining exposed tortilla with flour paste, then continue to roll it up tightly around filling. Press on edges firmly to seal.

Chicken Quesadillas with Roasted Peppers and Jack Cheese

Serves 4

☑ **WHY THIS RECIPE WORKS:** The perfect quesadilla is crisp and evenly browned outside with melted cheese and a warm, flavorful filling inside. For quesadillas that were substantial enough for a satisfying meal, we started with 10-inch flour tortillas. We wanted to make four quesadillas, but cooking them one at a time in a skillet was impractical. We turned to the oven to solve this problem. By placing the quesadillas on an oiled baking sheet and then brushing their tops with oil, we were able to achieve perfectly browned, crispy tortillas in only 15 minutes. To ensure that both sides browned evenly, we flipped the quesadillas partway through baking. With our cooking method down, we shifted our attention to creating a flavorful chicken filling. To keep the flavor uncluttered, we seasoned the chicken simply with salt and pepper and sautéed it until golden brown. Sautéed scallion whites, garlic, and cumin added plenty of background flavor. Roasted red peppers and hot sauce were a simple, quick way to give the filling some complex notes of smoke and subtle heat. Fresh cilantro and scallion greens gave the quesadillas a welcome freshness. Just the right amount of Monterey Jack cheese helped hold everything together and became perfectly melty in the oven. Serve with salsa and Mexican crema.

- 3 **tablespoons plus 1 teaspoon vegetable oil**
- 1 **pound boneless, skinless chicken breasts, trimmed**
  Salt and pepper
- 3 **scallions, white and green parts separated, sliced thin**
- 2 **garlic cloves, minced**
- 1 **teaspoon ground cumin**
- ½ **cup jarred roasted red peppers, patted dry and chopped**
- ¼ **cup minced fresh cilantro**
- 1 **teaspoon hot sauce**
- 8 **ounces Monterey Jack cheese, shredded (2 cups)**
- 4 **(10-inch) flour tortillas**

1. Adjust oven rack to middle position and heat oven to 450 degrees. Line rimmed baking sheet with aluminum foil and brush with 1 tablespoon oil.

2. Pat chicken dry with paper towels and season with salt and pepper. Heat 1 tablespoon oil in 12-inch nonstick skillet over medium-high heat until just smoking. Gently lay chicken in skillet and cook, turning as needed, until lightly golden on both sides and registers 160 degrees, about 12 minutes. Transfer chicken to cutting board and let cool slightly. Using 2 forks, shred into bite-size pieces.

3. Add 1 teaspoon oil, scallion whites, garlic, cumin, and ¼ teaspoon salt to now-empty skillet and cook over medium heat until softened, about 2 minutes. Transfer to medium bowl, add shredded chicken, peppers, cilantro, scallion greens, hot sauce, and cheese, and toss to combine.

4. Lay tortillas on counter. Spread chicken filling over half of each tortilla, leaving ½-inch border around edge. Fold other half of tortilla over top and press firmly to compact. Arrange quesadillas in single layer on prepared sheet with rounded edges facing center of sheet. Brush with remaining 1 tablespoon oil.

5. Bake until quesadillas begin to brown, about 10 minutes. Flip quesadillas over and press gently with spatula to compact. Continue to bake until crisp and golden brown on second side, about 5 minutes. Let quesadillas cool on wire rack for 5 minutes, then slice each into 4 wedges and serve.

Tequila-Lime Shrimp Quesadillas

Serves 4

✔ **WHY THIS RECIPE WORKS:** For a unique take on shrimp quesadillas, we turned to the classic Mexican flavor combination of tequila and lime. But achieving perfectly cooked shrimp in quesadillas proved to be a challenge: When we cooked the shrimp to perfection before filling the quesadillas, they overcooked as the quesadillas browned in the oven. But when we put raw shrimp in the quesadillas and then baked them, the shrimp released too much moisture and left the tortillas soggy and gummy. We solved this problem by parcooking the shrimp just slightly: We cooked aromatics and tequila in a pan, then tossed halved shrimp with the tequila mixture and cooked them very briefly. We found it was essential to cut the shrimp in half lengthwise so that they released most of their moisture in the pan. This prevented a wet filling and soggy tortillas. Cilantro, scallion greens, and lime zest provided welcome freshness, and Monterey Jack cheese offered melty richness.

3 tablespoons vegetable oil

12 ounces Monterey Jack cheese, shredded (3 cups)

¼ cup minced fresh cilantro

2 scallions, white and green parts separated, sliced thin

1½ pounds medium-large shrimp (31 to 40 per pound), peeled, deveined, tails removed, and halved lengthwise
Salt and pepper

2 garlic cloves, minced

1 teaspoon minced canned chipotle chile in adobo sauce

⅓ cup tequila

1 teaspoon grated lime zest

4 (10-inch) flour tortillas

1. Adjust oven rack to middle position and heat oven to 450 degrees. Line rimmed baking sheet with aluminum foil and brush with 1 tablespoon oil. Toss Monterey Jack with cilantro and scallion greens.

2. Pat dry shrimp with paper towels and season with salt and pepper. Heat 1 tablespoon oil in 12-inch nonstick skillet over medium heat until shimmering. Add scallion whites, garlic, chipotle, and ¼ teaspoon salt and cook until softened, about 2 minutes. Add tequila amd simmer until tequila has evaporated and pan is dry, about 5 minutes.

3. Add shrimp and cook, stirring often, until cooked through and opaque throughout, about 3 minutes. Transfer to bowl, stir in zest, and let cool for 5 minutes; drain well.

4. Lay tortillas on counter. Sprinkle half of cheese mixture over half of each tortilla, leaving ½-inch border around edge. Arrange shrimp on top in single layer, then sprinkle with remaining cheese mixture. Fold other half of each tortilla over top and press firmly to compact.

5. Arrange quesadillas in single layer on prepared sheet with rounded edges facing center of sheet. Brush with remaining 1 tablespoon oil. Bake until quesadillas begin to brown, about 10 minutes. Flip quesadillas over and press gently with spatula to compact. Continue to bake until crisp and golden brown on second side, about 5 minutes. Let quesadillas cool on wire rack for 5 minutes, then slice each into 4 wedges and serve.

TEST KITCHEN TIP **BAKING QUESADILLAS**

To fit quesadillas in single layer on baking sheet, arrange them with rounded edges facing center of sheet.

Mushroom and Swiss Chard Quesadillas

Serves 4

✓ **WHY THIS RECIPE WORKS:** We wanted a vegetable quesadilla filling with plenty of flavor, surrounded by a tortilla crunchy enough to rival any restaurant version. But putting raw vegetables and cheese in a tortilla resulted in a soggy, undercooked mess. Getting the filling to be as dry as possible was key. We first cooked onions and mushrooms, covered, until the mushrooms released their moisture. Once the moisture was released, we removed the cover and continued to cook until the mushrooms were deep golden brown. To add more flavor to the onions and mushrooms, we bloomed garlic, coriander, and pepper flakes with the vegetables. Swiss chard provided a delicate, earthy flavor counterpoint to the rich mushrooms and onions. A bit of cider vinegar added brightness. Cilantro provided freshness, and we liked Monterey Jack cheese for its mild tanginess and meltability. Serve with Mexican crema.

- ¼ **cup vegetable oil**
- 1 **onion, chopped fine**
- 1 **pound white mushrooms, trimmed and sliced thin**
  Salt and pepper
- 2 **garlic cloves, minced**
- 2 **teaspoons ground coriander**
- ¼ **teaspoon red pepper flakes**
- 1 **pound Swiss chard, stemmed, leaves sliced into ½-inch-wide strips**
- 1 **teaspoon cider vinegar**
- 8 **ounces Monterey Jack cheese, shredded (2 cups)**
- 2 **tablespoons minced fresh cilantro**
- 4 **(10-inch) flour tortillas**

1. Adjust oven rack to middle position and heat oven to 450 degrees. Line rimmed baking sheet with aluminum foil and brush with 1 tablespoon oil.

2. Heat 2 tablespoons oil in 12-inch nonstick skillet over medium-high heat until shimmering. Add onion and mushrooms and season with salt and pepper. Cover and cook, stirring occasionally, until mushrooms have released their moisture, 8 to 10 minutes. Uncover and cook, stirring occasionally, until liquid has evaporated and mushrooms are well browned, 8 to 10 minutes.

3. Stir in garlic, coriander, and pepper flakes and cook until fragrant, about 30 seconds. Add chard, cover, and cook until wilted but still bright green, 1 to 2 minutes. Uncover and cook, stirring often, until liquid evaporates, 4 to 6 minutes. Off heat, stir in vinegar. Let mixture cool slightly, then stir in Monterey Jack and cilantro.

4. Lay tortillas on counter. Spread vegetable filling over half of each tortilla, leaving ½-inch border around edge. Fold other half of tortilla over top and press firmly to compact. Arrange quesadillas in single layer on prepared sheet with rounded edges facing center of sheet. Brush with remaining 1 tablespoon oil.

5. Bake until quesadillas begin to brown, about 10 minutes. Flip quesadillas over and press gently with spatula to compact. Continue to bake until crisp and golden brown on second side, about 5 minutes. Let quesadillas cool on wire rack for 5 minutes, then slice each into 4 wedges and serve.

TEST KITCHEN TIP FILLING QUESADILLAS

Spread filling over half of each tortilla, being sure to leave ½-inch border around edge. Fold other half of tortilla over top and press firmly to compact.

CHEESE ENCHILADAS

Enchiladas and Casseroles

Beef Enchiladas

Serves 4 to 6

☑ **WHY THIS RECIPE WORKS:** For hearty, flavorful beef enchiladas, we turned to traditional slow-cooked and shredded chuck roast. Cubing and browning the meat first helped develop a flavorful base for our braising liquid. Sautéed onions and plenty of spices lent depth, while tomato sauce and wine provided rich color and just enough acidity to balance the beef's richness. Once the beef was fully tender, we strained the braising liquid to use as our sauce. Next, we needed to warm the tortillas to make them pliable enough to roll around our filling. Although traditional recipes call for frying the corn tortillas one at a time, we found that brushing them with oil and microwaving them briefly worked just as well. Tangy cheddar cheese stood up well to the rich beef filling, and a bit more sprinkled on top gave our enchiladas a rich finish. Be sure to trim the beef well before cooking or the enchiladas may be greasy. See page 148 for make-ahead information. See Learn How on page 144. Serve with sour cream, diced avocado, sliced radishes, minced cilantro, shredded romaine lettuce, and lime wedges.

2	pounds boneless beef chuck-eye roast, trimmed and cut into 1½-inch cubes
	Salt and pepper
3	tablespoons vegetable oil
2	onions, chopped fine
3	tablespoons chili powder
2	teaspoons ground cumin
2	teaspoons ground coriander
¼	teaspoon cayenne pepper
4	garlic cloves, minced
2	(15-ounce) cans tomato sauce
¼	cup red wine
8	ounces cheddar cheese, shredded (2 cups)
12	(6-inch) corn tortillas

1. Adjust oven rack to lower-middle position and heat oven to 300 degrees. Pat beef dry with paper towels and season with salt and pepper. Heat 1 tablespoon oil in Dutch oven over medium-high heat until just smoking. Brown half of beef well on all sides, 7 to 10 minutes; transfer to bowl. Repeat with remaining beef using fat left in pot.

2. Pour off all but 1 tablespoon fat from pot. Add onions and ½ teaspoon salt and cook over medium heat until softened, about 8 minutes. Stir in chili powder, cumin, coriander, cayenne, and ¼ teaspoon pepper and cook until spices darken, about 2 minutes. Stir in garlic and cook until fragrant, about 30 seconds. Stir in tomato sauce, wine, and browned beef and any accumulated juices and bring to simmer. Cover, transfer to oven, and cook until meat is fork-tender, 2 to 2½ hours.

3. Transfer beef to large bowl and let cool slightly. Using 2 forks, shred into bite-size pieces; refrigerate for 20 minutes. Strain sauce through fine-mesh strainer, discarding solids. Combine chilled beef, 1 cup cheddar, and ¼ cup reserved sauce in bowl.

4. Adjust oven rack to middle position and increase oven temperature to 450 degrees. Spread ¾ cup sauce over bottom of 13 by 9-inch baking dish. Brush both sides of tortillas with remaining 2 tablespoons oil. Stack tortillas, wrap in damp dish towel, and place on plate; microwave until warm and pliable, about 1 minute.

5. Working with 1 warm tortilla at a time, spread ⅓ cup beef filling across center of tortilla. Roll tortilla tightly around filling and place seam side down in baking dish; arrange enchiladas in 2 columns across width of dish.

6. Pour remaining sauce over top to cover completely and sprinkle remaining 1 cup cheddar over enchiladas. Cover dish tightly with greased aluminum foil. Bake until enchiladas are heated through and cheese is melted, 15 to 20 minutes. Let cool for 5 minutes and serve.

LEARN HOW **ENCHILADAS**

A flavorful filling and sauce are just part of great enchiladas. We found that the key to the most successful enchiladas is in the assembly: We spread sauce in the bottom of the baking dish so the enchiladas don't stick, and thoroughly coat the tops with sauce so the tortillas don't turn tough.

1. SPREAD SAUCE IN DISH: Spread some of the sauce in the bottom of a 13 by 9-inch baking dish. This prevents the enchiladas from sticking to the dish.

2. WARM TORTILLAS: Brush both sides of the tortillas with oil. Stack the tortillas, wrap them in a damp dish towel, and place the stack on a plate. Microwave the tortillas for about 1 minute, until they are warm and pliable. Using the microwave allows you to skip warming the tortillas in oil one at a time.

3. FILL TORTILLAS: Measure the filling onto each tortilla. Roll each tortilla tightly around the filling and place the rolled tortilla in the baking dish. It is important to carefully measure the filling to ensure that each enchilada is the same size.

4. ARRANGE ENCHILADAS: Place the filled and rolled tortillas seam side down in two columns across the width of the baking dish. Placing the rolled enchiladas seam side down ensures that they stay together while baking, and making two columns means that 12 enchiladas will fit in one dish.

5. TOP WITH SAUCE AND CHEESE: Pour the remaining sauce over the arranged enchiladas. Be sure to coat the tortillas evenly; the layer of sauce will protect the tortillas from drying out in the oven. Sprinkle cheese evenly over the sauce.

6. COVER AND BAKE: Cover the dish tightly with greased aluminum foil. Bake until the cheese is melted and the enchiladas are warmed through. Baking the enchiladas covered ensures that the tortillas don't dry out and the filling doesn't overcook.

Chicken Enchiladas with Red Chile Sauce

Serves 4 to 6

✓ **WHY THIS RECIPE WORKS:** Chicken enchiladas offer a rich and complex combination of flavors and textures, but traditional cooking methods require a whole day of preparation. We wanted a recipe for chicken enchiladas that could be made in 90 minutes from start to finish. We created a quick but flavorful red chile sauce with onion, garlic, spices, and tomato sauce. We poached the chicken directly in the sauce, which both enhanced the flavor of the sauce and ensured moist, flavorful meat for our enchilada filling. Sharp cheddar cheese complemented the rich filling nicely, while canned jalapeños and fresh cilantro rounded out the flavors and provided tang and brightness. As in our other enchilada recipes (pages 142–150), we brushed the tortillas with oil and microwaved them to make them pliable. After experimenting with oven temperatures and times, we found that baking the assembled enchiladas covered for 15 minutes resulted in perfectly melted cheese but didn't dry out the edges of the tortillas. See page 148 for make-ahead information. Serve with sour cream, diced avocado, sliced radishes, shredded romaine lettuce, and lime wedges.

- ¼ **cup vegetable oil**
- 1 **onion, chopped fine**
- 3 **tablespoons chili powder**
- 3 **garlic cloves, minced**
- 2 **teaspoons ground coriander**
- 2 **teaspoons ground cumin**
- 2 **teaspoons sugar**
- ½ **teaspoon salt**
- 1 **pound boneless, skinless chicken thighs, trimmed and cut into ¼-inch-wide strips**
- 2 **(8-ounce) cans tomato sauce**
- 1 **cup water**
- ½ **cup chopped fresh cilantro**
- ¼ **cup jarred jalapeños, chopped**
- 12 **ounces sharp cheddar cheese, shredded (3 cups)**
- 12 **(6-inch) corn tortillas**

1. Heat 2 tablespoons oil in medium saucepan over medium-high heat until shimmering. Add onion and cook until softened, 5 to 7 minutes. Stir in chili powder, garlic, coriander, cumin, sugar, and salt and cook until fragrant, about 30 seconds. Stir in chicken and coat thoroughly with spices. Stir in tomato sauce and water, bring to simmer, and cook until chicken is cooked through, about 8 minutes.

2. Drain mixture in fine-mesh strainer set over bowl, pressing on chicken and onion to extract as much sauce as possible; set sauce aside. Transfer chicken mixture to separate bowl, refrigerate for 20 minutes to chill, then stir in cilantro, jalapeños, and 2½ cups cheese.

3. Adjust oven rack middle position and heat oven to 450 degrees. Spread ¾ cup sauce over bottom of 13 by 9-inch baking dish. Brush both sides of tortillas with remaining 2 tablespoons oil. Stack tortillas, wrap in damp dish towel, and place on plate; microwave until warm and pliable, about 1 minute.

4. Working with 1 warm tortilla at a time, spread ⅓ cup chicken filling across center of tortilla. Roll tortilla tightly around filling and place seam side down in baking dish; arrange enchiladas in 2 columns across width of dish.

5. Pour remaining sauce over top to cover completely and sprinkle remaining ½ cup cheese over enchiladas. Cover dish tightly with greased aluminum foil. Bake until enchiladas are heated through and cheese is melted, 15 to 20 minutes. Let cool for 5 minutes and serve.

Chicken Enchiladas Verdes

Serves 4 to 6

✓ **WHY THIS RECIPE WORKS:** We love the bright, bold flavors of chicken *enchiladas verdes*. But too often, the green chile sauce that defines the dish is watery and lacks good chile flavor. We wanted memorable enchiladas verdes with moist, tender chicken wrapped in soft corn tortillas, covered by a sauce redolent with fresh citrusy flavors and topped with just the right amount of melted cheese. For easy, flavorful chicken, we poached boneless, skinless breasts in chicken broth enhanced with sautéed onion, garlic, and cumin. Next, we focused on the green sauce, which is based on tomatillos and green chiles. Although jalapeños and serranos added heat, we opted for the more complex herbal flavor of poblanos. For some characteristic char (which Mexican cooks achieve by roasting the vegetables on a *comal*), we broiled the tomatillos and the chiles until their skins blackened. For a chunky, well-seasoned sauce, we removed the bitter skins from the chiles and pulsed the tomatillos and chiles in the food processor. We also thinned the sauce with a bit of the chicken poaching broth for deep, chicken-y flavor. To enrich the filling, we chose pepper Jack cheese for its pleasant spice and mild flavor. Covering the bottom of the baking dish in a layer of sauce ensured that the enchiladas wouldn't stick, and arranging the filled enchiladas in two columns allowed us to fit 12 in a single baking dish. Since we wanted to melt the cheese and warm the enchiladas but not brown the tops, we baked them covered. See page 148 for make-ahead information. See Learn How on page 144. Serve with sour cream, diced avocado, sliced radishes, shredded romaine lettuce, and lime wedges.

3   tablespoons vegetable oil
1   onion, chopped fine
½   teaspoon ground cumin
3   garlic cloves, minced
1½ cups chicken broth
1   pound boneless, skinless chicken breasts, trimmed
1½ pounds tomatillos, husks and stems removed, rinsed well, dried, and halved
3   poblano chiles, halved lengthwise, stemmed, and seeded
1   teaspoon sugar, plus extra as needed
    Salt and pepper
½   cup chopped fresh cilantro
8   ounces pepper Jack or Monterey Jack cheese, shredded (2 cups)
12 (6-inch) corn tortillas
2   scallions, sliced thin

1. Heat 2 teaspoons oil in medium saucepan over medium heat until shimmering. Add onion and cook until golden, 6 to 8 minutes. Stir in cumin and two-thirds of garlic and cook until fragrant, about 30 seconds. Stir in broth and bring to simmer.

2. Nestle chicken into sauce. Cover, reduce heat to medium-low, and cook until chicken registers 160 degrees, 10 to 15 minutes, flipping chicken halfway through cooking. Transfer chicken to plate and let cool slightly. Using 2 forks, shred chicken into bite-size pieces; refrigerate for 20 minutes to chill. Reserve ¼ cup cooking liquid for sauce, discarding extra.

3. Meanwhile, adjust oven rack 6 inches from broiler element and heat broiler. Line rimmed baking sheet with aluminum foil. Toss tomatillos and poblanos with 1 teaspoon oil. Arrange tomatillos cut side down and poblanos skin side up on prepared sheet. Broil until vegetables are blackened and beginning to soften, 5 to 10 minutes. Transfer poblanos to bowl, cover with aluminum foil, and let steam until skins peel off easily, about 10 minutes. Using back of spoon, scrape loosened skins from poblanos.

4. Process broiled tomatillos with any accumulated juices, peeled poblanos, ¼ cup reserved cooking liquid, sugar, 1 teaspoon salt, and remaining garlic in food processor until sauce is somewhat chunky, about 8 pulses. Season with salt, pepper, and extra sugar to taste. Combine chilled chicken, cilantro, and 1½ cups cheese in bowl and season with salt and pepper to taste.

5. Adjust oven rack to middle position and heat oven to 450 degrees. Spread ¾ cup tomatillo sauce over bottom of 13 by 9-inch baking dish. Brush both sides of tortillas with remaining 2 tablespoons oil. Stack tortillas, wrap in damp dish towel, and place on plate; microwave until warm and pliable, about 1 minute.

6. Working with 1 warm tortilla at a time, spread ⅓ cup chicken filling across center of tortilla. Roll tortilla tightly around filling and place seam side down in baking dish; arrange enchiladas in 2 columns across width of dish.

7. Pour remaining sauce over top to cover completely and sprinkle remaining ½ cup cheese over enchiladas. Cover dish tightly with greased aluminum foil. Bake until enchiladas are heated through and cheese is melted, 15 to 20 minutes. Let cool for 5 minutes, sprinkle with scallions, and serve.

TEST KITCHEN TIP
ROASTING POBLANOS AND TOMATILLOS

Quickly charring the tomatillos and chiles under the broiler intensifies their flavor and adds smokiness.

TEST KITCHEN TIP PREPARING ENCHILADAS AHEAD OF TIME

The trick to making enchiladas ahead of time is to refrigerate the assembled enchiladas, the sauce, and the cheese topping separately. When assembling the enchiladas, don't spread any sauce over the bottom of the dish; instead, grease the dish. This prevents the tortillas from sticking; eliminating the layer of sauce ensures that the tortillas won't become soggy. You can store the assembled enchiladas for up to 24 hours. To bake, unwrap the dish of enchiladas, spray the tops with vegetable oil, and bake uncovered (without reserved sauce) in a 400-degree oven until lightly toasted on top, 10 to 15 minutes. Pour the sauce over the enchiladas, covering the tortillas completely, and sprinkle the reserved cheese down the center of the enchiladas. Cover the dish tightly with greased aluminum foil and bake until the enchiladas are hot throughout and bubbling around the edges and the cheese is melted, 20 to 25 minutes. Serve.

Roasted Poblano and Black Bean Enchiladas

Serves 4 to 6

✔ **WHY THIS RECIPE WORKS:** For great vegetarian enchiladas, we wanted a bright yet rich green sauce featuring sweet-tart tomatillos. We rounded out the flavor of the tomatillo sauce with onion, garlic, cilantro, and lime juice. A splash of heavy cream lent richness. For the filling, we started with roasted poblano chiles. We smashed canned black beans to create a quick "refried" bean base and stirred in a little of the tomatillo sauce, Monterey Jack cheese, and some heady seasonings. See Learn How on page 144. Serve with sour cream, diced avocado, sliced radishes, shredded romaine lettuce, and lime wedges.

- 1   **pound tomatillos, husks and stems removed, rinsed well, dried, and halved**
- 4   **poblano chiles, halved lengthwise, stemmed, and seeded**
- 1   **teaspoon plus ¼ cup vegetable oil**
- 2   **onions, chopped fine**
- 1   **cup fresh cilantro leaves**
- ⅓   **cup vegetable broth**
- ¼   **cup heavy cream**
- 4   **garlic cloves, minced**
- 1   **tablespoon lime juice**
- 1   **teaspoon sugar**
-     **Salt and pepper**
- 1   **teaspoon chili powder**
- ½   **teaspoon ground coriander**
- ½   **teaspoon ground cumin**
- 1   **(15-ounce) can black beans, rinsed, half of beans mashed smooth**
- 8   **ounces Monterey Jack cheese, shredded (2 cups)**
- 12   **(6-inch) corn tortillas**

1. Adjust oven rack 6 inches from broiler element and heat broiler. Line rimmed baking sheet with aluminum foil. Toss tomatillos and poblanos with 1 teaspoon oil. Arrange tomatillos cut side down and poblanos skin side up on prepared sheet. Broil until vegetables are blackened and beginning to soften, 5 to 10 minutes. Transfer poblanos to bowl, cover with aluminum foil, and let steam until skins peel off easily, about 10 minutes. Using back of spoon, scrape loosened skins from poblanos. Chop tomatillos and poblanos into ½-inch pieces.

2. Process broiled tomatillos, 1 cup onion, ½ cup cilantro, broth, cream, 1 tablespoon oil, half of garlic, lime juice, sugar, and 1 teaspoon salt in food processor until sauce is smooth, about 2 minutes. Season with salt and pepper to taste.

3. Heat 1 tablespoon oil in 12-inch skillet over medium heat until shimmering. Add remaining onion and cook until softened, 5 to 7 minutes. Stir in chili powder, coriander, cumin, and remaining garlic and cook until fragrant, about 30 seconds. Stir in mashed and whole beans and chopped poblanos and cook until warmed through, about 2 minutes. Transfer mixture to large bowl and let cool slightly. Stir in 1 cup Monterey Jack, ½ cup tomatillo sauce, and remaining ½ cup cilantro. Season with salt and pepper to taste.

4. Adjust oven rack to middle position and heat oven to 400 degrees. Spread ½ cup tomatillo sauce over bottom of 13 by 9-inch baking dish. Brush both sides of tortillas with remaining 2 tablespoons oil. Stack tortillas, wrap in damp dish towel, and place on plate; microwave until warm and pliable, about 1 minute.

5. Working with 1 warm tortilla at a time, spread ¼ cup bean-cheese filling across center of tortilla. Roll tortilla tightly around filling and place seam side down in baking dish; arrange enchiladas in 2 columns across width of dish.

6. Pour remaining sauce over top to cover completely and sprinkle remaining 1 cup cheese down center of enchiladas. Cover dish tightly with greased aluminum foil. Bake until enchiladas are heated through and cheese is melted, 15 to 20 minutes. Let cool for 5 minutes and serve.

Cheese Enchiladas

Serves 4 to 6

✔ **WHY THIS RECIPE WORKS:** Unlike their Mexican counterparts, Tex-Mex cheese enchiladas have no meat in the filling, and trade the tomatoey enchilada sauce for a smoky chile gravy. The gravy, a hallmark of Tex-Mex cooking, provides the bulk of flavor in the dish. Like beef or poultry gravy, it's based on broth thickened with a roux (in this case, flour cooked with vegetable oil or lard). But unlike other gravies, chile gravy gets its signature flavor not from meat drippings but from aromatics, spices, and, of course, dried chiles, either whole or powdered. Since the chile flavor is central to the gravy, we opted to work with dried chiles rather than chile powder; they gave the gravy a cleaner, more potent flavor. Dried ancho chiles, along with cumin, garlic, and oregano, were the perfect backbone for our roux-based gravy, and a splash of vinegar brightened it up. Instead of using the processed cheese typical of the dish, we opted for a combination of cheddar for big, bold flavor and Monterey Jack for smooth meltability. Finally, a sprinkling of raw onion over the finished enchiladas provided a sharp counterpoint to the rich spices and creamy cheese. See page 148 for make-ahead information. See Learn How on page 144. Serve with sour cream, diced avocado, sliced radishes, shredded romaine lettuce, and lime wedges. See the photo on page 140.

2 **dried ancho chiles, stemmed, seeded, and torn into ½-inch pieces (½ cup)**
1 **tablespoon cumin seeds**
1 **tablespoon garlic powder**
2 **teaspoons dried oregano**
5 **tablespoons vegetable oil**
3 **tablespoons all-purpose flour**
  Salt and pepper
2 **cups chicken broth**
2 **teaspoons distilled white vinegar**
8 **ounces Monterey Jack cheese, shredded (2 cups)**
6 **ounces sharp cheddar cheese, shredded (1½ cups)**
12 **(6-inch) corn tortillas**
1 **onion, chopped fine**

1. Toast anchos and cumin in 12-inch skillet over medium heat, stirring frequently, until fragrant, 2 to 6 minutes. Transfer to spice grinder and let cool slightly. Add garlic powder and oregano and grind to fine powder.

2. Heat 3 tablespoons oil in now-empty skillet over medium-high heat until shimmering. Whisk in flour, ½ teaspoon salt, ½ teaspoon pepper, and ground spices and cook until fragrant and slightly deepened in color, about 1 minute. Slowly whisk in broth and bring to simmer. Reduce heat to medium-low and cook, whisking often, until sauce has thickened and measures 1½ cups, about 5 minutes. Whisk in vinegar and season with salt and pepper to taste. Remove from heat, cover, and keep warm.

3. Adjust oven rack to middle position and heat oven to 450 degrees. Spread ½ cup sauce over bottom of 13 by 9-inch baking dish. Combine Monterey Jack and cheddar in bowl; set ½ cup cheese mixture aside for topping. Brush both sides of tortillas with remaining 2 tablespoons oil. Stack tortillas, wrap in damp dish towel, and place on plate; microwave until warm and pliable, about 1 minute.

4. Working with 1 warm tortilla at a time, spread ¼ cup cheese mixture across center of tortilla and sprinkle with 1 tablespoon onion. Roll tortilla tightly around filling and place seam side down in baking dish; arrange enchiladas in 2 columns across width of dish.

5. Pour remaining sauce over top to cover completely and sprinkle reserved cheese over enchiladas. Cover dish tightly with greased aluminum foil. Bake until enchiladas are heated through and cheese is melted, 15 to 20 minutes. Let cool for 5 minutes and sprinkle with remaining onion. Serve.

Beef Enchilada Casserole

Serves 8 to 10

✔ **WHY THIS RECIPE WORKS:** We love classic beef enchiladas, but making enough for a crowd poses a challenge. We set out to create a simple layered casserole that would feed a larger group of people and still have all the deep, meaty flavor of beef enchiladas. To keep things simple and streamlined, we chose ground beef over braised, shredded meat; tasters preferred the flavor of 85 percent lean ground beef. To get deep, full corn flavor from the tortillas and to prevent them from becoming tough and chewy in the casserole, we toasted them in a dry skillet, then used them in two ways: We blended some of them into a sauce mixture for the beef, and layered the rest into the casserole dish. We put all of the beef mixture in between the tortilla layers, which protected the meat from drying out in the oven. We then topped the casserole with some of our homemade enchilada sauce and let it bake for about 30 minutes. Finally, we sprinkled on Colby Jack cheese and minced jalapeño before returning the dish to the oven to bake until golden brown and bubbling. If you can't find Ro-Tel tomatoes, substitute 1¼ cups of canned diced tomatoes plus an additional jalapeño. Monterey Jack cheese may be substituted for the Colby Jack. Serve with sour cream, chopped scallions, and lime wedges.

20	(6-inch) corn tortillas
1	(10-ounce) can Ro-Tel tomatoes
1½	cups beef broth
2	pounds 85 percent lean ground beef
2	tablespoons vegetable oil
2	onions, chopped fine
8	garlic cloves, minced
2	tablespoons chili powder
1	teaspoon ground cumin
3	(15-ounce) cans tomato sauce
1	pound Colby Jack cheese, shredded (4 cups)
3	jalapeño chiles, stemmed, seeded, and minced
½	cup chopped fresh cilantro
1	tablespoon hot sauce
	Salt and pepper

1. Adjust oven rack to middle position and heat oven to 450 degrees. Toast tortillas, one at a time, in 12-inch nonstick skillet over medium-high heat until lightly browned, about 20 seconds per side; transfer to plate and cover with dish towel.

2. Tear 8 toasted tortillas into rough pieces and transfer to food processor. Add tomatoes and their juice and ¾ cup broth and process until smooth; transfer to large bowl. Add beef to now-empty skillet and cook over medium-high heat, breaking up meat with wooden spoon, until no longer pink, about 5 minutes. Drain beef in colander, then stir into processed tortilla mixture.

3. Add oil and onions to now-empty skillet and cook over medium heat until softened, about 5 minutes. Stir in garlic, chili powder, and cumin and cook until fragrant, about 30 seconds. Stir in tomato sauce and remaining ¾ cup broth and simmer until slightly thickened, 5 to 7 minutes; transfer to bowl.

4. Stir half of tomato sauce mixture, 1½ cups Colby Jack, half of jalapeños, cilantro, and hot sauce into beef mixture. Season with salt and pepper.

5. Arrange 6 toasted tortillas in bottom of greased 13 by 9-inch baking dish, overlapping them slightly. Spread beef mixture evenly into dish, then top with remaining 6 tortillas followed by remaining tomato sauce mixture. Bake until filling is bubbling around edges, about 30 minutes. Sprinkle with remaining 2½ cups Colby Jack and remaining jalapeños and continue to bake until cheese is browned, 15 to 20 minutes. Let casserole cool for 20 minutes before serving.

Pastel Azteca

Serves 6 to 8

✓ **WHY THIS RECIPE WORKS:** Traditional Mexican *pastel Azteca* (literally meaning "Aztec cake") bears a strong resemblance to familiar Mexican lasagna or enchilada casserole. This hearty casserole features corn tortillas layered with chicken, cheese, and a simple enchilada sauce. We added a bit of flour to our sauce, which allowed it to cling to the tortillas nicely. Toasting the tortillas in a dry skillet was preferable to using untoasted tortillas, which disintegrated, and it was less messy and greasy than frying them, as some pastel Azteca recipes do. A combination of melty Montery Jack and tangy *queso fresco* provided contrasting flavors and textures that helped bring the dish to life, and we topped the casserole with cilantro, scallions, and chopped tomatoes for a pop of bright freshness.

2 **dried ancho chiles, stemmed, seeded, and torn into ½-inch pieces (½ cup)**
1 **tablespoon vegetable oil**
1 **onion, chopped**
1 **tablespoon tomato paste**
3 **garlic cloves, minced**
2 **teaspoons dried oregano**
1 **teaspoon ground cumin**
1 **teaspoon ground coriander**
 Salt and pepper
3 **tablespoons all-purpose flour**
3 **cups chicken broth**
2½ **pounds boneless, skinless chicken breasts, trimmed**
5 **scallions, sliced thin**
⅓ **cup chopped fresh cilantro**
1 **tablespoon lime juice**
18 **(6-inch) corn tortillas**
8 **ounces Monterey Jack cheese, shredded (2 cups)**
8 **ounces queso fresco, crumbled (2 cups)**
2 **tomatoes, cored and chopped**

1. Adjust oven rack to middle position and heat oven to 425 degrees. Toast anchos in 12-inch skillet over medium heat, stirring frequently, until fragrant, 2 to 6 minutes; transfer to blender.

2. Heat oil in Dutch oven over medium-high heat until shimmering. Add onion and cook until softened, about 5 minutes. Stir in tomato paste, garlic, oregano, cumin, coriander, 1 teaspoon salt, and ½ teaspoon pepper and cook until fragrant, about 1 minute. Stir in flour and cook until slightly deepened in color, about 1 minute. Slowly whisk in broth and bring to simmer. Reduce heat to medium-low and cook, whisking often, until sauce is slightly thickened, about 3 minutes.

3. Add sauce to blender and process until smooth, about 30 seconds; return to now-empty pot. Nestle chicken into sauce, cover, and cook over medium-low heat until chicken registers 160 degrees, about 15 minutes. Transfer chicken to cutting board, let cool slightly, then shred into bite-size pieces using 2 forks; transfer to bowl. Add 1½ cups sauce, two-thirds of scallions, ¼ cup cilantro, and lime juice and toss to combine.

4. Meanwhile, toast tortillas, one at a time, in 8-inch skillet over medium-high heat until lightly browned, about 20 seconds per side; transfer to plate and cover with dish towel. Combine Monterey Jack and queso fresco in bowl.

5. Spread ½ cup remaining sauce over bottom of 13 by 9-inch baking dish. Lay 6 tortillas into dish, overlapping them slightly. Spread ½ cup sauce over tortillas and top with half of chicken mixture and one-third of cheese mixture. Repeat with 6 more tortillas, ½ cup sauce, remaining chicken mixture, and half of remaining cheese mixture. Top with remaining 6 tortillas, remaining sauce, and remaining cheese.

6. Cover dish with aluminum foil and bake until sauce is bubbling and cheese is melted, 15 to 20 minutes. Let casserole cool for 10 minutes. Sprinkle with tomatoes, remaining scallions, and remaining cilantro. Serve.

Chicken Chilaquiles

Serves 4

✅ **WHY THIS RECIPE WORKS:** *Chilaquiles* is a Mexican comfort food dish made from fried tortilla wedges that are tossed in a deeply flavored red or green chile sauce. The crisp chips soften slightly in the sauce, giving the dish a unique crunchy-chewy texture. The finished dish is topped with a variety of fresh garnishes along with a fried egg and served for breakfast. We loved this idea, but decided to swap the fried egg for shredded chicken to make the dish into a hearty main course. We quickly discovered that store-bought chips led to disappointing results; they either turned mushy or never softened properly. Although most recipes call for frying the chips, we opted to bake them, which was not only more hands-off but also prevented a greasy finished dish. We made a simple sauce by pureeing the chiles, vegetables, and aromatics in a blender and then simmering the mixture in a Dutch oven. Poaching the chicken directly in the sauce infused both with more depth of flavor. An assortment of fresh garnishes made the perfect counterpoint to the rich sauce, chips, and chicken. For the best texture, we prefer to use 100 percent corn tortillas in this recipe. Serve with Mexican crema and lime wedges.

16	(6-inch) corn tortillas, cut into 8 wedges
¼	cup olive oil
	Salt
5	dried guajillo chiles, stemmed, seeded, and torn into ½-inch pieces (⅔ cup)
1	(28-ounce) can whole peeled tomatoes
1	cup finely chopped onion
1	poblano chile, stemmed, seeded, and chopped
1	jalapeño chile, stemmed, seeded, and chopped
3	garlic cloves, peeled and chopped
8	sprigs fresh cilantro plus 2 tablespoons minced
1½	cups chicken broth
1½	pounds boneless, skinless chicken breasts, trimmed
4	ounces queso fresco, crumbled (1 cup)
1	avocado, halved, pitted, and cut into ½-inch pieces
2	radishes, trimmed and sliced thin

1. Adjust oven racks to upper-middle and lower-middle positions and heat oven to 425 degrees. Spread tortillas evenly over 2 rimmed baking sheets. Drizzle each sheet with 2 tablespoons oil and ¼ teaspoon salt and toss until evenly coated. Bake, stirring occasionally, until tortillas are golden brown and crisp, 15 to 20 minutes, switching sheets halfway through baking.

2. Toast guajillos in Dutch oven over medium heat, stirring frequently, until fragrant, 2 to 6 minutes. Transfer toasted guajillos to blender and process until finely ground, 60 to 90 seconds. Add tomatoes and their juice, ¾ cup onion, poblano, jalapeño, garlic, cilantro sprigs, and ¾ teaspoon salt to blender and process until very smooth, 60 to 90 seconds.

3. Combine guajillo-tomato mixture and broth in now-empty Dutch oven and bring to boil over medium-high heat. Nestle chicken into sauce. Cover, reduce heat to medium-low, and cook until chicken registers 160 degrees, 10 to 15 minutes, flipping halfway through cooking.

4. Transfer chicken to plate and let cool slightly. Using 2 forks, shred chicken into bite-size pieces. Meanwhile, increase heat to medium and simmer sauce until thickened and measures 4½ cups, about 5 minutes.

5. Stir in shredded chicken and cook until warmed through, about 2 minutes. Off heat, stir in tortillas, cover, and let sit until tortillas have softened slightly, 2 to 5 minutes. Transfer tortilla mixture to serving dish and sprinkle with queso fresco, avocado, radishes, remaining ¼ cup onion, and minced cilantro. Serve immediately.

Chiles Rellenos Casserole

Serves 6 to 8

✓ **WHY THIS RECIPE WORKS:** Traditional chiles rellenos are a long-standing Mexican favorite, but preparing them can be time-consuming and fussy. But the mild heat of the chiles, the beefy, cheesy filling, the crisp, light coating, and the spicy tomato sauce make this dish irresistible. We wanted all the multidimensional flavor and texture of traditional chiles rellenos without all the work, so we turned to chiles rellenos casserole. Fresh poblano chiles were favored for their mild vegetal flavor. To shortcut the traditional, time-consuming step of roasting and peeling whole chiles, we simply chopped them and sautéed them with the beef. We used 90 percent lean ground beef, since anything fattier made the casserole greasy. Spicy Ro-Tel tomatoes stood in for the traditional spicy tomato sauce. Finally, a combination of flour, egg whites, and milk made a topping that browned nicely in the oven. If you can't find Ro-Tel tomatoes, use 1 cup of drained diced tomatoes combined with one stemmed, seeded, and finely chopped jalapeño.

1	tablespoon vegetable oil
1	onion, chopped fine
2	pounds 90 percent lean ground beef
4	poblano chiles, stemmed, seeded, and chopped
2	garlic cloves, minced
2	teaspoons ground cumin
1	teaspoon dried oregano
¼	teaspoon cayenne pepper
	Salt and pepper
1	(10-ounce) can Ro-Tel tomatoes, drained
10	ounces Monterey Jack cheese, shredded (2½ cups)
½	cup all-purpose flour
¾	cup skim milk
2	large egg whites

1. Adjust oven rack to upper-middle position and heat oven to 450 degrees. Heat oil in 12-inch nonstick skillet over medium heat until shimmering. Add onion and cook until softened, about 5 minutes. Stir in beef, breaking up meat with wooden spoon, and cook until no longer pink, 8 to 10 minutes. Using slotted spoon, transfer beef mixture to paper towel–lined plate. Pour off all but 2 tablespoons fat from skillet.

2. Add poblanos to fat left in skillet and cook over medium-high heat until browned, 8 to 10 minutes. Stir in garlic, cumin, oregano, cayenne, ¾ teaspoon salt, ½ teaspoon pepper, and beef mixture and cook until fragrant, about 30 seconds. Stir in tomatoes and cook until mixture is dry, about 1 minute. Off heat, stir in 2 cups Monterey Jack. Scrape mixture into 13 by 9-inch baking dish and press into even layer.

3. Combine flour, ½ teaspoon salt, and ¼ teaspoon pepper in bowl. Slowly whisk in milk until smooth. Using stand mixer fitted with whisk, whip egg whites on medium-low speed until foamy, about 1 minute. Increase speed to medium-high and whip until stiff peaks form, about 3 minutes. Whisk one-third whipped egg whites into milk-flour batter to lighten. Gently fold in remaining whites, 1 scoop at a time, until combined.

4. Pour batter evenly over beef mixture. Bake until topping is light golden and puffed, about 15 minutes. Sprinkle with remaining ½ cup Monterey Jack and bake until golden brown, about 10 minutes. Let cool on wire rack for 10 minutes. Serve.

TEST KITCHEN TIP WHIPPING EGG WHITES

Whip egg whites on medium-high speed until stiff peaks form. Egg whites whipped to stiff peaks should stand up tall on their own.

Tamale Pie

Serves 6 to 8

✅ **WHY THIS RECIPE WORKS:** Tamale pie—lightly seasoned, tomatoey ground beef with cornbread topping—borrows the flavor of traditional Mexican tamales for an easy-to-make pie. But in many recipes, the filling either tastes bland and one-dimensional or turns heavy. As for the cornbread topping, it's usually from a mix—and tastes like it. We wanted a tamale pie with a rich, well-seasoned filling and a cornmeal topping reminiscent of real tamale dough with plenty of corn flavor. For the beef, we found that 90 percent lean ground beef gave us a good balance of richness and flavor. We bloomed chili powder, oregano, and garlic with some sautéed onion and jalapeño to intensify their flavors. The addition of canned black beans made our pie heartier, while corn and canned diced tomatoes contributed additional flavor and texture. We stirred Monterey Jack cheese into the mixture to enrich the filling and help thicken it. To finish our pie, we made a simple cornmeal batter which we spread over the filling before baking. After 30 minutes in the oven, our rich, hearty pie had a crunchy, flavorful topping that perfectly complemented the spicy filling. We like coarse cornmeal for the crust on this pie and had the best results using Goya Coarse Yellow Cornmeal. Ground pork or turkey can be substituted for the beef.

3   tablespoons vegetable oil
1   pound 90 percent lean ground beef
1   onion, chopped fine
1   jalapeño chile, stemmed, seeded, and minced
    Salt and pepper
2   tablespoons chili powder
1   tablespoon minced fresh oregano or 1 teaspoon dried

2   garlic cloves, minced
1   (15-ounce) can black beans, rinsed
1   (14.5-ounce) can diced tomatoes
1   cup fresh or frozen corn
2½ cups water
¾   cup coarse cornmeal
4   ounces Monterey Jack cheese, shredded (1 cup)

1. Adjust oven rack to lower-middle position and heat oven to 375 degrees. Heat 1 tablespoon oil in 12-inch skillet over medium-high heat until just smoking. Add beef and cook, breaking up meat with wooden spoon, until just beginning to brown, about 5 minutes.

2. Stir in onion, jalapeño, and ¼ teaspoon salt and cook until vegetables are softened, about 5 minutes. Stir in chili powder, oregano, and garlic and cook until fragrant, about 30 seconds. Stir in beans, tomatoes and their juice, and corn and simmer until most of liquid has evaporated, about 3 minutes. Off heat, season with salt and pepper to taste.

3. Bring water to boil in large saucepan. Add ¼ teaspoon salt and then slowly pour in cornmeal while whisking vigorously to prevent clumping. Turn heat to medium and cook, whisking constantly, until cornmeal thickens, about 3 minutes. Stir in remaining 2 tablespoons oil.

4. Stir Monterey Jack into beef mixture, then scrape into deep-dish pie plate (or other 3-quart baking dish). Spread cornmeal mixture over top and seal against edge of dish. Cover with aluminum foil and bake until crust has set and filling is hot throughout, about 30 minutes. Let casserole cool for 10 minutes. Serve.

SINALOA-STYLE GRILL-ROASTED CHICKENS

Poultry

Chicken Mole Poblano

Serves 4 to 6

✓ **WHY THIS RECIPE WORKS:** Hailing from the Puebla region of Mexico, *mole poblano* is a rich, deep red sauce made from chiles, nuts, spices, fruit, and chocolate. The most famous of Mexico's many moles, it's the style of mole you're apt to find on most restaurant menus. But the process to make traditional mole poblano is lengthy and complicated, taking several hours (or even several days) to complete. We set out to bring mole poblano to the American home kitchen without losing the rich, deeply complex flavor that makes mole so appealing. Although traditional mole poblano relies on as many as six types of chiles, we pared our recipe down to two: ancho, which lent a full chile flavor base, and chipotle, which amped up the intensity of the chile flavor and provided a hint of heat and smokiness. Breaking the chiles into small pieces and rehydrating them right in the sauce (rather than in plain water) ensured that our sauce was fully infused with chile flavor. As for the nuts and seeds, we liked the rich, creamy flavors of toasted almonds and sesame seeds. Using almond butter instead of ground almonds was a simple shortcut that lent a luxurious, velvety texture to the sauce. For the chocolate, just 1 ounce added richness and depth but didn't make the sauce taste chocolaty. To round out the flavor of our mole, we added warmth and a touch of sweetness with cinnamon, cloves, and raisins. Sautéing the chiles, chocolate, and spices along with the onion and garlic deepened the flavor of the final sauce, and we found that we could sauté everything together to streamline our prep work, although many traditional recipes called for sautéing each ingredient individually. Simmering the mole for just 10 minutes thickened the sauce to the perfect consistency. Bone-in chicken pieces worked perfectly with our mole, although removing the skin was essential since it turned inedibly soggy when covered in sauce. Feel free to substitute ½ teaspoon ground chipotle chile powder or ½ teaspoon minced canned chipotles in adobo sauce for the chipotle chile (we noted little difference in flavor) and add with the cinnamon in step 2. Serve with rice.

2 dried ancho chiles, stemmed, seeded, and torn into ½-inch pieces (½ cup)
½ dried chipotle chile, stemmed, seeded, and torn into ½-inch pieces (scant tablespoon)
3 tablespoons vegetable oil
1 onion, chopped fine
½ teaspoon ground cinnamon
⅛ teaspoon ground cloves
1 ounce bittersweet, semisweet, or Mexican chocolate, chopped coarse
2 garlic cloves, minced
2 cups chicken broth
1 (14.5-ounce) can diced tomatoes, drained
¼ cup raisins
¼ cup almond butter
2 tablespoons sesame seeds, plus extra for garnish, toasted
   Salt and pepper
   Sugar
3½ pounds bone-in chicken pieces (split breasts, legs, and/or thighs), skin removed, trimmed

1. Toast anchos and chipotle in 12-inch skillet over medium heat, stirring frequently, until fragrant, 2 to 6 minutes; transfer to plate. Add oil and onion to now-empty skillet and cook over medium-high heat until softened, 5 to 7 minutes.

2. Stir in cinnamon, cloves, chocolate, and toasted chiles and cook until chocolate is melted and bubbly, about 2 minutes. Stir in garlic and cook until fragrant, about 30 seconds. Stir in broth, tomatoes, raisins, almond butter, and sesame seeds and bring to simmer. Reduce heat to medium and simmer gently, stirring occasionally, until slightly thickened and measures about 2½ cups, about 10 minutes.

3. Transfer mixture to blender and process until smooth, about 20 seconds. Season with salt, pepper, and sugar to taste. (Sauce can be refrigerated for up to 3 days; loosen with water as needed before continuing.)

4. Adjust oven rack to middle position and heat oven to 400 degrees. Pat chicken dry with paper towels and season with salt and pepper. Arrange chicken in single layer in shallow baking dish and cover with mole sauce, turning to coat chicken evenly. Bake, uncovered, until breasts register 160 degrees, and thighs or drumsticks register 175 degrees, 35 to 45 minutes.

5. Remove chicken from oven, tent with aluminum foil, and let rest for 5 to 10 minutes. Sprinkle with sesame seeds and serve.

LEARN HOW **MOLE POBLANO SAUCE**

Mole poblano is a quintessential Mexican sauce, but traditional recipes can be very time-consuming. We streamlined the process by sautéing all of our aromatics together (rather than separately) and replacing ground almonds with almond butter for a mole with all the richness and depth of traditional versions.

1. TOAST CHILES: Stem, seed, and tear the chiles into ½-inch pieces. Toast the chiles in a 12-inch skillet over medium heat until fragrant, 2 to 6 minutes. Transfer the chiles to a plate.

2. BUILD SAUCE: Cook the onion, then add the chiles, spices, and chocolate. Stir in the garlic, then the broth, tomatoes, sesame seeds, raisins, and almond butter. Simmer until slightly thickened.

3. PUREE SAUCE: Transfer the sauce to a blender. Puree until smooth, about 20 seconds, then season it with salt, pepper, and sugar to taste.

Chicken Adobo

Serves 4

✔ **WHY THIS RECIPE WORKS:** The boldly flavored, vibrant Mexican sauce known as adobo is made by combining dried ground chiles, spices, herbs, and salt with vinegar. It is a popular seasoning for meat, but many recipes require a serious time commitment: an overnight marinade for the meat, plus simmering the sauce to concentrate flavors, not to mention preparing the actual dish. We wanted to achieve the same deeply flavorful results in much less time. We decided to quickly season our chicken (boneless thighs offered rich flavor and cooked quickly) with a salty, potently flavored rub made from chipotle chile in adobo, garlic, oregano, salt, and pepper. An unusual addition, espresso powder, heightened the flavors of our rub. While the chicken marinated, we built our sauce. First we sautéed onions and then added canned diced tomatoes, which we'd buzzed in a food processor to break up the pieces. Adding molasses to the sauce brought subtle bitter notes and gave us long-simmered flavor in only a few minutes. Cooking the chicken directly in the sauce allowed each to pick up flavor from the other. Some chopped cilantro added at the end brought a welcome note of freshness. Serve with rice.

1   **(14.5-ounce) can diced tomatoes, drained**
3   **tablespoons minced canned chipotle chile in adobo sauce**
3   **garlic cloves, minced**
2   **teaspoons dried oregano**
1½ **teaspoons instant espresso powder**
    Salt and pepper
1½ **pounds boneless, skinless chicken thighs, trimmed and cut into 2-inch pieces**
2   **tablespoons vegetable oil**
1   **onion, chopped**
3   **tablespoons molasses**
1   **tablespoon minced fresh cilantro or parsley**

1. Process tomatoes in food processor until smooth; set aside. Combine chipotle, garlic, oregano, espresso powder, ½ teaspoon salt, and ¼ teaspoon pepper in bowl. Pat chicken dry with paper towels, then coat completely with chipotle mixture.

2. Heat 1 tablespoon oil in 12-inch nonstick skillet over medium-high heat until just smoking. Cook chicken until golden brown on both sides, about 6 minutes; transfer to plate.

3. Heat remaining 1 tablespoon oil in now-empty skillet over medium heat until shimmering. Add onion and cook until softened and lightly browned, 6 to 8 minutes. Stir in molasses, processed tomatoes, and chicken with any accumulated juices. Cover and simmer until chicken registers 175 degrees and sauce has thickened, about 10 minutes.

4. Transfer chicken to platter, tent with aluminum foil, and let rest for 5 to 10 minutes. Season sauce with salt and pepper to taste, then spoon over chicken. Sprinkle with cilantro and serve.

TEST KITCHEN TIP
CUTTING UP CHICKEN THIGHS

Using chef's knife, trim boneless, skinless chicken thighs of excess fat, then cut into 2-inch pieces.

Chicken with Pumpkin Seed Sauce

Serves 4

✓ **WHY THIS RECIPE WORKS:** *Pipian verde*, or pumpkin seed sauce, is a traditional Pueblan sauce that can be served over anything from chicken to pork to fish. The sauce is made with tangy fresh tomatillos and nutty toasted pumpkin seeds. But, like many traditional Mexican sauces, it's one that requires an arsenal of cookware and hours, if not days, to make. We wanted to maintain the classic flavor profile but minimize the work. Our first move was to toast the sesame seeds and pumpkin seeds (we chose pepitas over unhulled pumpkin seeds, which made a smoother sauce) in a skillet, which we then used to build our sauce. Onion, garlic, and thyme gave the sauce an aromatic base, while fresh jalapeño gave it lively spice. We chopped the tomatillos so they would soften nicely. Poaching our chicken right in the sauce kept our recipe streamlined and ensured moist, flavorful chicken. Once the chicken was done, we pureed the sauce in the blender; lime juice, cilantro, and a pinch of sugar added at this point gave the sauce just the right brightness and rounded out the flavors. Serve with rice.

⅓ cup pepitas
¼ cup sesame seeds
2 tablespoons vegetable oil
1 onion, chopped fine
  Salt and pepper
1 jalapeño chile, stemmed, seeded, and chopped
3 garlic cloves, minced
1 teaspoon fresh minced thyme or ¼ teaspoon dried
6 ounces fresh tomatillos, husks and stems removed, rinsed well and dried, chopped
1½ cups chicken broth
4 (6- to 8-ounce) boneless, skinless chicken breasts, trimmed
1 cup fresh cilantro leaves
1 tablespoon lime juice
  Pinch sugar

1. Toast pepitas and sesame seeds in 12-inch nonstick skillet over medium heat until seeds are golden and fragrant, about 15 minutes; transfer to bowl. Reserve 1 tablespoon toasted seeds separately for garnish.

2. Add oil, onion, and ½ teaspoon salt to now-empty skillet and cook over medium-high heat until softened, 5 to 7 minutes. Stir in jalapeño, garlic, and thyme and cook until fragrant, about 30 seconds. Stir in tomatillos, broth, and toasted seeds, cover, and cook until tomatillos begin to soften, about 10 minutes.

3. Season chicken with salt and pepper, then nestle into skillet. Cover, reduce heat to medium-low, and cook until chicken registers 160 degrees, 10 to 15 minutes, flipping halfway through cooking. Transfer chicken to platter, tent with aluminum foil, and let rest for 5 to 10 minutes.

4. Carefully transfer mixture left in skillet to blender. Add cilantro, lime juice, and sugar and process until mostly smooth, about 1 minute. Season with salt and pepper to taste. Spoon some of sauce over chicken and sprinkle with reserved seeds. Serve with remaining sauce.

TEST KITCHEN TIP **TOASTING SEEDS**

Toast pepitas and sesame seeds in dry, 12-inch nonstick skillet over medium heat until seeds are golden and fragrant, about 15 minutes.

Chicken with Ancho-Peanut Sauce

Serves 4

✔ **WHY THIS RECIPE WORKS:** A specialty of the Puebla region, *pollo encacahuatado* is a chicken dish with a thick, hearty sauce made with tomatoes, ground peanuts, and chiles. A variation of a classic mole, the rich red sauce boasts deep chile flavor that is beautifully complemented by the sweetness of the tomatoes and the savory, nutty, peanut flavor. For our version, we settled on traditional ancho chiles; their naturally smoky, fruity, complex flavor and mild heat made them an excellent option. We also added a bit of chipotle chile in adobo for an even deeper, smokier flavor. As for the peanuts, we chose dry-roasted peanuts to save ourselves the time of roasting them ourselves. Toasted sesame seeds gave the sauce an even more complex nutty flavor. We blended the chiles, peanuts, and sesame seeds with tomatoes, warm spices, and aromatics to create a thick paste. We then fried the paste in oil to deepen its flavor; this also created a rich and flavorful fond. To this base, we added some savory chicken broth, which tasted better than plain water. The gentle, even heat of poaching left the chicken juicy and infused it with the complex chile-nut flavor. For some textural contrast, we dressed the finished dish with more chopped peanuts as well as some cilantro for freshness. Serve with rice.

- 3 dried ancho chiles, stemmed, seeded, and torn into ½-inch pieces (¾ cup)
- 1 onion, chopped fine
- 2 tomatoes, cored and chopped coarse
- 1 cup whole unsalted dry-roasted peanuts, plus ¼ cup chopped
- 1½ cups chicken broth
- 2 tablespoons sesame seeds, toasted
- 2 garlic cloves, minced
- 2 teaspoons cider vinegar
- 1 teaspoon sugar, plus extra as needed
- 1 teaspoon minced canned chipotle chile in adobo sauce
   Salt and pepper
- ½ teaspoon ground cinnamon
- ⅛ teaspoon ground cloves
- 3 tablespoons vegetable oil
- 4 (6- to 8-ounce) boneless, skinless chicken breasts, trimmed
- 2 tablespoons chopped fresh cilantro

1. Toast anchos in 12-inch skillet over medium heat, stirring frequently, until fragrant, 2 to 6 minutes; transfer to blender. Add onion, tomatoes, whole peanuts, ¼ cup broth, sesame seeds, garlic, vinegar, sugar, chipotle, ½ teaspoon salt, cinnamon, and cloves to blender and process until smooth, about 1 minute.

2. Heat oil in now-empty skillet over medium-high heat until shimmering. Add pureed chile mixture and cook, stirring often, until mixture has thickened and darkened in color, about 8 minutes.

3. Stir in remaining 1¼ cups broth, scraping up any browned bits, and bring to simmer. Season chicken with salt and pepper and nestle into sauce. Cover, reduce heat to medium-low, and cook until chicken registers 160 degrees, 10 to 15 minutes, flipping halfway through cooking.

4. Transfer chicken to platter, tent with aluminum foil, and let rest for 5 to 10 minutes. Season sauce with sugar, salt, and pepper to taste, and spoon over chicken. Sprinkle with cilantro and chopped peanuts and serve.

Orange-Annatto Glazed Chicken

Serves 4

✔ **WHY THIS RECIPE WORKS:** A take on the traditional Mexican entrée of chicken marinated with Seville oranges and annatto (a bright red seed with a subtle floral flavor), this dish features crispy-skinned chicken with an orange-annatto glaze. Chicken thighs worked well in this recipe; their rich, meaty flavor stood up nicely to the tangy sauce. Using a heavy, weighted Dutch oven, we pressed the thighs flat against the skillet to ensure even and direct contact of the skin with the hot pan. This resulted in ultracrisp, crunchy skin. As for the glaze, we complemented the annatto's flavor with spicy and smoky chipotle chile in adobo, earthy oregano, citrusy coriander, and aromatic garlic. A little bit of lime juice added extra tang, and a dab of cornstarch thickened the glaze nicely. We reduced the glaze to concentrate the flavors and achieve the perfect consistency, then simply coated our crisp chicken thighs with the tangy, flavorful glaze.

8	(5- to 7-ounce) bone-in chicken thighs, trimmed
	Salt and pepper
2	teaspoons vegetable oil
1½	cups orange juice (3 oranges)
¼	cup lime juice (2 limes)
2	tablespoons sugar, plus extra as needed
½	teaspoon cornstarch
4	garlic cloves, minced
2	teaspoons minced canned chipotle chile in adobo sauce
1½	teaspoons ground annatto
1	teaspoon ground coriander
¾	teaspoon dried oregano

1. Place several heavy cans inside Dutch oven. Pat chicken dry with paper towels and season with salt and pepper. Heat oil in 12-inch nonstick skillet over medium-high heat until just smoking. Place chicken skin side down in skillet. Place weighted Dutch oven on top of chicken and cook until skin is deep brown and very crisp, 16 to 20 minutes, checking browning after 10 minutes and adjusting heat as needed.

2. Remove pot and flip chicken. Reduce heat to medium and continue to cook (using splatter screen if necessary) until second side is well browned and chicken registers 175 degrees, 3 to 5 minutes. Transfer chicken to serving platter.

3. Whisk orange juice, lime juice, sugar, and cornstarch together in bowl. Pour off all but 2 teaspoons fat left in skillet. Add garlic, chipotle, annatto, coriander, and oregano and cook over medium heat until fragrant, about 30 seconds. Whisk in orange juice mixture. Increase heat to high and simmer, whisking often, until thickened, 8 to 10 minutes.

4. Return chicken and any accumulated juices to skillet and turn to coat with sauce. Return chicken to platter. Transfer sauce to bowl and season with salt, pepper, and sugar to taste. Serve.

TEST KITCHEN TIP

GETTING THE CRISPEST SKIN ON CHICKEN

1. Place chicken skin side down in skillet. Place Dutch oven, weighted with heavy cans, on top of chicken.

2. Cook until chicken is deep brown and crisp. Remove Dutch oven and flip chicken. Continue to cook without weight until done.

Sautéed Chicken with Cherry Tomato and Roasted Corn Salsa

Serves 4

✔ **WHY THIS RECIPE WORKS:** For a fast and easy meal with plenty of Mexican-inspired flavor, we turned to quick-cooking boneless chicken breasts. First, we gave the mild chicken a layer of spicy flavor by seasoning it with chili powder as well as salt and pepper. Next, we dredged the breasts in flour, which served two purposes: It created a barrier between the fat in the pan and the moisture in the cutlet so that the fat "spit" less, and it helped to produce a consistently brown and crispy crust. We used the same pan to whip up a simple and flavorful side dish from common Mexican ingredients. We toasted corn kernels in a bit of oil, which brought out their sweetness nicely. We then softened some tomatoes (cherry tomatoes were our favorite) and brightened up our salsa with cilantro and fresh lime juice. Garlic and shallot rounded out the flavor of the salsa. The bright salsa perfectly complemented our crispy chicken breasts. Be sure not to stir the corn when cooking in step 4 or it will not brown well. If using fresh corn, you will need three to four ears in order to yield 3 cups of kernels.

½	cup all-purpose flour
4	(6- to 8-ounce) boneless, skinless chicken breasts, trimmed and pounded to ½-inch thickness
1	teaspoon chili powder
	Salt and pepper
3	tablespoons vegetable oil
3	cups fresh or thawed frozen corn
1	shallot, minced
2	garlic cloves, minced
12	ounces cherry tomatoes, halved
¼	cup minced fresh cilantro
2	tablespoons lime juice

1. Spread flour into shallow dish. Pat chicken dry with paper towels and season with chili powder, salt, and pepper. Working with 1 chicken breast at time, dredge in flour, shaking off excess.

2. Heat 2 tablespoons oil in 12-inch nonstick skillet over medium-high heat until just smoking. Lay chicken in skillet and cook until well browned on first side, 6 to 8 minutes.

3. Flip chicken over, reduce heat to medium, and continue to cook until chicken registers 160 degrees, 6 to 8 minutes. Transfer chicken to plate and tent with aluminum foil.

4. Add remaining 1 tablespoon oil to now-empty skillet and place over medium-high heat until shimmering. Add corn and cook, without stirring, until well browned and roasted, 8 to 10 minutes. Stir in shallot and garlic and cook until fragrant, about 30 seconds. Stir in tomatoes, scraping up any browned bits, and cook until just softened, about 2 minutes.

5. Off heat, stir in cilantro and lime juice and season with salt and pepper to taste. Transfer vegetables to platter and serve with chicken.

TEST KITCHEN TIP

CUTTING KERNELS OFF THE COB

After removing husk and silk, stand ear upright in large bowl and use paring knife to slice kernels off cob.

Skillet Chicken Fajitas

Serves 4

✓ **WHY THIS RECIPE WORKS:** In the early 20th century, Mexican ranch hands living in Texas made fajitas with grilled skirt steak (the word "fajita" is derived from the Spanish word *faja*, meaning strip or girdle). Today, fajitas are made with everything from steak to shrimp to chicken. But too often, the protein is buried under gobs of sour cream and shredded cheese. We wanted to figure out a way to make appealingly simple chicken fajitas (indoors, so we could prepare them year-round) without all the extraneous toppings—just the essential peppers and onions. We chose to work with quick-cooking chicken breasts, but knew we needed to punch up their sometimes-bland flavor. We mixed up an oil-based marinade that contained lime juice, garlic, cumin, smoked paprika, and cayenne pepper, as well as salt (to help the meat stay moist) and sugar (to encourage quick browning). After marinating the chicken for 30 minutes, we browned the breasts on one side and then let them finish cooking in the gentle heat of the oven. For the vegetables, we took a cue from traditional *rajas con crema*, strips of pepper and onion cooked down with tangy Mexican *crema*. We broiled poblanos for nice charred flavor and removed most of their skin to avoid bitterness. We then sautéed onions with garlic, thyme, and oregano for complex, earthy flavors. Heavy cream made a rich, creamy base and didn't curdle in the heat. We tossed the onion mixture with the poblanos and some lime juice for brightness. Serve with queso fresco and Spicy Pickled Radishes (recipe follows).

CHICKEN

- ¼ cup vegetable oil
- 2 tablespoons lime juice
- 4 garlic cloves, peeled and smashed
- 1½ teaspoons smoked paprika
- 1 teaspoon sugar
- 1 teaspoon salt
- ½ teaspoon ground cumin
- ½ teaspoon pepper
- ¼ teaspoon cayenne pepper
- 1½ pounds boneless, skinless chicken breasts, trimmed and pounded to ½-inch thickness

RAJAS CON CREMA

- 1 pound poblano chiles, stemmed, halved, and seeded
- 1 tablespoon vegetable oil
- 1 onion, halved and sliced ¼ inch thick
- 2 garlic cloves, minced
- ¼ teaspoon dried thyme
- ¼ teaspoon dried oregano
- ½ cup heavy cream
- 1 tablespoon lime juice
- ½ teaspoon salt
- ¼ teaspoon pepper
- 12 (6-inch) flour tortillas, warmed
- ¼ cup minced fresh cilantro
  Lime wedges

1. FOR THE CHICKEN: Whisk 3 tablespoons oil, lime juice, garlic, paprika, sugar, salt, cumin, pepper, and cayenne together in bowl. Add chicken, toss to coat, cover, and refrigerate for at least 30 minutes or up to 1 hour.

2. FOR THE RAJAS CON CREMA: Meanwhile, adjust oven rack 6 inches from broiler element and heat broiler. Arrange poblanos skin side up on aluminum foil–lined rimmed baking sheet and broil until blackened and beginning to soften, 4 to 10 minutes, rotating baking sheet halfway through cooking.

3. Transfer poblanos to bowl, cover, and let steam for 10 minutes. Remove majority of skin from poblanos (preserving some skin for flavor) and slice peppers into ¼-inch-thick strips.

4. Adjust oven racks to middle and lowest positions and heat oven to 200 degrees. Heat oil in 12-inch ovensafe nonstick skillet over high heat until just smoking. Add onion and cook until just softened, about 3 minutes. Stir in garlic, thyme, and oregano and cook until fragrant, about 15 seconds. Stir in cream and cook, stirring often, until reduced and cream lightly coats onion, 1 to 2 minutes. Stir in lime juice, salt, pepper, and poblanos. Transfer vegetables to bowl, cover, and place on upper oven rack.

5. Wipe out now-empty skillet. Remove chicken from marinade and wipe off excess. Heat remaining 1 tablespoon oil in skillet over high heat until just smoking. Add chicken and cook without moving until well charred on bottom, about 4 minutes. Flip chicken, transfer skillet to lower oven rack, and cook until chicken registers 160 degrees, 7 to 10 minutes.

6. Transfer chicken to cutting board, let rest for 5 minutes, then slice crosswise into ¼-inch-thick strips; return chicken to skillet and toss with pan juices. Serve with warmed tortillas, rajas con crema, cilantro, and lime wedges.

Spicy Pickled Radishes
MAKES ABOUT 1¾ CUPS

These easy-to-make spicy pickled radishes are the perfect garnish for numerous Mexican dishes including stews, tacos, tostadas, sopes, braised beans, and more.

10 radishes, trimmed and sliced thin
½ cup lime juice (4 limes)
½ jalapeño chile, stemmed and sliced thin
1 teaspoon sugar
¼ teaspoon salt

Combine all ingredients in bowl, cover, and let stand at room temperature for 30 minutes. (Mixture can be refrigerated for up to 24 hours).

TEST KITCHEN TIP COOKING CHICKEN FOR SKILLET FAJITAS

1. Sear marinated chicken until well charred on bottom, about 4 minutes.

2. Flip breasts and finish in 200-degree oven to ensure juicy, tender meat.

3. After resting and slicing chicken, return it to skillet and toss with flavorful juices.

Classic Arroz con Pollo

Serves 4 to 6

✓ **WHY THIS RECIPE WORKS:** Mexican *arroz con pollo*, literally meaning "rice with chicken" is a satisfying one-dish meal. The traditional method calls for stewing marinated chicken slowly with aromatic herbs and vegetables, creating a rich broth in which the rice is cooked once the chicken is fall-off-the-bone tender. We set out to streamline the traditional method without sacrificing its deep, rich chicken flavor. We opted for flavorful dark-meat chicken thighs and removed any visible pockets of fat and some of the skin before cooking to prevent the dish from becoming greasy. Once the chicken was done, we removed the skin; although it protected the meat during cooking, it didn't crisp in the moist environment of the closed pot. Using spoons rather than forks to pull the meat apart ensured that we ended up with chunks, not shreds. Moving the pot to the oven while the rice cooked and stirring it twice during cooking ensured that every grain of rice cooked evenly. To keep the dish from becoming greasy, it is important to remove excess fat from the chicken thighs and most of the skin, leaving just enough to protect the meat. To use long-grain rice instead of medium-grain, increase the amount of water to ¾ cup.

- 6 garlic cloves, minced
- 5 teaspoons distilled white vinegar
  Salt and pepper
- ½ teaspoon dried oregano
- 4 pounds bone-in chicken thighs, trimmed
- 2 tablespoons olive oil
- 1 onion, chopped fine
- 1 small green bell pepper, stemmed, seeded, and chopped fine
- ¼ teaspoon red pepper flakes
- ¼ cup minced fresh cilantro
- 1¾ cups chicken broth
- 1 (8-ounce) can tomato sauce
- ¼ cup water, plus extra as needed
- 3 cups medium-grain white rice
- ½ cup green Manzanilla olives, pitted and halved
- 1 tablespoon capers, rinsed
- ½ cup jarred whole pimentos, cut into 2 by ¼-inch strips
  Lemon wedges

1. Adjust oven rack to middle position and heat oven to 350 degrees. Combine garlic, 1 tablespoon vinegar, 1 teaspoon salt, ½ teaspoon pepper, and oregano in large bowl. Add chicken, toss to coat, and marinate for 15 minutes.

2. Heat 1 tablespoon oil in Dutch oven over medium heat until shimmering. Add onion, bell pepper, and pepper flakes and cook until beginning to soften, about 5 minutes. Stir in 2 tablespoons cilantro.

3. Clear center of pot and increase heat to medium-high. Add chicken, skin side down, to center of pot and cook until outer layer of meat becomes opaque, 2 to 4 minutes per side, reducing heat if chicken begins to brown. Stir in broth, tomato sauce, and water. Bring to simmer, cover, reduce heat to medium-low, and simmer for 20 minutes.

4. Stir in rice, olives, capers, and ¾ teaspoon salt and bring to simmer. Cover pot, transfer to oven, and cook, stirring every 10 minutes, until chicken register 175 degrees, about 30 minutes. (If, after 20 minutes of cooking, rice appears dry and bottom of pot begins to scorch, stir in additional ¼ cup water.)

5. Transfer chicken to cutting board; cover pot and set aside. Using 2 spoons, pull chicken into large chunks, discarding skin and bones. Place chicken in large bowl, toss with pimentos, remaining 2 teaspoons vinegar, remaining 1 tablespoon oil, and remaining 2 tablespoons cilantro and season with salt and pepper to taste. Place chicken on top of rice, cover, and let stand until warmed through, about 5 minutes. Serve with lemon wedges.

LEARN HOW **CLASSIC ARROZ CON POLLO**

Traditional versions of this comforting, hearty dish can take hours to prepare, but quick versions often sacrifice flavor for speed. We get all of the flavor in a fraction of the time by using a few savvy shortcuts.

1. MARINATE CHICKEN: Add the chicken to the marinade and toss to fully coat. Let the chicken marinate for 15 minutes. Although traditional recipes often call for marinating overnight, we found it worked best to marinate quickly before cooking and then mix the cooked chicken with more flavorful marinade.

2. SAUTÉ, THEN SIMMER CHICKEN: Add the chicken to the pot with the onions and peppers and cook, skin side down, until the outer layer of meat is just opaque. Stir in the liquids and simmer for about 20 minutes. Cooking the chicken with aromatics creates a flavorful base for the dish without the need for homemade stock.

3. ADD RICE, OLIVES, AND CAPERS AND TRANSFER POT TO OVEN: Stir in the rice, olives, and capers. Cover and transfer the pot to the oven; cook for 30 minutes, stirring twice. The direct heat of the stovetop can scorch the bottom layer of rice; the diffuse heat of the oven ensures that everything cooks evenly.

4. PULL CHICKEN INTO CHUNKS: Remove the chicken from the pot. Using two spoons, pull the chicken into chunks; discard the skin and bones. The skin protects the chicken during cooking, but it becomes flabby in the moist environment of the pot and is better removed.

5. TOSS CHICKEN WITH EXTRA MARINADE: Transfer the cooked chicken to a large bowl and toss with additional vinegar, oil, cilantro, and pimentos. This postcooking "marinade" boosts the flavor of the chicken dramatically and makes the dish taste brighter and cleaner.

6. WARM THROUGH AND SERVE: Place the dressed chicken on top of the rice. Cover the pot and let stand until the dish is warmed through. Letting the chicken sit on top of the rice (rather than stirring it in) ensures that the rice doesn't become gummy and starchy from overstirring.

Chile-Rubbed Roast Chicken

Serves 4

✓ **WHY THIS RECIPE WORKS:** We wanted a juicy, tender roast chicken infused with Mexican flavors that would be easy enough to make any day of the week. This meant that we needed the right mix of spices, a technique that ensured the spices flavored the chicken throughout, and a simple, foolproof cooking method. First, we turned our attention to the spices. A combination of New Mexican and chipotle chiles gave us lots of deep, smoky, earthy flavors. To round out our chile rub, we toasted and coarsely ground some nutty cumin seeds and citrusy coriander seeds; using whole seeds rather than preground powders gave the rub much deeper flavor and texture. Onion powder and garlic powder added more aromatic depth, warm cinnamon and cloves gave a hint of sweetness, and cayenne and black pepper provided some extra piquant flavor. We tested our recipe with gradually increasing amounts of spice rub; by the time our tasters were satisfied with the flavor, we were left with a thoroughly spice-crusted chicken. To keep the cooking method foolproof, we roasted the chicken in a preheated skillet. This jump-started the cooking of the chicken thighs, which normally take longer to cook than the breasts. About halfway through the cooking time, we shut the oven off, which allowed the chicken to cook through gently in the residual heat, resulting in moist, tender meat. Feel free to substitute ½ teaspoon ground chipotle chile powder for the dried chipotle chile (we noted little difference in flavor) and add to spice grinder with other spices. If using table salt, reduce the amount of salt in the spice rub to 1½ teaspoons.

4 **dried New Mexican chiles, stemmed, seeded, and torn into ½-inch pieces (1 cup)**
1 **dried chipotle chile, stemmed, seeded, and torn into ½-inch pieces (1½ tablespoons)**
1 **tablespoon cumin seeds**
1 **tablespoon coriander seeds**
½ **teaspoon pepper**
½ **teaspoon onion powder**
½ **teaspoon garlic powder**
¼ **teaspoon ground cloves**
¼ **teaspoon ground cinnamon**
⅛ **teaspoon cayenne pepper**
¼ **cup vegetable oil**
1 **tablespoon kosher salt**
2 **teaspoons sugar**
1 **(3- to 4-pound) whole chicken, giblets discarded**
   Lime wedges

1. Toast New Mexican and chipotle chiles, cumin seeds, and coriander seeds in 12-inch ovensafe skillet over medium heat, stirring frequently, until fragrant, 2 to 6 minutes. Transfer mixture to spice grinder and let cool slightly. Add pepper, onion powder, garlic powder, cloves, cinnamon, and cayenne to grinder and process until coarsely ground, 5 to 10 seconds. Transfer spice mixture to bowl and stir in oil, salt, and sugar.

2. Wipe out now-empty skillet, place on middle rack of oven, and heat oven to 450 degrees. Pat chicken dry with paper towels, then gently separate skin from meat. Rub 3 tablespoons spice paste underneath skin over breast, thighs, and legs. Rub remaining spice paste over top and sides of chicken (do not rub bottom of chicken). Tuck wings behind back and tie legs together loosely with kitchen twine.

3. Transfer chicken, breast side up, to preheated skillet in oven. Roast chicken until breast registers 120 degrees and thighs register 135 degrees, 25 to 35 minutes. Turn off oven and leave chicken in oven until breast registers 160 degrees and thighs register 175 degrees, 25 to 35 minutes.

4. Transfer chicken to carving board and let rest, uncovered, for 15 minutes. Carve and serve with lime wedges.

Grilled Chipotle Chicken Kebabs with Cilantro Dipping Sauce

Serves 4

✓ **WHY THIS RECIPE WORKS:** While kebabs are generally known as a Middle Eastern dish, they also have a place in Mexican cuisine. Here we coated chunks of boneless, skinless chicken breast in a potent chile-spice rub and then married them with a cooling and flavorful sauce. Three types of chiles gave us well-rounded chile flavor in our rub. We added cumin seeds, oregano, and garlic powder for depth. To ensure the delicate white meat stayed moist in the intense heat of the grill, we briefly brined the meat. To complement the spicy, boldly flavored chicken, we created a cool, creamy sauce. A combination of sour cream and mayonnaise gave us the perfect creaminess, while lime juice provided extra tang and brightness. Feel free to substitute 2 teaspoons ground chipotle chile powder for the chipotle chiles (we noted little difference in flavor) and add it to the spice grinder with the toasted chiles and spices. You will need four 12-inch metal skewers for this recipe.

	Salt and pepper
2	pounds boneless, skinless chicken breasts, trimmed and cut into 1-inch pieces
2	dried New Mexican chiles, stemmed, seeded, and torn into ½-inch pieces (½ cup)
4	dried chipotle chiles, stemmed, seeded, and torn into ½-inch pieces (6 tablespoons)
2	dried guajillo chiles, stemmed, seeded, and torn into ½-inch pieces (¼ cup)
1	teaspoon cumin seeds
½	teaspoon dried oregano
½	teaspoon garlic powder
3	tablespoons vegetable oil
1½	teaspoons sugar
6	tablespoons sour cream
¼	cup chopped fresh cilantro
2	tablespoons mayonnaise
2	tablespoons lime juice, plus extra as needed
1	scallion, minced

1. Dissolve 2 tablespoons salt in 1 quart cold water. Submerge chicken in brine, cover, and refrigerate for 30 minutes.

2. Meanwhile, toast New Mexican, chipotle, and guajillo chiles and cumin seeds in 10-inch skillet, stirring frequently, until fragrant, 2 to 6 minutes. Transfer mixture to spice grinder and let cool slightly. Add oregano and garlic powder to grinder and process until finely ground, about 20 seconds. Transfer spice mixture to bowl and stir in oil and sugar.

3. Remove chicken from brine and pat dry with paper towels. Toss chicken with spice mixture and thread onto four 12-inch metal skewers.

4A. FOR A CHARCOAL GRILL: Open bottom vent completely. Light large chimney starter filled with charcoal briquettes (6 quarts). When top coals are partially covered with ash, pour evenly over grill. Set cooking grate in place, cover, and open lid vent completely. Heat grill until hot, about 5 minutes.

4B. FOR A GAS GRILL: Turn all burners to high, cover, and heat grill until hot, about 15 minutes. Leave all burners on high.

5. Clean and oil cooking grate. Place chicken skewers on grill. Cook (covered if using gas), turning as needed, until chicken is lightly charred on all sides and registers 160 degrees, about 8 minutes. Transfer skewers to platter, tent with aluminum foil, and let rest for 5 to 10 minutes.

6. Mix sour cream, cilantro, mayonnaise, lime juice, scallion, and ⅛ teaspoon pepper together in bowl and season with extra lime juice, salt, and pepper to taste. Using tongs, remove chicken from skewers and serve with cilantro dipping sauce.

Grilled Tequila Chicken with Orange, Avocado, and Pepita Salad

Serves 4

☑ **WHY THIS RECIPE WORKS:** We set out to create a fresh, bright salad that paired juicy grilled chicken with authentic Mexican flavors. A simple tequila-lime marinade boosted the chicken's flavor both before and after cooking. Grilled avocados gave the salad more smoky depth. To bring the salad together, we created a bright, tangy vinaigrette by combining lime juice and olive oil with cayenne and honey for well-rounded flavor. Ripe but firm avocados are critical for successful grilling. If your avocados are overripe, skip seasoning and grilling and simply peel and slice the avocados before assembling the salad. Do not marinate the chicken longer than an hour or it will turn mushy.

½   **cup tequila**
½   **cup water**
6   **tablespoons lime juice (3 limes)**
4   **garlic cloves, minced**
    Salt and pepper
4   **(6- to 8-ounce) boneless, skinless chicken breasts, trimmed**
3   **oranges, peeled and cut into ½-inch pieces**
5   **tablespoons extra-virgin olive oil**
1   **tablespoon honey**
¼   **teaspoon cayenne pepper**
2   **ripe but firm avocados, halved and pitted**
6   **ounces (6 cups) watercress, chopped coarse**
⅓   **cup pepitas, toasted**
1   **shallot, sliced thin**

1. Whisk tequila, water, 3 tablespoons lime juice, garlic, and 2 teaspoons salt together in bowl until salt is dissolved. Transfer ½ cup marinade to small saucepan. Pour remaining marinade into 1-gallon zipper-lock bag, add chicken, and toss to coat. Press out as much air as possible, seal bag, and refrigerate for 30 minutes to 1 hour, flipping bag occasionally.

2. Let oranges drain in colander set over large bowl, reserving juice. In large bowl, whisk ¼ cup oil, honey, cayenne, ¼ teaspoon salt, ¼ pepper, and remaining 3 tablespoons lime juice together; set aside for salad.

3. Before grilling, brush avocado halves with remaining 1 tablespoon oil and season with salt and pepper. Remove chicken from marinade, let excess marinade drip off, and transfer to plate.

4A. FOR A CHARCOAL GRILL: Open bottom vent completely. Light large chimney starter filled with charcoal briquettes (6 quarts). When top coals are partially covered with ash, pour two-thirds evenly over half of grill, then pour remaining coals over other half of grill. Set cooking grate in place, cover, and open lid vent completely. Heat grill until hot, about 5 minutes.

4B. FOR A GAS GRILL: Turn all burners to high, cover, and heat grill until hot, about 15 minutes. Leave primary burner on high and turn other burner(s) to medium.

5. Clean and oil cooking grate. Place chicken on hotter side of grill. Cook (covered if using gas), turning as needed, until chicken is nicely charred and registers 160 degrees, 8 to 12 minutes. Meanwhile, place avocados cut side down on cooler side of grill and cook until lightly charred, 3 to 5 minutes. Transfer chicken and avocados to cutting board and tent with aluminum foil.

6. Add drained orange juice to reserved marinade in saucepan, bring to simmer over medium-high heat, and cook until reduced to ¼ cup, 3 to 5 minutes. Whisk dressing to recombine, then add watercress, pepitas, shallots, and drained oranges and toss gently to coat; transfer to platter. Peel grilled avocado, slice thin, and lay on top of salad. Slice chicken on bias into ½-inch-thick pieces, lay on top of salad, and drizzle with reduced marinade. Serve.

Grilled Chicken Fajitas

Serves 4

✔ **WHY THIS RECIPE WORKS:** We wanted to create a simple fajita recipe with the perfect combination of smoky grilled vegetables and tender chicken. To boost the flavor of the chicken, we made a brightly flavored marinade and added a surprising ingredient—Worcestershire sauce—which lent a subtle but complex savory note. To prepare the vegetables for grilling, we quartered the bell peppers so they'd lie flat on the grill, and cut the onion into thick rounds that would hold together during cooking. A two-level fire enabled us to grill the chicken and vegetables at the same time, the latter on the cooler part so they wouldn't burn. We reserved some of the marinade to toss with everything at the end for a bright burst of flavor. You can use red, yellow, orange, or green bell peppers in this recipe. Serve with your favorite fajita toppings, including guacamole, salsa, sour cream, shredded cheddar or Monterey Jack cheese, lime wedges, and Spicy Pickled Radishes (page 171).

6	tablespoons vegetable oil
⅓	cup lime juice (3 limes)
1	jalapeño chile, stemmed, seeded, and minced
1½	tablespoons minced fresh cilantro
3	garlic cloves, minced
1	tablespoon Worcestershire sauce
1½	teaspoons packed brown sugar
	Salt and pepper
1½	pounds boneless, skinless chicken breasts, trimmed and pounded to ½-inch thickness
2	large bell peppers, quartered, stemmed, and seeded
1	large red onion, peeled and cut into ½-inch-thick rounds (do not separate rings)
12	(6-inch) flour tortillas

1. Whisk ¼ cup oil, lime juice, jalapeño, cilantro, garlic, Worcestershire, sugar, 1 teaspoon salt, and ¾ teaspoon pepper together in bowl. Measure out and reserve ¼ cup marinade separately for serving. Whisk 1 teaspoon salt into remaining marinade and transfer to 1-gallon zipper-lock bag. Add chicken to bag and toss to coat. Press out as much air as possible, seal bag, and refrigerate for 15 minutes, flipping bag occasionally.

2. Brush bell peppers and onion with remaining 2 tablespoons oil and season with salt and pepper. Remove chicken from marinade, let excess marinade drip off, and transfer to plate.

3A. FOR A CHARCOAL GRILL: Open bottom vent completely. Light large chimney starter filled with charcoal briquettes (6 quarts). When top coals are partially covered with ash, pour coals over two-thirds of grill, leaving remaining one-third empty. Set cooking grate in place, cover, and open lid vent completely. Heat grill until hot, about 5 minutes.

3B. FOR A GAS GRILL: Turn all burners to high, cover, and heat grill until hot, about 15 minutes. Leave primary burner on high and turn other burner(s) to medium.

4. Clean and oil cooking grate. Place chicken on hotter side of grill and vegetables on cooler side of grill. Cook (covered if using gas), turning chicken and vegetables as needed, until chicken is well browned and registers 160 degrees and vegetables are tender and slightly charred, 8 to 12 minutes. Transfer chicken and vegetables to cutting board and tent with aluminum foil.

5. Working in batches, grill tortillas, turning as needed, until warm and lightly browned, about 40 seconds; transfer to plate and cover with foil.

6. Slice bell peppers into ¼-inch strips, separate onion into rings, and toss together with 2 tablespoons reserved marinade. Slice chicken on bias into ¼-inch-thick slices and toss with remaining 2 tablespoons marinade in separate bowl. Transfer chicken and vegetables to platter and serve with warmed tortillas.

Sinaloa-Style Grill-Roasted Chickens

Serves 4

✓ **WHY THIS RECIPE WORKS:** In the coastal region of Sinaloa, chickens are split in half; marinated with bitter orange, garlic, and herbs; and slow-roasted over smoky embers. We wanted a foolproof way to bring all the flavor of this dish to the American home kitchen. We first tried marinating the chicken with an orange juice–garlic mixture, but the results proved lackluster. After several tests, we discovered that the best way to ramp up the flavor of the marinade was to swap fresh orange juice for frozen orange juice concentrate. To help the marinade thoroughly penetrate the chicken, we scored the meat with a knife before marinating it for at least 2 hours. Butterflying, halving, and skewering the chicken allowed it to hold its shape and made it easier to maneuver on the grill. To further boost the chicken's flavor and help keep the meat moist, we reserved a little less than a cup of the marinade to baste the chicken during grilling. Oregano, thyme, and chipotle chile in adobo rounded out the flavor of our basting liquid. The sugars in the marinade and the basting liquid caramelized to produce a crisp, well-charred exterior. Adding a wood chip packet to the grill infused the chicken with savory, smoky flavor. A squeeze of lime juice perfectly complemented the bold, smoky, earthy flavors in the chicken. You will need four 12-inch metal skewers for this recipe. If you'd like to use wood chunks instead of wood chips when using a charcoal grill, substitute 1 medium wood chunk, soaked in water for 1 hour, for the wood chip packet. See the photo on page 158.

2   (3½- to 4-pound) whole chickens, giblets discarded
2   onions, chopped
1   (12-ounce) can frozen orange juice concentrate, thawed
¼   cup extra-virgin olive oil
2   garlic heads, cloves separated and peeled (20 cloves)
     Salt and pepper

1   tablespoon chopped fresh oregano
1   tablespoon minced fresh thyme
2   teaspoons minced canned chipotle chile in adobo sauce
1½   cups wood chips
     Lime wedges

1. With chickens breast side down, use kitchen shears to cut out backbone and butterfly chicken. Flip chickens over and split chickens in half lengthwise through breastbones using chef's knife. Cut ½-inch-deep slits across breasts, thighs, and legs, about ½ inch apart. Tuck wingtips behind backs.

2. Blend onions, orange juice concentrate, oil, garlic, and 2 tablespoons salt in blender until smooth, about 1 minute. Transfer ¾ cup mixture to bowl and stir in oregano, thyme, and chipotle; set aside for grilling. Divide remaining marinade among two 1-gallon zipper-lock bags. Add chickens to bags and toss to coat. Press out as much air as possible, seal bags, and refrigerate for at least 2 hours or up to 24 hours, flipping occasionally.

3. Just before grilling, soak wood chips in water for 15 minutes, then drain. Using large piece of heavy-duty aluminum foil, wrap soaked chips in foil packet and cut several vent holes in top. Remove chickens from marinade and pat dry with paper towels; discard marinade. Insert 1 skewer lengthwise through thickest part of breast down through thigh of each chicken half.

4A. FOR A CHARCOAL GRILL: Open bottom vent halfway. Light large chimney starter filled with charcoal briquettes (6 quarts). When top coals are partially covered with ash, pour into steeply banked pile against side of grill. Place wood chip packet on coals. Set cooking grate in place, cover, and open lid vent halfway. Heat grill until hot and wood chips are smoking, about 5 minutes.

4B. FOR A GAS GRILL: Remove cooking grate and place wood chip packet directly on primary burner.

Set grate in place, turn all burners to high, cover, and heat grill until hot and wood chips are smoking, about 15 minutes. Leave primary burner on high and turn off other burner(s). (Adjust primary burner as needed to maintain grill temperature between 350 to 375 degrees.)

5. Clean and oil cooking grate. Place chicken halves skin side up on cooler side of grill with legs pointing toward fire. Cover and cook for 45 minutes, basting every 15 minutes with reserved marinade.

6. Switch placement of chickens, with legs still pointing toward fire, and continue to cook, covered, until breasts register 160 degrees and thighs register 175 degrees, 30 to 45 minutes longer. Transfer chicken to carving board, tent with foil, and let rest for 20 minutes. Carve and serve with lime wedges.

LEARN HOW **SINALOA-STYLE GRILL-ROASTED CHICKENS**

To ensure that our Sinaloa-style chicken was ultraflavorful and perfectly cooked, we halved the chickens to make them easier to handle, slashed the meat before marinating, and grilled the chickens over indirect heat.

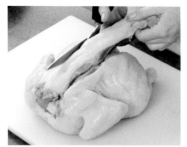

1. BUTTERFLY CHICKENS: With the chickens breast side down, use kitchen shears to cut out the backbones; press the birds flat.

2. HALVE CHICKENS: Flip the chickens over and split them in half lengthwise through their breast-bones using a chef's knife. This makes the chickens easier to grill.

3. SCORE CHICKENS: To allow the marinade to penetrate the meat, cut ½-inch-deep slits across the breasts, thighs, and legs, about ½ inch apart.

4. MARINATE CHICKENS: Divide the chickens and orange juice concentrate marinade between two 1-gallon zipper-lock bags and refrigerate for 2 to 24 hours.

5. SKEWER CHICKENS: To help the chickens hold their shape on the grill, insert a skewer lengthwise through the thickest part of each breast and down through the thigh.

6. GRILL CHICKENS: Place the chickens skin side up on the cooler side of the grill with legs pointing toward the fire. Cover and cook, basting with reserved marinade.

Turkey Breast en Cocotte with Mole

Serves 6 to 8

✓ **WHY THIS RECIPE WORKS:** Turkey is a popular meat in Mexico, and it's frequently paired with a rich, dark mole sauce. For our recipe, we decided to work with a turkey breast, since it's easier to handle than a whole bird but still provides a substantial amount of meat. For perfectly cooked, moist, tender meat, we chose to use an *en cocotte* method, meaning cooking in a covered pot over low heat. We opted for a bone-in breast, which retained moisture and had more flavor than a boneless breast. We browned the meat to develop deep flavor and then added some aromatics and cooked it until it was perfectly tender and juicy. To make our mole, we first bloomed aromatics and an abundance of warm spices in the same pot we had used to cook the turkey, allowing us to pick up the flavorful browned bits from the bottom of the pot. Using the turkey juices as well as canned tomatoes for our liquid base gave us a balanced sauce with meaty flavor. In place of the ground nuts used in many moles, we used creamy peanut butter, which gave our sauce a luxurious texture. Many supermarkets sell "hotel-style" turkey breasts. Try to avoid these, as they still have the wings attached. If this is the only type of breast you can find, you will need to remove the wings before proceeding with the recipe. Don't buy a turkey breast larger than 7 pounds; it won't fit in the pot. For a smaller turkey breast, reduce the cooking time as necessary. Be sure to use a 7- to 8-quart Dutch oven. Serve with rice.

1	(6- to 7-pound) whole bone-in turkey breast
	Salt and pepper
5	tablespoons vegetable oil
1	onion, chopped
9	garlic cloves, peeled (6 crushed, 3 minced)
2	sprigs fresh thyme
1	bay leaf
2	tablespoons chili powder
2	tablespoons unsweetened cocoa powder
½	teaspoon ground cinnamon
⅛	teaspoon ground cloves
1	(14.5-ounce) can diced tomatoes, drained
¼	cup raisins
2	tablespoons creamy peanut butter

1. Adjust oven rack to lowest position and heat oven to 250 degrees. Using kitchen shears, trim rib bones and excess fat from edges of turkey breast. Pat turkey dry with paper towels and season with salt and pepper.

2. Heat 2 tablespoons oil in Dutch oven over medium-high heat until just smoking. Add turkey, breast side down, to pot. Scatter onion, crushed garlic, thyme, and bay leaf around turkey. Cook, turning turkey on its sides and stirring vegetables as needed, until turkey and vegetables are well browned, 12 to 16 minutes, reducing heat if pot begins to scorch.

3. Off heat, place large piece aluminum foil over pot and press to seal, then cover tightly with lid. Transfer pot to oven and cook until turkey registers 160 degrees, 1½ to 1¾ hours.

4. Remove pot from oven. Transfer turkey to cutting board, tent with foil, and let rest while making sauce. Strain juices from pot into fat separator, reserving strained vegetables. Let juices settle for about 5 minutes, then defat juices; set aside.

5. Add remaining 3 tablespoons oil, minced garlic, chili powder, cocoa powder, cinnamon, and cloves to now-empty pot and cook over medium heat until fragrant, about 1 minute. Stir in defatted juices, strained vegetables, any accumulated juices from turkey, tomatoes, raisins, and peanut butter and simmer over medium-high heat, stirring occasionally, until slightly thickened, 8 to 10 minutes.

6. Discard thyme and bay leaf, then puree sauce in blender until smooth, about 20 seconds. Season sauce with salt and pepper to taste. Remove and discard turkey skin, carve turkey, and serve with sauce.

MEATBALLS IN CHIPOTLE SAUCE

Beef and Pork

Mexican-Style Picadillo

Serves 4 to 6

✓ **WHY THIS RECIPE WORKS:** The Spanish word *picadillo* comes from the word *picar*, "to mince"; in Mexico, the dish consists of finely chopped beef stewed with a combination of minced peppers, tomatoes, and sometimes vegetables such as potatoes and carrots. It's Mexican comfort food at its best. Authentic recipes call for finely chopping the beef and vegetables by hand, but we wanted a quick weeknight option, which meant switching to more convenient ground beef. We also decided to pulse the vegetables in the food processor rather than chop them by hand. Not only was this method faster, but tasters also preferred the rustic texture of the processed onion, red bell pepper, carrots, and potatoes. We kept our onion and pepper separate from the root vegetables as we processed them so that we could bloom the aromatics and concentrate their flavor before cooking the beef. We then added the potatoes and carrots, which we gently simmered until just tender. With our food processor already on the counter, we made a quick tomato and jalapeño puree to serve as the sauce for our picadillo. The fresh tomatoes had a vibrant flavor, but the consistency of the finished sauce was watery. By blending a few corn tortillas into our sauce, we achieved a nice thick texture along with a welcome subtle corn flavor. We stirred fresh cilantro into the finished dish to provide a refreshing note to balance the spiced meat and vegetables. Serve with warm tortillas or rice.

- **1   onion, cut into 1-inch pieces**
- **1   red bell pepper, stemmed, seeded, and cut into 1-inch pieces**
- **6   ounces red potatoes, unpeeled, cut into 1-inch pieces**
- **2   carrots, peeled and cut into 1-inch pieces**
- **1½ pounds tomatoes, cored and quartered**
- **3   (6-inch) corn tortillas, torn into 1-inch pieces**
- **1   jalapeño chile, stemmed, halved, and seeded**
- **   Salt and pepper**
- **1   tablespoon vegetable oil**
- **1½ tablespoons chili powder**
- **3   garlic cloves, minced**
- **1   pound 85 percent lean ground beef**
- **¼   cup chopped fresh cilantro**

1. Pulse onion and bell pepper in food processor until broken down into rough ¼-inch pieces, about 12 pulses, scraping down sides of bowl as needed; transfer mixture to bowl. Pulse potatoes and carrots in now-empty food processor until broken down into rough ¼-inch pieces, about 12 pulses; transfer mixture to separate bowl. Process tomatoes, tortillas, jalapeño, and 1½ teaspoons salt in now-empty food processor until smooth, about 1 minute.

2. Heat oil in 12-inch skillet over medium heat until shimmering. Add onion mixture and cook until softened, about 5 minutes. Stir in chili powder and garlic and cook until fragrant, about 30 seconds. Stir in ground beef and cook, breaking up meat with wooden spoon, until no longer pink, about 5 minutes.

3. Stir in potato mixture and tomato mixture and bring to simmer. Cover, reduce heat to low, and simmer gently, stirring occasionally, until potatoes and carrots are tender, about 30 minutes. Stir in cilantro and season with salt and pepper to taste. Serve.

Beef Taco Salad

Serves 4

✓ **WHY THIS RECIPE WORKS:** Golden and ultra-crunchy, tortilla "bowls" make a perfect contrast to a saucy, spicy beef filling and crisp salad fixings. We microwaved flour tortillas to make them pliable and coated them with vegetable oil spray to ensure they crisped up in the oven. We found dressing unnecessary; the saucy meat and a bit of lime juice provided plenty of flavor. To avoid dried-out taco filling, be careful not to cook the meat beyond pink before adding the liquid ingredients, or it will overcook as it simmers. Serve with lime wedges and Mexican *crema*.

TACO MEAT

1   tablespoon vegetable oil
1   onion, chopped fine
2   tablespoons chili powder
3   garlic cloves, minced
1   pound 90 percent lean ground beef
1   (8-ounce) can tomato sauce
½   cup chicken broth
2   teaspoons cider vinegar
1   teaspoon packed light brown sugar
     Salt and pepper

SALAD

4   (10-inch) flour tortillas
     Vegetable oil spray
2   romaine lettuce hearts (12 ounces), shredded
1   (15-ounce) can black beans, rinsed
8   ounces cherry or grape tomatoes, quartered
2   scallions, sliced thin
¼   cup chopped fresh cilantro
2   tablespoons lime juice
     Salt and pepper
2   ounces shredded Mexican cheese blend (½ cup)

1. FOR THE TACO MEAT: Heat oil in 12-inch nonstick skillet over medium-high heat until shimmering. Add onion and cook until softened, about 5 minutes. Stir in chili powder and garlic and cook until fragrant, about 30 seconds. Add ground beef and cook, breaking up meat with wooden spoon, until almost cooked through but still slightly pink, about 2 minutes. Stir in tomato sauce, broth, vinegar, and sugar and simmer until slightly thickened, about 5 minutes; mixture will be saucy. Off heat, season with salt and pepper to taste.

2. FOR THE SALAD: Adjust oven racks to upper-middle and lower-middle positions and heat oven to 425 degrees. Arrange 4 ovensafe soup bowls (or 4 slightly flattened 3-inch aluminum foil balls) upside down on 2 rimmed baking sheets. Place tortillas on plate, cover with damp paper towel, and microwave until warm and pliable, about 30 seconds.

3. Generously spray both sides of warm tortillas with oil spray. Drape tortillas over soup bowls, pressing top flat and pinching sides to create 4-sided bowl. Bake until tortillas are golden and crisp, 10 to 15 minutes, switching and rotating sheets halfway through baking. Let cool upside down.

4. Combine lettuce, beans, tomatoes, scallions, and 2 tablespoons cilantro in large bowl; toss with lime juice and season with salt and pepper to taste. Place tortilla bowls on individual plates. Divide salad among bowls, top with taco meat, and sprinkle with cheese and remaining 2 tablespoons cilantro. Serve.

TEST KITCHEN TIP MAKING TORTILLA BOWLS

Place ovensafe soup bowls upside down on rimmed baking sheets. Drape prepared tortillas over bowls. Press tops flat; pinch sides to create shells.

Meatballs in Chipotle Sauce

Serves 4 to 6

✓ **WHY THIS RECIPE WORKS:** *Albóndigas en chipotle* is a classic Mexican dish that features a smoky, spicy, chipotle chile–infused tomato sauce and tender meatballs. Usually the meatballs also contain rice. Our goal was to create a recipe with big flavors and perfectly cooked rice and meatballs. We borrowed a method from our recipe for Meatball Soup with Rice and Cilantro (page 58) and parcooked the rice to ensure that it became fully tender by the time the meatballs finished cooking. Next, we focused on the flavor and texture of the meatballs. Instead of utilizing a laundry list of ingredients to flavor our meatballs, we looked to a commonly used Mexican ingredient with plenty of its own seasoning: Mexican chorizo. By substituting chorizo for a portion of the ground beef, we were able to quickly infuse our meatballs with spicy, rich flavor. A panade, a mixture of milk and bread, kept the meatballs tender. To develop a rich sauce, we used canned fire-roasted tomatoes, which echoed the deep smoky flavors of the chipotle chile. The addition of red wine vinegar and brown sugar helped to balance the sauce with tart and sweet notes. Canned chipotle chile in adobo sauce was easy to use and provided heat, smokiness, and a bit of acidity. Covering the meatballs during baking ensured that they stayed moist in the oven. See the photo on page 184.

½ **cup long-grain white rice**
Salt and pepper
2 **tablespoons extra-virgin olive oil**
1 **onion, chopped fine**
3 **garlic cloves, minced**
1 **tablespoon minced fresh oregano or 1 teaspoon dried**
¼ **teaspoon ground cumin**
1 **(14.5-ounce) can crushed fire-roasted tomatoes**
1 **cup chicken broth**
2 **tablespoons red wine vinegar**

1 **tablespoon minced canned chipotle chile in adobo sauce**
1 **tablespoon packed brown sugar**
1 **bay leaf**
2 **slices hearty white sandwich bread, torn into 1-inch pieces**
½ **cup whole milk**
12 **ounces Mexican-style chorizo sausage, casings removed**
12 **ounces 90 percent lean ground beef**
2 **tablespoons chopped fresh cilantro**

1. Adjust oven rack to middle position and heat oven to 350 degrees. Bring 4 cups water to boil in medium saucepan. Add rice and 1 teaspoon salt and cook, stirring occasionally, for 8 minutes. Drain rice in fine-mesh strainer, rinse with cold water, and drain again; set aside.

2. Heat oil in now-empty saucepan over medium heat until shimmering. Add onion and cook until softened, about 5 minutes. Stir in garlic, oregano, and cumin and cook until fragrant, about 30 seconds. Stir in tomatoes, broth, vinegar, chipotle, sugar, and bay leaf and bring to simmer; transfer sauce to 13 by 9-inch baking dish.

3. Mash bread and milk to paste with fork in large bowl. Add chorizo, ground beef, parcooked rice, 1 teaspoon pepper, and ½ teaspoon salt and mix with your hands until thoroughly combined.

4. Pinch off and roll mixture into 16 meatballs (¼ cup each) and nestle into sauce. Spoon some sauce over meatballs, cover tightly with aluminum foil, and bake until meatballs are cooked through, about 1 hour.

5. Remove dish from oven and let meatballs rest in sauce, covered, for 15 minutes. Transfer meatballs to serving platter. Discard bay leaf, skim any fat off surface of sauce, and season with salt and pepper to taste. Pour sauce over meatballs, sprinkle with cilantro, and serve.

Oaxacan-Style Beef Brisket

Serves 6

✔ **WHY THIS RECIPE WORKS:** We wanted a recipe for tender, juicy beef brisket full of bold Mexican flavor. To ensure that our brisket turned out tender, we cooked it fat side up so it would self-baste as it cooked, and we covered it with foil to hold in moisture. We infused our aromatic cooking liquid with toasted pasilla chiles and lots of Mexican spices; we blended the cooking liquid to a smooth consistency to make an ample quantity of sauce to spoon over the rich meat. You will need 18-inch-wide heavy-duty aluminum foil for this recipe.

1	(3½-pound) beef brisket, flat cut, fat trimmed to ¼ inch
	Salt and pepper
4	pasilla chiles, stemmed, seeded, and torn into ½-inch pieces (1 cup)
1	tablespoon vegetable oil
2	onions, chopped
8	garlic cloves, peeled and smashed
1	tablespoon dried oregano
2	teaspoons ground cumin
2	teaspoons dried thyme
1	teaspoon ground coriander
¼	teaspoon ground cloves
1	cup chicken broth
1	(28-ounce) can diced tomatoes

1. Poke holes all over brisket with fork and rub with 1 tablespoon salt. Wrap brisket in plastic wrap and refrigerate for at least 6 or up to 24 hours.

2. Adjust oven rack to lower-middle position and heat oven to 325 degrees. Pat brisket dry with paper towels and season with pepper. Toast pasillas in 12-inch skillet over medium heat, stirring frequently, until fragrant, 2 to 6 minutes; transfer to bowl.

3. Heat oil in now-empty skillet over medium-high heat until just smoking. Lay brisket in skillet, place heavy Dutch oven on top, and cook until well browned on both sides, about 4 minutes per side; transfer to platter.

4. Pour off all but 1 tablespoon fat from skillet. Add onions and cook over medium heat until softened, 8 to 10 minutes. Stir in garlic, oregano, cumin, thyme, coriander, cloves, and 1 teaspoon pepper and cook until fragrant, about 1 minute. Stir in broth, tomatoes and their juice, and toasted chiles, scraping up any browned bits, and bring to simmer. Transfer to 13 by 9-inch baking dish.

5. Nestle browned brisket, fat side up, into dish and spoon some sauce over top. Cover dish tightly with aluminum foil and bake until tender and fork easily slips in and out of meat, 3½ to 4 hours. Remove dish from oven and let brisket rest, covered, for 1 hour.

6. Transfer brisket to carving board and tent loosely with foil. Strain cooking liquid through fine-mesh strainer into bowl; transfer solids to blender. Let liquid settle for 5 minutes, then skim fat from surface. Add defatted liquid to blender and puree until smooth, about 2 minutes. Season sauce with salt and pepper to taste.

7. Slice brisket against grain into ¼-inch-thick slices and return to baking dish. Pour sauce over top and serve. (Brisket can be refrigerated for up to 2 days; reheat, covered, in 350 degree oven for 45 minutes before serving.)

TEST KITCHEN TIP BROWNING BRISKET

To achieve deep browning, weight brisket with heavy Dutch oven to ensure thorough and even contact with hot pan.

Braised Short Ribs with Peppers and Onions

Serves 4

☑ **WHY THIS RECIPE WORKS:** *Bistec ranchero* is a traditional dish of beef braised in an aromatic mixture of peppers, onions, tomatoes, and spices. Hailing from the northwestern Mexican state of Sonora, the minimalist preparation is indicative of the local cuisine, which is straightforward and uncomplicated. Though there are very few ingredients, the flavor is vibrant and satisfying. We began with beef short ribs, which became meltingly tender with long, slow cooking. Searing the meat over medium-high heat quickly browned the exterior, giving it a flavorful crust, and developed flavorful fond, which added rich meatiness to the braise. Once we removed the ribs from the pan, we sautéed the onions and peppers to concentrate their flavors before we continued building our sauce. We included jalapeños, garlic, oregano, cumin, ancho chile powder, coriander, and a pinch of ground cloves to round out the flavor profile. A can of diced tomatoes gave the sauce some heft and allowed us to scrape up the flavorful browned bits from the bottom of the pan. When we returned the meat to the pan, we covered the braise and transferred it a 325-degree oven to slowly and evenly simmer our steak and vegetables until tender. After setting the beef aside, we stirred chopped fresh cilantro into the vegetable mixture to provide freshness and color. A small amount of lime juice cut through the richness and provided just enough acidity to balance the sauce. Serve with rice.

2   **pounds boneless beef short ribs, trimmed**
    Salt and pepper
2   **tablespoons vegetable oil**
2   **onions, halved and sliced thin**

2   **red bell peppers, stemmed, seeded, and cut into ½-inch-wide strips**
1   **jalapeño chile, stemmed and sliced thin**
1½   **tablespoons minced fresh oregano or 1½ teaspoons dried**
4   **garlic cloves, minced**
1   **teaspoon ground cumin**
1   **teaspoon ancho chile powder**
½   **teaspoon ground coriander**
    Pinch ground cloves
1   **(14.5-ounce) can diced tomatoes**
2   **tablespoons chopped fresh cilantro**
2   **teaspoons lime juice**

1. Adjust oven rack to lower-middle position and heat oven to 325 degrees. Pat beef dry with paper towels and season with salt and pepper. Heat 1 tablespoon oil in 12-inch ovensafe skillet over medium-high heat until just smoking. Brown beef well, 4 to 5 minutes per side; transfer to plate.

2. Add onions, bell peppers and ¼ teaspoon salt to fat left in skillet and cook over medium-high heat until softened, 8 to 10 minutes. Stir in jalapeño, oregano, garlic, cumin, chile powder, coriander, and cloves and cook until fragrant, about 30 seconds. Stir in tomatoes and their juice, scraping up any browned bits. Nestle browned beef into skillet along with any accumulated juices. Cover, transfer skillet to oven, and cook until fork slips easily in and out of meat, about 2 hours.

3. Remove skillet from oven. Transfer beef to serving platter and tent with aluminum foil. Let vegetable mixture settle for 5 minutes, then skim any fat off surface. Stir in cilantro and lime juice and season with salt and pepper to taste. Spoon vegetable mixture over beef and serve.

Indoor Steak Fajitas

Serves 4

✔ **WHY THIS RECIPE WORKS:** Although the grill is great for achieving a crisp, nicely charred crust on steak for fajitas, we wanted a recipe that we could make indoors that would produce the same deeply flavorful results. Flank steak worked well, with its beefy flavor and tender texture when sliced, and pan-searing gave the steak a good crust. Traditionally, the steak for fajitas is marinated in lime juice before being cooked, but when we tried pan-searing the marinated steak, it steamed rather than seared. To avoid this, we skipped the marinade and simply drizzled the lime juice on the cooked steak. To keep our recipe simple, we cooked the peppers and onions in the same pan we had used to cook the steak. This had the added benefits of allowing the vegetables to pick up flavorful fond from the pan and giving the steak time to rest while we cooked the vegetables. We prefer the flank steak cooked to medium-rare, but if you prefer it more or less done, see the chart. Serve the fajitas as is or with salsa, shredded cheese, sour cream, and/or lime wedges.

1	(1½-pound) flank steak, trimmed
	Salt and pepper
2	tablespoons vegetable oil
2	tablespoons lime juice
2	red bell peppers, stemmed, seeded, and sliced thin
1	large red onion, halved and sliced thin
2	tablespoons water
1	teaspoon chili powder
1	teaspoon hot sauce
½	teaspoon ground cumin
8–12	(6-inch) flour tortillas, warmed

1. Pat steak dry with paper towels and season with salt and pepper. Heat 1 tablespoon oil in 12-inch skillet over medium-high heat until just smoking. Cook steak until well browned on both sides and meat registers 120 to 125 degrees (for medium-rare), 4 to 6 minutes per side. Transfer steak to carving board, drizzle with lime juice, and tent with aluminum foil.

2. While steak rests, heat remaining 1 tablespoon oil in now-empty skillet over medium-high heat until shimmering. Add bell peppers, onion, water, chili powder, hot sauce, cumin, and ½ teaspoon salt. Cook, scraping up any browned bits, until peppers are softened and onion is browned, about 8 minutes. Transfer vegetables to serving platter and season with salt and pepper to taste.

3. Slice steak against grain into ¼-inch-thick slices and transfer to serving platter with vegetables. Serve with warm tortillas.

TEST KITCHEN TIP

KNOWING WHEN MEAT IS DONE

For the most accurate measurement, use an instant-read thermometer. The temperature of the meat will continue to rise as it rests, an effect called carryover cooking; the temperatures listed below are the temperatures at which you should remove the meat from the heat. Be sure to let meat rest before slicing or serving.

TYPE OF MEAT	COOK UNTIL IT REGISTERS
Beef	
Rare	115°–120°
Medium-Rare	120°–125°
Medium	130°–135°
Medium-Well	140°–145°
Well-Done	150°–155°
Pork	
Chops and Tenderloin	145°
Loin Roasts	140°

Pork Chops with Chile-Peanut Rice

Serves 4

✔ **WHY THIS RECIPE WORKS:** Peanuts with chile and lime are a classic bar snack that can be found in a number of regions across Mexico. Inspired by these flavors, we set out to create a simple one-pan weeknight meal using pork chops and rice as the backbone of the dish. To keep the pork chops flat during cooking, we cut small slits through the fat and silverskin. To ensure that the delicate chops didn't overcook, we seared just one side to develop deep flavor while keeping the cooking time to a minimum. We parcooked the rice in the microwave to ensure that the rice and pork were done cooking at the same time. After removing the chops from the pan, we sautéed an aromatic mixture of onion, garlic, tomato paste, oregano, ancho chile powder, coriander, and cayenne pepper to develop a complex, flavorful base for the dish. Letting the pork and rice simmer in a covered skillet infused them both with flavor. A quick vinaigrette of cilantro, lime zest, lime juice, and honey brought bright, fresh flavor to the finished dish. While the pork was resting, we folded ⅓ cup of dry-roasted peanuts into the rice; adding them at this late point preserved their crunch and gave the rice lots of peanut flavor.

2½	cups chicken broth
1	cup long-grain white rice, rinsed
4	(6- to 8-ounce) boneless pork chops, ¾ to 1 inch thick, trimmed
	Salt and pepper
3	tablespoons extra-virgin olive oil
1	onion, chopped fine
3	garlic cloves, minced
1	tablespoon tomato paste
1	tablespoon minced fresh oregano or 1 teaspoon dried
1	teaspoon ancho chile powder
¼	teaspoon ground coriander
	Pinch cayenne pepper
⅓	cup unsalted dry-roasted peanuts, chopped
¼	cup chopped fresh cilantro
1	tablespoon honey
2	teaspoons grated lime zest plus 3 tablespoons juice (2 limes)

1. Combine 1¼ cups broth and rice in bowl, cover, and microwave until liquid is absorbed, about 12 minutes. Fluff rice with fork.

2. Meanwhile, cut 2 slits, about 2 inches apart, through fat on edges of each chop. Pat chops dry with paper towels and season with salt and pepper. Heat 1 tablespoon oil in 12-inch skillet over medium-high heat until just smoking. Brown chops until well browned on 1 side, about 5 minutes; transfer to plate.

3. Pour off all but 1 tablespoon fat from skillet. Add onion and cook until softened, about 5 minutes. Stir in garlic, tomato paste, oregano, chile powder, coriander, and cayenne and cook until fragrant, about 30 seconds. Stir in remaining 1¼ cups broth and microwaved rice, scraping up any browned bits, and bring to simmer.

4. Nestle chops browned side up into rice along with any accumulated juices. Cover, reduce heat to medium-low, and simmer gently until pork registers 145 degrees, rice is tender, and liquid is absorbed, 6 to 8 minutes.

5. Transfer chops to carving board, tent with aluminum foil, and let rest for 5 to 10 minutes. Gently fold peanuts and 2 tablespoons cilantro into rice and season with salt and pepper to taste; cover to keep warm.

6. Whisk honey, lime zest and juice, remaining 2 tablespoons oil, remaining 2 tablespoons cilantro, and ⅛ teaspoon salt together in bowl. Slice chops into ½-inch-thick slices. Transfer rice to platter, arrange pork over top, and spoon vinaigrette over pork. Serve.

Braised Pork Loin with Black Mole Sauce

Serves 6

☑ **WHY THIS RECIPE WORKS:** Hailing from the state of Oaxaca, black mole is also known as *mole negro*. This thick, complexly flavored sauce consists of dried chiles, spices, tomatillos, tomatoes, cocoa, dried or fresh fruit, nuts, and seeds. Its intense, subtly bitter flavor and deep brown, almost black color sets it apart from other moles. Usually paired with meat or poultry, it functions as both a sauce and a cooking medium. For our version, we chose to pair the mole with pork, which is one of the most commonly used proteins of the Oaxaca region. Pork loin was particularly well suited to the moist cooking environment; tying the roast at 1½-inch intervals ensured that it cooked evenly. We quickly browned the pork in a Dutch oven to deepen the meat's flavor and create flavorful fond in the pot. After removing the roast, we sautéed onion until it was a very deep brown, which contributed to the color and complex flavor of the mole. We then added garlic, oregano, cloves, and cinnamon for aromatic, warm spice notes. Next, the tomato and tomatillos went into the pot to concentrate their flavors. Adding chicken broth allowed us to scrape up the flavorful browned bits on the bottom of the pot. We then finished the sauce with toasted pasilla chiles, peanuts, sesame seeds, raisins, and cocoa powder; black cocoa powder (cocoa powder that has been heavily Dutched) worked especially well for its intense flavor and deep, dark color. Cooking the nuts, seeds, and cocoa along with the pork gave them plenty of time to hydrate and soften, making it easier to blend them into a smooth sauce later. You can find black cocoa powder in specialty stores or online. While we prefer the deeper flavor of black cocoa powder in this recipe, Dutch-processed cocoa powder also works well. Serve with rice.

4   **pasilla chiles, stemmed, seeded, and torn into ½-inch pieces (1 cup)**

1   **(2½- to 3-pound) boneless pork loin roast, fat trimmed to ¼ inch, tied at 1½-inch intervals**
     Salt and pepper

2   **tablespoons vegetable oil**

1   **onion, chopped**

2   **garlic cloves, peeled**

2   **teaspoons minced fresh oregano or ½ teaspoon dried**

⅛   **teaspoon ground cloves**

⅛   **teaspoon ground cinnamon**

2   **tomatillos, husks and stems removed, rinsed well, dried, and cut into 1-inch pieces**

1   **tomato, cored and cut into 1-inch pieces**

2   **cups chicken broth**

¼   **cup unsalted dry-roasted peanuts**

3   **tablespoons black or Dutch-processed cocoa powder**

3   **tablespoons sesame seeds, toasted**

2   **tablespoons raisins**

1. Adjust oven rack to lowest position and heat oven to 250 degrees. Toast pasilla chiles in Dutch oven over medium-high heat, stirring frequently, until fragrant, 2 to 6 minutes; transfer to bowl.

2. Pat roast dry with paper towels and season with salt and pepper. Heat oil in now-empty pot over medium-high heat until just smoking. Brown roast well on all sides, 7 to 10 minutes; transfer to plate.

3. Add onion to fat left in pot and cook over medium heat until softened and well browned, about 5 minutes. Stir in garlic, oregano, cloves, and cinnamon and cook until fragrant, about 30 seconds. Stir in tomatillos and tomato and cook until softened, about 5 minutes. Stir in broth, scraping up any browned bits. Stir in peanuts, cocoa, 2 tablespoons sesame seeds, raisins, toasted pasillas, 1 teaspoon salt, and ½ teaspoon pepper and bring to simmer.

4. Nestle browned pork fat side up into pot along with any accumulated juices. Cover, transfer pot to oven, and cook until pork registers 140 degrees, 40 minutes to 1 hour.

5. Transfer pork to carving board, tent with aluminum foil, and let rest for 15 to 20 minutes. Meanwhile, process cooking liquid in blender until smooth, 1 to 2 minutes. Season sauce with salt and pepper to taste.

6. Remove twine from roast, slice into ¼-inch-thick slices, and transfer to serving platter. Spoon 1 cup sauce over pork, sprinkle with remaining 1 tablespoon sesame seeds, and serve with remaining sauce.

LEARN HOW **BRAISED PORK LOIN WITH BLACK MOLE SAUCE**

We use our rich, intense black mole sauce as both a braising liquid and a serving sauce.

1. TOAST CHILES: Toast the pasilla chiles in a Dutch oven over medium-high heat until fragrant, 2 to 6 minutes. Toasting brings out the chiles' full flavor.

2. BROWN PORK: Pat the roast dry, season with salt and pepper, and brown on all sides. Transfer the roast to a plate. The fond left in the pot boosts the flavor of the sauce.

3. MAKE SAUCE: Cook the aromatics, then add the tomatillos and tomato. Add the broth, nuts, seeds, cocoa, raisins, and chiles; bring the sauce to a simmer.

4. BRAISE PORK: Nestle the roast, fat side up, into the sauce, cover, and transfer the pot to the oven. The fat drips down and bastes the meat as it cooks. Braising in the oven promotes even cooking.

5. CHECK FOR DONENESS: Cook until the pork registers 140 degrees, 40 minutes to 1 hour. Transfer to a carving board and let it rest. Don't let the pork overcook or it will become tough.

6. PUREE SAUCE: Process the cooking liquid in a blender until smooth. Slice the pork and serve with the sauce. Blending the sauce is not only traditional, it also helps to meld the distinct flavors.

Pork Tenderloin with Garlic Sauce

Serves 4

☑ **WHY THIS RECIPE WORKS:** We wanted to create a recipe that would infuse quick-cooking pork tenderloin with big Mexican flavor. We first browned the tenderloins in a skillet, then let them gently finish cooking in the oven. Since mild pork tenderloin calls out for a deeply flavorful sauce, we found inspiration in traditional Mexican *mojo de ajo*, or garlic sauce. This simple sauce is prepared by slowly browning garlic in oil and butter until it becomes soft and sweet. Since our skillet was still warm from searing the pork, we used the residual heat to gently start cooking the garlic, scraping up the flavorful fond in the skillet as the garlic cooked. A bit of brown sugar brought out the sweetness in the garlic and provided molasses undertones that complemented the pork nicely. Lime juice, cilantro, and chives provided much-needed brightness and freshness, while red pepper flakes tempered the sweetness with some background spice. Butter, added at the end, made our sauce rich and silky. To ensure the tenderloins don't curl during cooking, remove the silverskin—the swath of connective tissue that covers the meat. A rasp-style grater makes quick work of turning the garlic into a paste.

2	(12- to 16-ounce) pork tenderloins, trimmed
	Salt and pepper
2	tablespoons vegetable oil
10	garlic cloves, minced to paste
2	tablespoons water
2	teaspoons packed light brown sugar
¼	teaspoon red pepper flakes
¼	cup chopped fresh cilantro
3	tablespoons lime juice (2 limes)
1	tablespoon chopped fresh chives
4	tablespoons unsalted butter, cut into 4 pieces and chilled

1. Adjust oven rack to middle position and heat oven to 400 degrees. Pat tenderloins dry with paper towels and season with salt and pepper. Heat 1 tablespoon oil in 12-inch skillet over medium-high heat until just smoking. Brown tenderloins well on all sides, about 10 minutes. Transfer tenderloins to rimmed baking sheet and roast in oven until pork registers 145 degrees, 10 to 16 minutes, flipping pork halfway through roasting.

2. Meanwhile, combine garlic and water in bowl. Add remaining 1 tablespoon oil and garlic mixture to now-empty skillet. Cook using skillet's residual heat, scraping up any browned bits, until sizzling subsides, about 2 minutes. Place skillet over low heat and cook, stirring often, until garlic is sticky, 8 to 10 minutes; remove from heat and set aside.

3. Transfer tenderloins to carving board, tent with aluminum foil, and let rest for 5 to 10 minutes. Stir sugar and pepper flakes into skillet and cook over medium heat until sticky and sugar is dissolved, about 1 minute. Stir in cilantro, lime juice, and chives and simmer until flavors meld, 1 to 2 minutes. Stir in any accumulated pork juices and simmer for 1 minute. Off heat, whisk in butter, 1 piece at a time. Season with salt and pepper to taste.

4. Slice tenderloins into ½-inch-thick slices, arrange on serving platter or individual plates, and spoon sauce over top. Serve.

TEST KITCHEN TIP

REMOVING PORK SILVERSKIN

To remove silverskin from pork tenderloin, slip knife underneath, angle knife slightly upward, and use gentle back-and-forth motion to cut away from meat.

Chiles Rellenos with Pork

Serves 4

✔ WHY THIS RECIPE WORKS: *Chiles rellenos* are poblano chiles that are stuffed with a savory filling, enrobed in an airy batter and deep-fried. Traditional recipes take hours to prepare; we wanted a streamlined recipe for exceptional chiles rellenos. The fillings for chiles rellenos vary widely, but we were drawn to a boldly flavored ground pork filling seasoned with tomatoes, almonds, raisins, and warm spices. Although we loved the authentic flavor of the stuffing, a few tasters preferred the cheese-filled versions commonly found stateside, so we also developed a simple cheese variation. Although most recipes call for peeling the peppers before stuffing them, we found this step unnecessary; we simply broiled the peppers to soften them. Instead of the traditional (and fussy) egg white batter, we opted for an easy-to-make batter of flour, cornstarch, and seltzer. A quick dredge in cornstarch dried out the surface of the chiles and helped the batter to adhere. If using poblano chiles smaller than 4 ounces, increase the total number of chiles to 12 to accommodate the filling. Use a Dutch oven that holds 6 quarts or more. Serve with hot sauce.

FILLING

- 1 tablespoon vegetable oil
- 2 garlic cloves, minced
- 1 teaspoon minced fresh oregano or ¼ teaspoon dried
- ½ teaspoon minced canned chipotle chile in adobo sauce
- ½ teaspoon ground cinnamon
- ⅛ teaspoon ground cloves
- 1 pound ground pork
- 1 (8-ounce) can tomato sauce
- ¼ cup raisins
- 1 tablesoon cider vinegar
  Salt and pepper
- 2 ounces Monterey Jack cheese, shredded (½ cup)
- ¼ cup slivered almonds, toasted and chopped

POBLANOS

- 8 poblano chiles (4 ounces each)
- 1⅓ cups cornstarch
- 5 cups vegetable oil
- ⅔ cup all-purpose flour
- 1 teaspoon baking powder
- 1 teaspoon salt
- 1 cup seltzer

1. FOR THE FILLING: Cook oil, garlic, oregano, chipotle, cinnamon, and cloves in 12-inch non-stick skillet over medium heat until fragrant, about 1 minute. Stir in ground pork and cook, breaking up meat with wooden spoon, until no longer pink, about 5 minutes. Stir in tomato sauce, raisins, vinegar, and ¼ teaspoon salt and simmer until most of liquid has evaporated, 3 to 5 minutes.

2. Transfer meat mixture to bowl and mash into fine pieces with potato masher. Let meat cool slightly, then stir in Monterey Jack and almonds. Season with salt and pepper to taste.

3. FOR THE POBLANOS: Position oven rack 4 inches from broiler element and heat broiler. Line rimmed baking sheet with aluminum foil. Lay poblanos on sheet and broil until skin is charred and puffed but flesh is still firm, about 8 minutes, flipping after 5 minutes. Transfer poblanos to bowl, cover, and steam for 10 minutes. Gently remove any loosened pieces of poblano skin, cut off stem end, and remove seeds; you do not need to remove all of skin or seeds.

4. Set wire rack in rimmed baking sheet. Stuff poblanos with meat mixture, leaving ½ inch room at top. Seal open end by weaving toothpick through top of chile. Place ⅔ cup cornstarch in shallow bowl; coat stuffed poblanos thoroughly with cornstarch and place on prepared wire rack.

5. Add oil to large Dutch oven and bring to 375 degrees over medium-high heat. Whisk flour, baking powder, salt, and remaining ⅔ cup cornstarch together in large bowl. Slowly whisk in seltzer until just combined (some lumps will remain). Coat 1 poblano with batter and add to hot oil; repeat with 3 more poblanos. Fry chiles, turning as needed, until golden and crisp, about 6 minutes, adjusting burner as needed to maintain oil temperature of 325 degrees.

6. Transfer fried chiles to prepared rack and remove toothpicks. Repeat with remaining chiles. (Chiles can be held in 200-dgree oven for 30 minutes.)

Chiles Rellenos with Cheese

Omit filling and skip steps 1 and 2. Toss 8 ounces shredded Monterey Jack cheese with 3 thinly sliced scallions and 3 tablespoons minced fresh cilantro; substitute cheese mixture for meat filling when stuffing poblanos.

LEARN HOW **CHILES RELLENOS WITH PORK**

Chiles rellenos are a labor of love, but this ultraflavorful traditional dish is well worth the time.

1. COOK FILLING: Cook the ground pork with the aromatics, tomato sauce, vinegar, and raisins until most of the of liquid has evaporated. Vinegar prevents the filling from becoming too sweet.

2. BROIL CHILES: Heat the broiler. Broil the chiles on an aluminum foil–lined baking sheet until the skin is charred but the flesh is still firm. This makes the poblanos pliable enough to stuff.

3. STEM AND SEED: Let the broiled chiles rest, covered, for 10 minutes. Remove any loosened pieces of skin, cut off the stem ends, and scoop out most of the seeds.

4. STUFF AND CLOSE ENDS: Carefully stuff the chiles. Weave a toothpick through the open end of each chile to close it. This keeps the filling in while frying.

5. DREDGE IN CORNSTARCH, THEN BATTER: Spread ⅔ cup cornstarch in a shallow dish. Dredge each chile in cornstarch to thoroughly dry the exterior. Coat each chile with batter.

6. FRY CHILES: Fry the chiles, four at a time, until they are golden and crisp. Frying in batches ensures the chiles cook evenly.

Grilled Steak Fajitas

Serves 4

✔ **WHY THIS RECIPE WORKS:** We wanted a recipe that would take fajitas back to their traditional roots: steak grilled over an open flame, sliced thin, and served in soft tortillas. To make sure our steak was packed with meaty flavor, we started with a marinade that included soy sauce. This helped brine the steak, keeping the meat moist. Pricking the steak with a fork helped the marinade penetrate the meat in just 30 minutes. After the steak was cooked, we drizzled it with some reserved marinade for a last-minute flavor boost. Don't marinate the steak for longer than 2 hours or it will begin to turn mushy. We prefer the flank steak cooked to medium-rare, but if you prefer it more or less done, see the chart on page 195. Serve the fajitas as is or with salsa, shredded cheese, sour cream, and/or lime wedges.

½   cup lime juice (4 limes)
¼   cup vegetable oil
1   jalapeño chile, stemmed, seeded, and minced
2   tablespoons soy sauce
3   garlic cloves, minced
2   teaspoons ground cumin
2   teaspoons packed brown sugar
1   tablespoon chopped fresh cilantro
1   (1½-pound) flank steak, trimmed
2   bell peppers, stemmed, seeded, and quartered
1   onion, sliced into ½-inch-thick rounds (do not separate rings)
    Salt and pepper
12   (6-inch) flour tortillas

1. Combine lime juice, 2 tablespoons oil, jalapeño, soy sauce, garlic, cumin, and sugar in bowl. Transfer ¼ cup of marinade to separate bowl and stir in cilantro; set aside for serving. Poke each side of steak about 25 times with fork. Pour remaining marinade into 1-gallon zipper-lock bag, add steak, and toss to coat. Press out as much air as possible, seal bag, and refrigerate for at least 30 minutes or up to 2 hours, flipping bag occasionally.

2. Just before grilling, remove steak from bag and pat dry with paper towels. Brush bell peppers and onion rounds with remaining 2 tablespoons oil and season with salt and pepper.

3A. FOR A CHARCOAL GRILL: Open bottom vent completely. Light large chimney starter filled with charcoal briquettes (6 quarts). When top coals are partially covered with ash, pour two-thirds evenly over half of grill, then pour remaining coals over other half of grill. Set cooking grate in place, cover, and open lid vent completely. Heat grill until hot, about 5 minutes.

3B. FOR A GAS GRILL: Turn all burners to high, cover, and heat grill until hot, about 15 minutes. Leave primary burner on high and turn other burner(s) to medium.

4. Clean and oil cooking grate. Place steak on hotter side of grill and place bell peppers and onion rounds on cooler side of grill. Cook (covered if using gas), turning as needed, until vegetables are nicely charred on both sides and meat registers 120 to 125 degrees (for medium-rare), 8 to 12 minutes. As they finish cooking, transfer steak and vegetables to carving board and tent loosely with aluminum foil. Let steak rest for 5 to 10 minutes.

5. Working in batches, grill tortillas over cooler part of grill, turning as needed, until warmed and lightly browned, about 40 seconds. As tortillas finish cooking, wrap in dish towel or large sheet of foil.

6. Separate onion rings and slice bell peppers into ¼-inch-wide strips; toss together in bowl with half of reserved marinade. Slice steak against grain into ¼-inch-thick slices and toss with remaining reserved marinade in separate bowl. Arrange steak and vegetables on serving platter and serve with tortillas.

Spicy Grilled Beef and Chorizo Kebabs

Serves 4 to 6

✓ **WHY THIS RECIPE WORKS:** *Alambre Mexicano,* a dish of skewered meat, chiles, and vegetables grilled over an open flame, is popular in northern Mexico. The word *alambre* literally means "wire" or "cable," referring to the metal skewers that hold the ingredients together on the grill. For the meat, we chose richly marbled steak tips for their beefy flavor and tender texture, as well as chorizo for its spice and assertive flavor profile. We tossed the beef in a mixture of olive oil and spices; we chose oregano for a peppery bite, garlic powder to add savoriness, and cumin for depth. We rounded out our kebabs with spicy jalapeños and sweet red onion. We briefly parcooked the vegetables in the microwave to ensure they would finish cooking at the same time as the meat. Stemming and seeding the jalapeños allowed us to enjoy their flavor without making the dish overly spicy. If you can't find steak tips, sometimes labeled flap meat, substitute 1¼ pounds blade steaks (if using, cut the steak in half and remove the gristle that runs through it). If you have long, thin pieces of meat, roll or fold them into approximate 2-inch cubes. You will need four 12-inch metal skewers for this recipe. We prefer these steak kebabs cooked to medium, but if you prefer them more or less done, see the chart on page 195. Serve with warm tortillas or rice.

1   **large red onion, cut into 1-inch pieces, 3 layers thick**

4   **jalapeño chiles, stemmed, halved, seeded, and cut into 1-inch pieces**

3   **tablespoons extra-virgin olive oil**

1   **tablespoon minced fresh oregano or 1 teaspoon dried**

½   **teaspoon garlic powder**
     Salt and pepper

¼   **teaspoon ground cumin**

1   **pound sirloin steak tips, trimmed and cut into 2-inch pieces**

1   **pound Mexican-style chorizo sausage, cut into 2-inch lengths**

2   **tablespoons chopped fresh cilantro**
     Lime wedges

1. Gently toss onion and jalapeños with 1 tablespoon oil in bowl. Cover vegetables and microwave until just tender, 3 to 5 minutes. In large bowl, combine oregano, garlic powder, ½ teaspoon salt, ¼ teaspoon pepper, cumin, and remaining 2 tablespoons oil. Add steak and toss to coat. Thread steak, chorizo, onion, and jalapeños tightly onto four 12-inch metal skewers in alternating pattern.

2A. FOR A CHARCOAL GRILL: Open bottom vent completely. Light large chimney starter filled with charcoal briquettes (6 quarts). When top coals are partially covered with ash, pour evenly over grill. Set cooking grate in place, cover, and open lid vent completely. Heat grill until hot, about 5 minutes.

2B. FOR A GAS GRILL: Turn all burners to high, cover, and heat grill until hot, about 15 minutes. Leave all burners on high.

3. Clean and oil cooking grate. Place kebabs on grill and cook (covered if using gas), turning as needed, until well browned and meat registers 130 to 135 (for medium), 10 to 15 minutes. Transfer kebabs to serving platter, tent loosely with aluminum foil, and let rest for 5 to 10 minutes. Sprinkle with cilantro and serve with lime wedges.

TEST KITCHEN TIP

PREPARING ONIONS FOR KEBABS

Peel onion, trim off stem and root ends, then quarter onion. Pull onion apart into sections that are 3 layers thick; discard core. Cut each section into 1-inch pieces.

Carne Asada

Serves 4 to 6

✔ **WHY THIS RECIPE WORKS:** *Carne asada* (literally meaning "grilled meat") is the Mexican answer to steak on the grill. Generally, a thin steak is marinated with lime juice and salt, cooked until well charred on the outside, and served with a bevy of sides—rice, beans, and salsa are common. It was first served at the Tampico Club in Mexico City, and nowadays the steak is eaten both as an entrée unto itself and as a filling for tacos, burritos or other composed dishes. In keeping with tradition, we wanted our steak to have a nicely charred exterior. We also wanted the interior to be reasonably tender and well seasoned. Many recipes call for skirt steak, and we found that this cut worked perfectly since it is already thin and has good flavor and texture when cooked to medium (which we preferred over the well-done steak called for in many recipes). We found that the traditional marinade was interfering with our ability to achieve a good sear because of the excess moisture it left on the steaks. Instead, we opted for a dry rub of salt and cumin, and we also let the steak dry out in the refrigerator for 45 minutes. In order to achieve maximum char before the interior overcooked, we needed the hottest possible grill fire, so we corralled the coals using a disposable roasting pan with the bottom cut out. To work in the traditional lime flavor, we squeezed lime juice on the steaks just before serving, and rubbed them with a clove of garlic for a layer of pungent flavor. If you can't find skirt steak, substitute 2 pounds of sirloin steak tips, sometimes labeled flap meat. If using table salt, reduce the amount of salt to 1 teaspoon. We prefer the skirt steak cooked to medium, but if you prefer it more or less done, see the chart on page 195. Serve with fresh salsa, refried beans, rice, and/or warm tortillas.

2 teaspoons kosher salt
¾ teaspoon ground cumin
1 (2-pound) skirt steak, trimmed, cut with grain into 4 equal steaks, and pounded ¼-inch thick
1 (13 by 9-inch) disposable aluminum roasting pan (if using charcoal)
1 garlic clove, peeled and smashed
 Lime wedges

1. Combine salt and cumin and sprinkle evenly over both sides of steaks. Transfer steaks to wire rack set in rimmed baking sheet and refrigerate, uncovered, for at least 45 minutes or up to 24 hours. Meanwhile, if using charcoal, use kitchen shears to remove and discard bottom of roasting pan; reserve pan collar.

2A. FOR A CHARCOAL GRILL: Open bottom vent completely. Light large chimney starter filled with charcoal briquettes (6 quarts). When top coals are partially covered with ash, place roasting pan collar in center of grill, oriented over bottom vents, and pour coals into even layer in collar. Set cooking grate in place, cover, and open lid vent completely. Heat grill until hot, about 5 minutes.

2B. FOR A GAS GRILL: Turn all burners to high, cover, and heat grill until hot, about 15 minutes. Leave all burners on high.

3. Clean and oil cooking grate. Place steaks on grill (over coals if using charcoal). Cook, uncovered, until well browned on both sides and meat registers 130 to 135 degrees (for medium), 2 to 4 minutes per side. Transfer steaks to carving board, tent with aluminum foil, and let rest for 5 minutes.

4. Rub garlic clove thoroughly over 1 side of steaks. Slice steaks against grain into ¼-inch-thick slices and serve with lime wedges.

LEARN HOW **CARNE ASADA**

This quintessential Mexican steak preparation is full of flavor. But to get a good, hard sear on a perfectly cooked steak, it's important to start with the driest steak possible. We forgo the traditional marinating step and infuse our steak with flavor in other ways.

1. SPRINKLE STEAKS WITH SALT AND CUMIN: Combine salt and cumin in a small bowl. Sprinkle the mixture evenly over the steaks. Rather than marinating, using a dry rub of salt and cumin keeps the meat tender and flavorful without adding extra moisture.

2. REFRIGERATE STEAKS: Transfer the steaks to a wire rack set in a rimmed baking sheet and refrigerate, uncovered. The naturally dry, cool environment of the refrigerator helps to further dry out the steaks' exteriors, and the wire rack allows full air circulation.

3. MAKE A HOT GRILL FIRE: If using a charcoal grill, place the disposable pan collar in the center of the grill over the bottom vent. Pour the coals in an even layer into the collar. Coralling the coals concentrates the heat, allowing the steaks to get a good sear quickly before the insides can overcook.

4. GRILL STEAKS: Place the steaks directly over the coals. Cook until they are well browned on the first side, then flip them and cook until the meat registers 130 degrees, for medium. Although steak is often cooked to medium-rare, skirt steak is more tender at the higher temperature.

5. RUB STEAKS WITH GARLIC: Once the steak has rested, rub one side with a peeled and smashed garlic clove. Since minced garlic burns in the intense heat of the grill, rubbing the steak with garlic after grilling is a better way to infuse it with garlic flavor.

6. SLICE STEAKS AND SERVE WITH LIME WEDGES: Slice the steak thin against the grain into ¼-inch-thick slices. It is important to slice skirt steak in this way to maximize tenderness. A squeeze of lime juice is a simple way to achieve the lime flavor that is typical of this dish.

Grilled Citrus-Marinated Pork Cutlets

Serves 4 to 6

✔ **WHY THIS RECIPE WORKS:** A signature dish of the Yucatán, *poc chuc* begins with thinly sliced pork cutlets marinated in sour orange juice, annatto powder, and a combination of other spices and aromatics. The pork is quickly grilled over a hot fire and then served with tortillas and a variety of raw vegetable garnishes, which often include avocado, radishes, and tomatoes. Although traditional recipes often call for ham steaks, they can be difficult to find; we decided to use boneless country-style pork ribs, which boasted rich pork flavor and stayed moist during cooking (even when pounded into thin cutlets). We briefly marinated our cutlets in a simple lime juice mixture. Placing the cutlets over a concentrated fire allowed the meat to quickly brown without overcooking. Per tradition, we scattered diced avocado and tomato, sliced radishes, and fresh cilantro over the cutlets before serving. For more information on building a concentrated fire, see step 3 on page 207. Serve with warm tortillas or rice.

- 1½ **pounds boneless country-style pork ribs, trimmed**
- ⅓ **cup lime juice (3 limes)**
- ⅓ **cup extra-virgin olive oil**
- 3 **garlic cloves, minced**
- 1 **tablespoon annatto powder**
- ¾ **teaspoon brown sugar**
- **Salt and pepper**
- ½ **teaspoon ground coriander**
- 1 **(13 by 9-inch) disposable aluminum roasting pan (if using charcoal)**
- 1 **avocado, halved, pitted, and cut into ½-inch pieces**
- 1 **tomato, cored and cut into ½-inch pieces**
- 2 **radishes, trimmed and sliced thin**
- 2 **tablespoons chopped fresh cilantro**

1. Cut each rib lengthwise to create 2 or 3 cutlets about ⅜-inch-wide. Place cutlets cut side down between 2 sheets of plastic wrap and gently pound to even ¼-inch thickness.

2. Combine lime juice, oil, garlic, annatto powder, sugar, ¾ teaspoon salt, ½ teaspoon pepper, and coriander in 1-gallon zipper-lock bag. Add pork to bag and toss to coat. Press out as much air as possible, seal bag, and refrigerate for at least 30 minutes or up to 2 hours, flipping bag occasionally.

3. Just before grilling, remove cutlets from bag and pat dry with paper towels; discard marinade. If using charcoal, use kitchen shears to remove and discard bottom of roasting pan; reserve pan collar.

4A. FOR A CHARCOAL GRILL: Open bottom vent completely. Light large chimney starter filled with charcoal briquettes (6 quarts). When top coals are partially covered with ash, place roasting pan collar in center of grill, oriented over bottom vents, and pour coals into even layer in collar. Set cooking grate in place, cover, and open lid vent completely. Heat grill until hot, about 5 minutes.

4B. FOR A GAS GRILL: Turn all burners to high, cover, and heat grill until hot, about 15 minutes. Leave all burners on high.

5. Clean and oil cooking grate. Place cutlets on grill (over coals if using charcoal), Cook, uncovered, until lightly browned on first side, about 2 minutes. Flip cutlets and continue to cook until just cooked through, about 30 seconds. Transfer cutlets to serving platter, top with avocado, tomato, radishes, and cilantro, and serve immediately.

TEST KITCHEN TIP MAKING CUTLETS

Cut each rib lengthwise into 2 or 3 cutlets about ⅜ inch thick. Place cutlets between 2 sheets of plastic wrap and gently pound to even ¼-inch thickness.

Grilled Ancho-Rubbed Pork Chops

Serves 4

✓ **WHY THIS RECIPE WORKS:** The reality of many grilled pork chops is burnt exteriors, tough meat, and barely a hint of flavor. We wanted a recipe for pork chops with perfectly seared crusts, juicy and tender meat, and bold Mexican-inspired flavor. Rib chops were our top choice for their intense porky flavor and juiciness. Brining the chops in a solution of water, salt, and sugar seasoned the pork throughout and kept it juicy on the grill. A dry rub was the best way to give the brined pork deep flavor: Two different kinds of dried chiles added layers of flavor and a subtle heat, while brown sugar encouraged browning and rounded out the flavor of the pork. If the pork is enhanced (injected with a salt solution), do not brine, but increase the salt amount in the spice rub to 2 teaspoons.

    Salt
3   tablespoons granulated sugar
4   (12-ounce) bone-in pork rib or center-cut chops, 1½ inches thick, trimmed
1   dried chipotle chile, stemmed, seeded, and torn into ½-inch pieces (1½ tablespoons)
½   dried ancho chile, stemmed, seeded, and torn into ½-inch pieces (2 tablespoons)
1   teaspoon dried oregano
¼   teaspoon garlic powder
2   teaspoons packed brown sugar

1. Dissolve 3 tablespoons salt and granulated sugar in 1½ quarts cold water in large container. Submerge chops in brine, cover, and refrigerate for at least 30 minutes or up to 1 hour.

2. Meanwhile, toast chipotle and ancho chiles in 8-inch skillet over medium heat, stirring frequently, until fragrant, 2 to 6 minutes. Transfer chiles to spice grinder and let cool slightly. Add oregano and garlic powder and process until finely ground, about 10 seconds. Transfer mixture to bowl and stir in brown sugar and ¼ teaspoon salt.

3. Just before grilling, remove chops from brine, pat dry with paper towels, and rub with spice rub.

4A. FOR A CHARCOAL GRILL: Open bottom vent completely. Light large chimney starter filled with charcoal briquettes (6 quarts). When top coals are partially covered with ash, pour two-thirds evenly over grill, then pour remaining coals over half of grill. Set cooking grate in place, cover, and open lid vent completely. Heat grill until hot, about 5 minutes.

4B. FOR A GAS GRILL: Turn all burners to high, cover, and heat grill until hot, about 15 minutes. Leave primary burner on high and turn off other burner(s).

5. Clean and oil cooking grate. Place chops on hotter side of grill and cook (covered if using gas) until well browned on both sides, 2 to 4 minutes per side. Move chops to cooler side of grill, cover, and continue to cook until pork registers 145 degrees, 7 to 9 minutes, flipping chops halfway through cooking. Transfer chops to serving platter, tent with aluminum foil, and let rest for 5 to 10 minutes. Serve.

TEST KITCHEN TIP

MAKING A TWO-LEVEL GRILL FIRE

Evenly distribute two-thirds of lit coals evenly over grill, then pour remaining coals over half of grill.

Yucatán-Style Barbecued Pork

Serves 8

☑ **WHY THIS RECIPE WORKS:** Traditionally prepared in the Yucatán peninsula, *cochinita pibil* is a whole suckling pig that is marinated in citrus and earthy spices, wrapped in banana leaves, and pit-roasted. Smoky and tangy, the pork turns out tender and full of flavor. We wanted a version that we could re-create at home using a grill instead of a roasting pit and that wouldn't require handling a whole suckling pig. Our first step was to settle on the cut of meat. We chose pork shoulder, since its rich marbling would keep the meat tender and moist on the grill. Many modern recipes call for wrapping the pork in banana leaves before cooking, but tests revealed that any flavor from the banana leaves was easily overpowered by the traditional citrus marinade; plus, wrapping the meat prevented the smoke from flavoring the pork. After a little research, we realized that the banana leaves were traditionally used to protect the meat from the pit, not to flavor the pork; we decided to forgo them. Next we focused on boosting the flavor of the marinade. To re-create the sweet and sour flavor profile of traditional sour orange juice (which can be hard to come by), we used a combination of lime juice and orange juice. We rounded out our marinade with garlic, oregano, cinnamon, cumin, cloves, and a local favorite, annatto powder. We let our pork rest in the tangy, earthy marinade for an hour before smoking. After an hour on the grill the pork had plenty of smoke flavor so we moved the cooking indoors to the oven. Once the pork was tender, we put it under the broiler for a few minutes to give it a crisp crust. We tossed the shredded pork with a couple tablespoons of lime juice to bring the fresh citrus flavors back into focus. Pork butt roast is often labeled Boston butt in the supermarket. Annatto powder, also called achiote, can be found with the Latin American foods at your supermarket. If you'd like to use wood chunks instead of wood chips when using a charcoal grill, substitute 2 medium wood chunks, soaked in water for 1 hour, for the wood chip packet. Serve with Pickled Onions and Jalapeños (recipe follows) and warm tortillas.

½ cup plus 2 tablespoons lime juice (5 limes)
¼ cup orange juice
2 tablespoons annatto powder
1 tablespoon minced canned chipotle chile in adobo sauce
3 garlic cloves, minced
1 tablespoon dried oregano
Salt and pepper
2 teaspoons ground cinnamon
1 teaspoon ground cumin
¼ teaspoon ground cloves
1 (4- to 5-pound) boneless pork butt roast, trimmed and quartered
2 cups wood chips

1. Combine ½ cup lime juice, orange juice, annatto powder, chipotle, garlic, oregano, 1 table-spoon salt, 2 teaspoons pepper, cinnamon, cumin, and cloves in 1-gallon zipper-lock bag. Place pork in bag, press out as much air as possible, and seal. Turn bag to distribute marinade, then refrigerate pork for at least 1 hour or up to 2 hours, flipping occasionally.

2. Just before grilling, soak wood chips in water for 15 minutes, then drain. Using large piece of heavy-duty aluminum foil, wrap soaked chips in foil packet and cut several vent holes in top.

3A. FOR A CHARCOAL GRILL: Open bottom vent halfway. Light large chimney starter three-quarters filled with charcoal briquettes (4½ quarts). When top coals are partially covered with ash, pour into steeply banked pile against side of grill. Place wood chip packet on coals. Set cooking grate in place, cover, and open lid vent halfway. Heat grill until hot and wood chips are smoking, about 5 minutes.

3B. FOR A GAS GRILL: Remove cooking grate and place wood chip packet directly on primary burner. Set grate in place, turn all burners to high, cover, and heat grill until hot and wood chips are smoking, about 15 minutes. Turn primary burner to medium-high and turn off other burner(s). (Adjust primary burner as needed to maintain grill temperature around 325 degrees.)

4. Clean and oil cooking grate. Remove pork from marinade and pat dry with paper towels; discard marinade. Place pork on cooler side of grill, cover (position lid vent over meat if using charcoal), and cook for 1 hour. During final 20 minutes of grilling, adjust oven racks to upper-middle (at least 6 inches below broiler) and lower-middle positions and heat oven to 325 degrees. Line rimmed baking sheet with foil.

5. Transfer pork to prepared sheet, cover with foil, and crimp edges tightly to seal. Roast pork on lower rack in oven until fork slips easily in and out of meat, 1 to 2 hours.

6. Remove top layer of foil and place sheet on upper rack. Turn on broiler and broil pork until well browned and crispy in spots, 5 to 10 minutes.

Transfer pork to cutting board and let cool slightly. Using 2 forks, shred into bite-size pieces; discard excess fat. Toss shredded pork with remaining 2 tablespoons lime juice in bowl. Season with salt and pepper to taste. Serve.

Pickled Onions and Jalapeños
MAKES 2 CUPS

2 red onions, halved and sliced thin
4 jalapeño chiles, stemmed and sliced thin
¼ cup lime juice (2 limes)
¼ cup distilled white vinegar
2 teaspoons sugar
1 teaspoon salt

Combine onions and jalapeños in large bowl. Bring lime juice, vinegar, sugar, and salt to boil in small saucepan. Pour vinegar mixture over onion mixture and let sit for at least 30 minutes, or refrigerate for up to 2 days.

TEST KITCHEN TIP
MAKING A WOOD CHIP PACKET

Place soaked and drained wood chips on 15 by 12-inch piece of heavy-duty aluminum foil and fold to seal edges. Cut several vent holes in top of packet.

ARROZ CON CAMARONES

Seafood

Fish Veracruz

Serves 4

WHY THIS RECIPE WORKS: Originally from the seaside town of Veracruz, traditional *pescado a la Vercruzana* is now a common fish preparation throughout Mexico. The dish is usually made with white fish served in a light yet aromatic tomato sauce. For our brothy, flavorful sauce, we began by sautéing onion and garlic with chili powder for subtle heat and cumin for extra depth of flavor. Canned diced tomatoes gave our sauce a satisfyingly chunky consistency, and a bit of white wine brightened everything up. Braising mild-flavored cod in this savory sauce both gave the fish a deeper flavor and infused the sauce with seafood flavor. The key to successful braising was twofold: We used low heat (so that the delicate fish wouldn't burn), and we made sure to have a skillet with a tight-fitting lid to trap the heat, so that the fish partially simmered and partially steamed. Halibut, snapper, bluefish, monkfish, and sea bass fillets are good substitutes for the cod.

- 2 tablespoons extra-virgin olive oil, plus extra for serving
- 1 onion, halved and sliced thin
  Salt and pepper
- 4 garlic cloves, minced
- 1 teaspoon chili powder
- ½ teaspoon ground cumin
- 1 (14.5-ounce) can diced tomatoes, drained
- ½ cup dry white wine
- 1 teaspoon minced fresh thyme or ¼ teaspoon dried
- 4 (6- to 8-ounce) skinless cod fillets, 1 to 1½ inches thick
- 2 tablespoons minced fresh cilantro

1. Heat oil in 12-inch nonstick skillet over medium-high heat until shimmering. Add onion and ½ teaspoon salt and cook until softened, about 5 minutes. Stir in garlic, chili powder, and cumin and cook until fragrant, about 30 seconds. Stir in tomatoes, wine, and thyme and bring to simmer.

2. Season cod with salt and pepper. If using any tail-end fillets, tuck tail under. Nestle cod into skillet and spoon some sauce over fish. Cover, reduce heat to medium-low, and cook until fish flakes apart when gently prodded with paring knife and registers 140 degrees, about 10 minutes.

3. Transfer fish to individual plates. Stir cilantro into sauce and season with salt and pepper to taste. Spoon sauce over fish and drizzle with extra oil before serving.

TEST KITCHEN TIP **TUCKING A FISH TAIL**

If using any tail-end fillets, tuck thinner tail piece under before cooking so that it will cook at same rate as thicker fillets.

Pan-Roasted Cod with Amarillo Sauce

Serves 4

✓ **WHY THIS RECIPE WORKS:** Classic *amarillo* is a mole-style sauce from Oaxaca. Although amarillo literally means "yellow," the sauce is more of a light rust orange in color (the name's origin is debated and could come from the inclusion of tomatillos, from the masa harina that's commonly used as a thickener, or from the old Oaxacan tradition of using amarillo chiles in the sauce). We wanted a version of this lively, tangy, slightly spicy sauce to dress up mild white fish. We started by choosing the type of chiles. Most modern recipes use guajillo chiles, which we found gave the mole a pleasant, mild heat. Some warm spices complemented the chile's flavor nicely without overpowering it. Our aromatic base benefited from the addition of clam broth, which provided a subtle seafood backbone. For the cod, we cooked the fillets simply, sprinkling them with just a bit of sugar to accelerate browning. This shortened the cooking time and ensured that the fish didn't dry out. Be sure to immediately remove each fillet when it reaches 140 degrees. You will need a 12-inch ovensafe nonstick skillet for this recipe. Serve with rice or warmed tortillas.

3   **guajillo chiles, stemmed, seeded, and torn into ½-inch pieces (6 tablespoons)**
2   **tablespoons vegetable oil**
1   **onion, chopped**
4   **garlic cloves, peeled**
½   **teaspoon dried oregano**
¼   **teaspoon whole cumin seeds**
⅛   **teaspoon ground cloves**
⅛   **teaspoon ground allspice**
3   **tablespoons masa harina**
1   **(8-ounce) bottle clam broth**
8   **ounces tomatillos, husks and stems removed, rinsed well, dried, and cut into ½-inch pieces**

6   **sprigs cilantro**
     Salt and pepper
4   **(6- to 8-ounce) skinless cod fillets, 1 to 1½ inches thick**
½   **teaspoon sugar**

1. Toast guajillos in medium saucepan over medium heat, stirring frequently, until fragrant, 2 to 6 minutes; transfer to bowl. Heat 1 tablespoon oil in now-empty pot over medium heat until shimmering. Add onion and cook until softened, about 5 minutes. Stir in garlic, oregano, cumin seeds, cloves, and allspice, and cook until fragrant, about 30 seconds. Stir in masa harina and cook for 1 minute. Slowly whisk in clam broth, scraping up any browned bits and smoothing out any lumps.

2. Stir in tomatillos, cilantro sprigs, toasted chiles, ½ teaspoon salt, and ¼ teaspoon pepper, bring to simmer, and cook until tomatillos begin to soften, about 3 minutes. Carefully transfer mixture to blender and process until smooth, 1 to 2 minutes. Return to pot and cover to keep warm.

3. Adjust oven rack to middle position and heat oven to 425 degrees. Pat fish dry with paper towels and season both sides with salt and pepper. If using any tail-end fillets, tuck tail under. Sprinkle sugar evenly over 1 side of fish.

4. Heat remaining 1 tablespoon oil in 12-inch ovensafe nonstick skillet over high heat until just smoking. Place fillets in skillet, sugar side down, and press lightly to ensure even contact with pan. Cook until browned, about 2 minutes. Using 2 spatulas, flip fillets. Transfer skillet to oven and roast fish until centers are just opaque and register 140 degrees, 5 to 10 minutes.

5. Using potholders (skillet handle will be hot), remove skillet from oven. Transfer fish to serving platter or individual dishes. Serve with sauce.

Pan-Seared Trout with Salsa Borracha

Serves 4

☑ **WHY THIS RECIPE WORKS:** For a fish preparation with deep flavor and a bit of pizzazz, we turned to *salsa borracha*, or "drunken sauce." Often served with grilled meats, salsa borracha is an assertive sauce made with pasilla chiles. It gets its name from the addition of beer or tequila (or both). For our version, we chose a robust combination of tequila, orange juice, and aromatics along with the pasilla chiles. To meld all of the flavors and cook off some of the alcohol in the tequila, we simmered the sauce for just a few minutes. The sweet orange juice nicely tempered the bold tequila flavor. A bit of sugar rounded out the bitter undertones, and a few tablespoons of extra-virgin olive oil gave our full-bodied sauce the perfect drizzling consistency. A splash of fresh lime juice tempered the heat of the chiles and added welcome brightness. For the fish, we chose trout, which is found in many Mexican waters and has a mild flavor and pleasantly firm flesh. Simply pan-searing the trout fillets allowed their fresh flavor to shine, and a bit of sugar sprinkled over the fillets encouraged browning. The fish needed just a drizzle of sauce to create a finished dish with big, bold flavor. Serve with rice or warmed tortillas.

3	dried pasilla chiles, stemmed, seeded, and torn into ½-inch pieces (¾ cup)
⅓	cup orange juice
3	tablespoons tequila
3	scallions, white parts chopped, green parts sliced thin
6	tablespoons extra-virgin olive oil
1	tablespoon plus ½ teaspoon sugar
1	garlic clove
½	teaspoon ground coriander
	Salt and pepper
4	(6- to 8-ounce) trout fillets, ¼ to ½ inch thick
2	tablespoons lime juice, plus lime wedges for serving

1. Toast pasillas in small saucepan over medium heat, stirring frequently, until fragrant, 2 to 6 minutes; transfer to blender. Add orange juice, tequila, scallion whites, 3 tablespoons oil, 1 tablespoon sugar, garlic, coriander, and ¼ teaspoon salt to blender and process until smooth, about 1 minute. Return sauce to now-empty pot and simmer over medium heat, stirring often, until slightly thickened, 2 to 4 minutes. Remove from heat; cover to keep warm.

2. Meanwhile, pat fish dry with paper towels and season both sides with salt and pepper. Sprinkle remaining ½ teaspoon sugar evenly over 1 side of fish.

3. Heat 1 tablespoon oil in 12-inch nonstick skillet over high heat until shimmering. Lay half of fish in skillet, sugar side down, and press lightly to ensure even contact with pan. Cook until edges of fillets are opaque and bottoms are lightly browned, 2 to 3 minutes. Using 2 spatulas, flip fillets. Cook on second side until thickest part of fillets is firm to touch and fish flakes easily, 2 to 3 minutes. Transfer fish to platter and tent with aluminum foil. Repeat with 1 tablespoon oil and remaining fish.

4. Stir lime juice and remaining 1 tablespoon oil into sauce and season with salt and pepper to taste. Transfer fish to individual serving plates, leaving any accumulated juices behind on platter. Spoon small amount of sauce over fish and sprinkle with scallion greens. Serve with remaining sauce and lime wedges.

TEST KITCHEN TIP **FLIPPING FISH**

Using 2 spatulas, gently flip fish over in skillet to cook on second side.

Salmon with Roasted Salsa Verde

Serves 4

✓ **WHY THIS RECIPE WORKS:** We wanted a fuss-free recipe for rich salmon with a light, vibrant tomatillo sauce. To make easy work of both fish and sauce, we turned to the oven. Roasting a salmon fillet can create a beautifully browned exterior, but often the price is an overcooked interior. To avoid this, we used a hybrid roasting method: We preheated the oven and baking sheet to 500 degrees, then turned down the heat just before placing the fish in the oven. The initial blast of high heat firmed the exterior and rendered some excess fat (we further encouraged the fat to render by cutting slashes in the skin), while the lower heat cooked the fish through gently. Since we were already turning the oven all the way up, we simply switched on the broiler to roast the tomatillos, poblanos, and aromatics for our sauce. If your knife is not sharp enough to cut through the skin easily, try a serrated knife. It is important to keep the skin on during cooking; remove it afterward if desired.

- 8 ounces tomatillos, husks and stems removed, rinsed well, dried, and quartered
- 1 poblano chile, stemmed, seeded, and chopped
- 1 jalapeño chile, stemmed, halved, and seeded
- 2 tablespoons plus 2 teaspoons extra-virgin olive oil
- 3 garlic cloves, peeled
- 2 teaspoons chopped fresh oregano
- 1 teaspoon ground coriander
    Salt and pepper
- ¼ cup minced fresh cilantro
- 3 scallions, chopped
- 1 tablespoon lime juice, plus lime wedges for serving
- 1 (1¾- to 2-pound) skin-on salmon fillet, 1½ inches thick

1. Adjust oven racks to lowest position and 6 inches from broiler element and heat broiler. Line baking sheet with aluminum foil. Toss tomatillos, poblano, jalapeño, 1 tablespoon oil, garlic, oregano, coriander, ¼ teaspoon salt, and ¼ teaspoon pepper together, then spread onto prepared sheet. Broil vegetables on upper rack until tomatillos and jalapeños are browned, 10 to 12 minutes, stirring occasionally.

2. Transfer broiled vegetables to blender and let cool slightly. Add 2 tablespoons cilantro, scallions, lime juice, and 1 tablespoon oil and blend until smooth, about 1 minute. Meanwhile, place clean rimmed baking sheet on lower oven rack and heat oven to 500 degrees.

3. Cut salmon crosswise into 4 fillets. Using sharp knife, make 4 or 5 shallow slashes, about 1 inch apart, through skin of each fillet, being careful not to cut into flesh. Pat salmon dry with paper towels, rub with remaining 2 teaspoons oil, and season with salt and pepper.

4. Reduce oven temperature to 275 degrees and remove preheated baking sheet. Carefully place salmon, skin side down, on baking sheet. Roast on lower rack until center is still translucent when checked with tip of paring knife and registers 125 degrees (for medium-rare), 9 to 13 minutes. Transfer salmon to plates, spoon some of sauce over top and sprinkle with remaining 2 tablespoons minced cilantro. Serve with remaining sauce and lime wedges.

TEST KITCHEN TIP

PREPARING SALMON FILLETS FOR ROASTING

Cut salmon fillet into 4 equal pieces, then cut 4 or 5 shallow slashes, about 1 inch apart, through skin on each piece. Be careful not to cut into flesh.

Shrimp a la Diabla

Serves 4 to 6

✔ **WHY THIS RECIPE WORKS:** Classic Mexican shrimp *a la diabla*, or "devilish shrimp," features tender shrimp cooked in a fiery tomato-chile sauce. The smooth sauce is traditionally made with guajillo chiles, which add a little heat and a lot of deep chile flavor. To coax the most possible flavor from the chiles, we toasted them and then simmered them with an aromatic blend of onion, garlic, oregano, and tomato sauce. Simmering the chiles not only infused their flavor into the sauce but also softened their tough skins, making it easy to blend the sauce to a silky smooth consistency. For the tomato component of the sauce, we found that canned tomato sauce gave us better texture and more consistent results than cooking down fresh tomatoes. For even more "devilish" spice, we added a full tablespoon of spicy, smoky chipotle chile in adobo sauce. Cooking the shrimp directly in the sauce not only kept this a one-pot dish, but also allowed the shrimp to pick up all the rich, spicy flavors of the sauce. Serve with rice.

8 dried guajillo chiles, stemmed, seeded and torn into ½-inch pieces (1 cup)
2 tablespoons extra-virgin olive oil, plus extra for serving
1 onion, chopped fine
   Salt and pepper
3 garlic cloves, minced
1 tablespoon minced canned chipotle chile in adobo sauce
2 teaspoons dried oregano
1 (8-ounce) can tomato sauce
1 cup water
2 pounds extra-large shrimp (21 to 25 per pound), peeled and deveined
¼ cup chopped fresh cilantro or parsley
1 tablespoon lime juice, plus lime wedges for serving

1. Toast guajillo chiles in Dutch oven over medium heat, stirring frequently, until fragrant, 2 to 6 minutes; transfer to bowl.

2. Heat oil in now-empty pot over medium-high heat until shimmering. Add onion and ½ teaspoon salt and cook until softened, about 5 minutes. Stir in garlic, chipotle, and oregano and cook until fragrant, about 30 seconds. Stir in tomato sauce, water, and toasted chiles, bring to simmer, and cook until chiles are softened, about 10 minutes.

3. Transfer mixture to blender and process until smooth, about 30 seconds. Return sauce to now-empty pot and stir in shrimp. Cover and cook over medium-low heat until shrimp are cooked through and completely opaque, 5 to 7 minutes.

4. Transfer shrimp to individual plates. Stir cilantro and lime juice into sauce and season with salt and pepper to taste. Spoon sauce over shrimp, drizzle with extra oil, and serve with lime wedges.

TEST KITCHEN TIP POACHING SHRIMP

Return blended sauce to pan. Add shrimp and poach gently in sauce over medium-low heat, covered, until cooked through and completely opaque, 5 to 7 minutes.

Garlicky Shell-On Shrimp with Cilantro and Lime

Serves 4 to 6

☑ **WHY THIS RECIPE WORKS:** Shell-on shrimp make for a rustic and flavorful (if slightly messy) meal; the shells give the shrimp lots of deep seafood flavor that peeled shrimp simply don't have. We wanted to create a simple, Mexican-inspired preparation that would accentuate the shell-on shrimp's tender, briny sweetness. To keep our shrimp moist through cooking, we briefly brined them in the refrigerator. To complement the flavor of the shrimp, we tossed the brined shrimp with a flavorful oil-based mixture of garlic, lime, and spices like coriander and annatto. We broiled the shrimp just briefly; the shells browned quickly under the concentrated heat of the broiler and infused the shrimp with roasty flavor. The shells also helped to protect the delicate shrimp from the intense heat. Don't be tempted to use smaller shrimp with this cooking technique as they will be overseasoned and prone to overcook. Serve with warmed tortillas.

¼   cup salt
2   pounds shell-on jumbo shrimp (16 to 20 per pound)
½   cup vegetable oil
¼   cup minced fresh cilantro
6   garlic cloves, minced
2   teaspoons coriander seeds, lightly crushed
2   teaspoons grated lime zest, plus lime wedges for serving
1   teaspoon annatto powder
½   teaspoon red pepper flakes

1. Dissolve salt in 1 quart cold water in large container. Using kitchen shears or sharp paring knife, cut through shells of shrimp and devein but do not remove shells. Using paring knife, continue to cut shrimp ½ inch deep, taking care not to cut in half completely. Submerge shrimp in brine, cover, and refrigerate for 15 minutes.

2. Adjust oven rack 4 inches from broiler element and heat broiler. Set wire rack in rimmed baking sheet. Combine oil, cilantro, garlic, coriander seeds, lime zest, annatto, and pepper flakes in large bowl. Remove shrimp from brine, pat dry with paper towels, and add to oil mixture. Toss well, making sure mixture gets into interior of shrimp. Arrange shrimp in single layer on prepared rack.

3. Broil shrimp until opaque and shells are beginning to brown, 2 to 4 minutes, rotating sheet halfway through broiling. Flip shrimp and continue to broil until second side is opaque and shells are beginning to brown, 2 to 4 minutes, rotating sheet halfway through broiling. Transfer shrimp to serving platter and serve with lime wedges.

TEST KITCHEN TIP BUTTERFLYING SHRIMP

1. Using kitchen shears or sharp paring knife, cut through shell of shrimp. Do not remove shell.

2. Using tip of paring knife, remove and discard vein. Continue to cut shrimp ½ inch deep, taking care not to cut in half completely.

Seared Shrimp with Tomatoes, Lime, and Avocado

Serves 4

✔ **WHY THIS RECIPE WORKS:** This dish of flavorfully seasoned, perfectly browned shrimp tossed with a fresh tomato sauce and rich avocado brings classic Mexican flavors to the fore. Searing the shrimp produced the ultimate combination of well-caramelized exteriors and moist, tender interiors. This cooking method also preserved the shrimp's juiciness and trademark briny sweetness. To promote caramelization and to accentuate the shrimp's natural sweetness, we tossed them with sugar in addition to salt and pepper. To prevent overcooking, we seared the shrimp on one side, then removed them from the pan while we cooked the second batch. After the second batch was seared and removed from the pan, we made our smoky, slightly spicy sauce. Later, we returned the shrimp to the pan with the sauce to heat through and finish cooking. The cooking times are for extra-large shrimp. If this size is not available in your market, buy large shrimp and shorten the cooking time slightly. To make this dish spicier, use the larger amount of chipotle.

1	pound tomatoes, cored, seeded, and cut into ½-inch pieces
6	scallions, white and green parts separated and sliced thin
¼	cup minced fresh cilantro
3	garlic cloves, minced
1–2	teaspoons minced canned chipotle chile in adobo sauce
	Salt and pepper
1½	pounds extra-large shrimp (21 to 25 per pound), peeled and deveined

⅛	teaspoon sugar
2	tablespoons vegetable oil
1	tablespoon lime juice, plus lime wedges for serving
1	avocado, halved, pitted, and diced

1. Toss tomatoes, scallion whites, cilantro, garlic, chipotle, and ¾ teaspoon salt together in bowl. In separate bowl, toss shrimp with sugar, ¼ teaspoon salt, and ¼ teaspoon pepper.

2. Heat 1 tablespoon oil in 12-inch skillet over high heat until just smoking. Add half of shrimp to pan in single layer and cook, without moving, until spotty brown on one side, about 1 minute. Transfer shrimp to large bowl (they will be underdone). Repeat with remaining 1 tablespoon oil and shrimp.

3. Return now-empty skillet to high heat, add tomato mixture and lime juice, and cook until tomatoes are slightly softened, about 1 minute. Stir in shrimp with any accumulated juices and cook until shrimp are cooked through and hot, about 1 minute. Transfer shrimp to large platter and sprinkle with avocado and scallion greens. Serve with lime wedges.

TEST KITCHEN TIP PAN-SEARING SHRIMP

To achieve maximum browning on shrimp, make sure shrimp are in single layer in pan and cook without moving for about 1 minute.

Shrimp Fajitas

Serves 4

✓ **WHY THIS RECIPE WORKS:** Too often, restaurant versions of shrimp fajitas are heavy and flavorless, loaded with a seemingly random assortment of vegetables and bland guacamole. Plus, continued exposure to heat in the sizzling serving pan inevitably leads to overcooked, rubbery shrimp. We wanted great shrimp fajitas with flavorful, perfectly cooked shrimp that we could drape with simple onions and peppers and wrap in warm flour tortillas. To make our recipe suitable for year-round preparation, we decided to skip grilling and develop an indoor cooking method. To infuse our shrimp with flavor, we marinated them briefly in an aromatic mixture of garlic, lime, cumin seeds, and a small amount of chipotle in adobo sauce for some smoky spice. Searing the shrimp on the stovetop turned them golden brown and succulent. Plus, to keep dishes to a minimum and to ensure the recipe was simple and streamlined, we used the same skillet to sauté the peppers and onions and cook the shrimp. A sprinkling of cilantro, a drizzle of Mexican *crema*, and a squeeze of lime juice brightened up the shrimp and vegetables and brought all the flavors together perfectly.

6	tablespoons vegetable oil
2	tablespoons lime juice, plus lime wedges for serving
4	garlic cloves, peeled and smashed
1	teaspoon minced canned chipotle chile in adobo sauce
1	teaspoon sugar
1	teaspoon cumin seeds
	Salt and pepper
⅛	teaspoon cayenne pepper
1½	pounds medium-large shrimp (31 to 40 per pound), peeled, deveined, and tails removed
2	red bell peppers, stemmed, seeded, and sliced thin
1	large red onion, halved and sliced thin
2	tablespoons water
¼	cup minced fresh cilantro
12	(6-inch) flour tortillas, warmed
½	cup Mexican crema

1. Whisk 3 tablespoons oil, lime juice, garlic, chipotle, sugar, ½ teaspoon cumin seeds, 1 teaspoon salt, ½ teaspoon pepper, and cayenne together in large bowl. Add shrimp and toss to coat. Cover and refrigerate for 30 minutes.

2. Heat 1 tablespoon oil in 12-inch nonstick skillet over medium-high heat until shimmering. Add bell peppers, onion, water, remaining ½ teaspoon cumin seeds, and ½ teaspoon salt and cook until peppers are soft and onion is browned, about 8 minutes. Transfer to serving bowl and season with salt and pepper to taste.

3. Wipe out skillet with paper towels. Remove garlic from shrimp marinade and discard. Heat 1 tablespoon oil in now-empty skillet over high heat until just smoking. Add half of shrimp to pan in single layer and cook until spotty brown and edges turn pink, 1 to 2 minutes. Remove pan from heat and flip each shrimp over using tongs. Cover and let shrimp stand off heat until just cooked through, 1 to 2 minutes; transfer to bowl and cover to keep warm.

4. Repeat with remaining 1 tablespoon oil and remaining shrimp. Toss shrimp with cilantro and serve with vegetables, warm tortillas, crema, and lime wedges.

Arroz con Camarones

Serves 4 to 6

✔ **WHY THIS RECIPE WORKS:** This simple one-pot Mexican staple is made by cooking rice, vegetables, and shrimp in a flavorful stock. Although this simplicity is part of the dish's appeal, we found that there was a fine line between simple and boring. To coax as much flavor as possible out of our shrimp, we marinated them briefly and also made a quick but rich-tasting shrimp stock by sautéing the shrimp shells with onion and guajillo chiles, then adding water, peppercorns, cilantro sprigs, and bay leaves for layers of herbal flavor. Toasting the rice in olive oil helped the grains stay firm and not turn mushy when cooked. Some garlic and oregano added with the rice gave it an extra flavor boost. To achieve perfectly tender shrimp, we nestled the shrimp into the rice during the last few minutes of cooking. See the photo on page 214.

6   tablespoons extra-virgin olive oil

1½   pounds extra-large shrimp (21 to 25 per pound), peeled and deveined, shells reserved

2   onions, chopped

4   guajillo chiles, stemmed, seeded, and torn into ½-inch pieces (½ cup)

     Salt and pepper

4   cups water

1   tablespoon black peppercorns

5   sprigs fresh cilantro plus 2 tablespoons minced

2   bay leaves

5   garlic cloves, minced

     Pinch cayenne pepper

1   green bell pepper, stemmed, seeded, and chopped

2   cups long-grain white rice

1   tablespoon minced fresh oregano or ¾ teaspoon dried

1   (14.5-ounce) can diced tomatoes

     Lime wedges

1. Heat 1 tablespoon oil in large saucepan over medium heat. Add shrimp shells, 1 cup onion, guajillos, and 1 teaspoon salt and cook, stirring occasionally, until shells are spotty brown, about 10 minutes. Add water, peppercorns, cilantro sprigs, and bay leaves, increase heat to high, and bring to boil. Reduce heat to low, cover, and simmer for 30 minutes. Strain shrimp stock through fine-mesh strainer into large liquid measuring cup; you should have 3 cups stock. (If you have extra, reserve for another use.)

2. Meanwhile, whisk 2 tablespoons oil, half of garlic, cayenne, and ½ teaspoon pepper together in large bowl. Add shrimp and toss to coat. Cover and refrigerate for 30 minutes.

3. Heat remaining 3 tablespoons oil in Dutch oven over medium heat until shimmering. Add bell pepper, remaining onion, and ½ teaspoon salt and cook until vegetables begin to soften, 5 to 7 minutes. Stir in rice, remaining garlic, and oregano and cook until fragrant and rice is translucent, about 2 minutes. Stir in tomatoes and their juice and 3 cups shrimp stock. Bring to boil, then reduce heat to low, cover, and cook for 20 minutes.

4. Nestle shrimp attractively into rice, in concentric circles, with tails sticking up out of rice. Cover and cook until shrimp are opaque, 8 to 10 minutes. Remove pot from heat and let sit, covered, until shrimp are cooked through, about 5 minutes. Sprinkle with minced cilantro and serve with lime wedges.

TEST KITCHEN TIP **MAKING SHRIMP AND RICE**

Nestle shrimp into partially cooked rice in attractive concentric circles with tails sticking out of rice. Cover and cook until shrimp are opaque.

Steamed Clams with Chorizo

Serves 4

✔ **WHY THIS RECIPE WORKS:** Clams are a popular ingredient in Mexico's vast coastal regions. Often, they are prepared simply by steaming in a flavorful broth. For our version, we chose littleneck clams for their wide availability and ease of preparation. To make this dish satisfying enough for a meal, we sautéed chorizo sausage with some onion and garlic before adding our steaming liquid and a hearty 4 pounds of clams. We used a large can of diced tomatoes with their juice as the base for our broth, as well as another ingredient we found in many Mexican clam recipes: beer. Beer added rounder, richer flavor than water would have; plus, it helped cut the acidity of the tomatoes. Two sliced serrano chiles added the perfect amount of heat to our broth. After just a few minutes, the clams had released lots of briny flavor, further enriching the broth. As a final touch, we stirred some fresh cilantro into the broth before pouring it over the clams for serving. To make this dish spicier, you can use spicy chorizo in place of the regular chorizo. You can serve this dish over rice or with tortillas, but we prefer soft rolls, such as Mexican *bolillos* (similar to soft French bread), to sop up all the flavorful broth.

1 tablespoon vegetable oil

8 ounces Mexican-style chorizo sausage, casings removed

1 onion, chopped fine

2 serrano chiles, stemmed and sliced thin

3 garlic cloves, minced

1 (28-ounce) can diced tomatoes

1 cup beer

4 pounds littleneck clams, scrubbed

2 tablespoons minced fresh cilantro

Lime wedges

1. Heat oil in Dutch oven over medium heat until shimmering. Add chorizo and cook, breaking into ½-inch pieces with wooden spoon, until beginning to brown, about 5 minutes. Transfer chorizo to paper towel–lined plate, leaving fat in pot.

2. Add onion to fat left in pot and cook over medium-high heat until softened, 5 to 7 minutes. Stir in serranos and garlic and cook until fragrant, about 30 seconds. Stir in tomatoes and their juice and beer. Reduce heat to medium and simmer until slightly thickened, 8 to 10 minutes.

3. Increase heat to high and stir in clams and reserved chorizo. Cover and cook, stirring once, until clams have opened, 4 to 8 minutes.

4. Using slotted spoon, transfer clams to serving bowl or individual bowls; discard any clams that haven't opened. Stir cilantro into broth, then pour broth over clams. Serve with lime wedges.

TEST KITCHEN TIP SCRUBBING CLAMS

Before cooking clams, scrub away any bits of sand using stiff brush.

Spicy Grilled Shrimp Skewers

Serves 4

✓ **WHY THIS RECIPE WORKS:** For a great Mexican-inspired grilled shrimp recipe, we created a bold marinade of jalapeño, lime, garlic, and spices to flavor the shrimp both before and after cooking. Butterflying the shrimp allowed the marinade to flavor the shrimp deeply and thoroughly. To get good char on the shrimp without overcooking them, we packed them tightly onto skewers and sprinkled one side with sugar to encourage browning. We started the shrimp over a hot fire, then finished them over low heat to allow them to cook through gently. Finally, we tossed our cooked shrimp with more marinade, which packed a fresh, bright punch. You will need four 12-inch metal skewers for this recipe.

1	teaspoon lime zest plus 5 tablespoons juice (3 limes)
3	tablespoons extra-virgin olive oil
1	jalapeño chile, stemmed, seeded, and chopped
1	tablespoon chopped fresh cilantro
6	garlic cloves, minced
½	teaspoon ground cumin
½	teaspoon salt
¼	teaspoon cayenne pepper
1½	pounds extra-large shrimp (21 to 25 per pound), peeled, deveined, and butterflied
½	teaspoon sugar

1. Combine lime zest and juice, oil, jalapeño, cilantro, garlic, cumin, salt, and cayenne in large bowl. Measure out 2 tablespoons marinade and set aside for serving.

2. Pat shrimp dry with paper towels, add to remaining marinade, and toss to coat. Cover and refrigerate for 15 minutes. Thread marinated shrimp tightly onto four 12-inch metal skewers, alternating direction of heads and tails. Sprinkle 1 side of shrimp skewers with sugar.

3A. FOR A CHARCOAL GRILL: Open bottom vent completely. Light large chimney starter filled with charcoal briquettes (6 quarts). When top coals are partially covered with ash, pour evenly over half of grill. Set cooking grate in place, cover, and open lid vent completely. Heat grill until hot, about 5 minutes.

3B. FOR A GAS GRILL: Turn all burners to high, cover, and heat grill until hot, about 15 minutes. Leave primary burner on high and turn other burner(s) to low.

4. Clean cooking grate, then repeatedly brush grate with well-oiled paper towels until black and glossy, 5 to 10 times. Place shrimp, sugar side down, on hotter part of grill and cook until lightly charred, 3 to 4 minutes. Flip skewers and slide to cooler part of grill. Cover and continue to cook until shrimp are uniformly pink, 1 to 2 minutes.

5. Holding skewers with potholder, use tongs to slide shrimp off skewers into medium bowl. Add reserved marinade and toss to coat. Transfer shrimp to platter and serve.

TEST KITCHEN TIP MAKING SHRIMP SKEWERS

1. Using paring knife, make ½-inch-deep cut down back of peeled shrimp, taking care not to cut in half completely.

2. Thread marinated shrimp tightly onto four 12-inch metal skewers, alternating direction of heads and tails.

Grilled Salmon Steaks with Lime-Cilantro Sauce

Serves 4

✔ **WHY THIS RECIPE WORKS:** Salmon steaks are rich and sturdy, making them particularly well suited to the heat of the grill. To make the process foolproof, we turned the oblong steaks into medallions and used a two-level cooking approach. We first seared the fish over high heat, then transfered the browned steaks to a disposable pan on the grill to simmer in our flavorful sauce. Bright, citrusy lime juice and fresh cilantro paired well with the meaty salmon. Before eating, lift out the small circular bone from the center of each steak.

4   **(10-ounce) skin-on salmon steaks, 1 to 1½ inches thick**
      Salt and pepper
2   **tablespoons vegetable oil**
1   **teaspoon grated lime zest plus 6 tablespoons juice (3 limes)**
3   **tablespoons unsalted butter**
2   **garlic cloves, minced**
½   **teaspoon ground cumin**
1   **(13 by 9-inch) disposable aluminum roasting pan**
2   **tablespoons chopped fresh cilantro**

1. Pat salmon steaks dry with paper towels. Working with 1 steak at a time, carefully trim 1½ inches of skin from 1 tail. Tightly wrap other tail around skinned portion and tie steaks with kitchen twine. Season salmon with salt and pepper and brush both sides with oil. Combine lime zest and juice, butter, garlic, cumin, and ⅛ teaspoon salt in disposable pan.

2A. FOR A CHARCOAL GRILL: Open bottom vent completely. Light large chimney starter filled with charcoal briquettes (6 quarts). When top coals are partially covered with ash, pour evenly over half of grill. Set cooking grate in place, cover, and open lid vent completely. Heat grill until hot, about 5 minutes.

2B. FOR A GAS GRILL: Turn all burners to high, cover, and heat grill until hot, about 15 minutes. Leave primary burner on high and turn off other burner(s).

3. Clean cooking grate, then repeatedly brush grate with well-oiled paper towels until black and glossy, 5 to 10 times. Place salmon on hotter part of grill. Cook until browned on both sides, 2 to 3 minutes per side. Meanwhile, set disposable pan on cooler part of grill and cook until butter has melted, about 2 minutes.

4. Transfer salmon to pan and gently turn to coat. Cook salmon (covered if using gas) until center is still translucent when checked with tip of paring knife and registers 125 degrees (for medium-rare), 6 to 14 minutes, flipping salmon and rotating pan halfway through grilling.

5. Transfer salmon to platter; remove twine. Whisk cilantro into sauce left in pan. Drizzle sauce over salmon and serve.

TEST KITCHEN TIP

MAKING SALMON MEDALLIONS

1. Working with 1 steak at a time, carefully trim 1½ inches of skin from 1 tail.

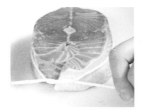

2. Tightly wrap other tail around skinned portion and tie steaks with kitchen twine.

Grilled Swordfish, Lime, and Red Onion Skewers

Serves 4

☑ **WHY THIS RECIPE WORKS:** We wanted a recipe for grilled swordfish that would highlight the clean flavor and meaty texture of the fish. To make the swordfish easier to grill and serve, we cut it into 1¼-inch chunks and strung the chunks onto skewers. For some aromatic flavor, we coated the fish with a simple mixture of ground coriander, cumin, salt, pepper, and sugar. Grilling the limes along with the swordfish transformed their flavor from tart and acidic to deeply rich and sweet; plus, the grilled limes could be eaten, peel and all. Once the fish was cooked, we brushed it with a mixture of oil, cilantro, and shallot for a pop of freshness. You can substitute other sturdy, firm-fleshed fish such as mahi-mahi or halibut for the swordfish. You will need four 12-inch metal skewers for this recipe.

1	large red onion, cut into 1-inch pieces, 3 layers thick
5	tablespoons extra-virgin olive oil
1	tablespoon ground coriander
1	teaspoon ground cumin
1	teaspoon sugar
	Salt and pepper
1	(1½-pound) skinless swordfish steak, cut into 1¼-inch pieces
3	limes, halved, then each half quartered
2	tablespoons chopped fresh cilantro
1½	teaspoons minced shallot

1. Gently toss onion with 1 tablespoon oil in bowl, cover, and microwave until just tender, about 2 minutes. Combine 2 tablespoons oil, coriander, cumin, sugar, ½ teaspoon salt, and ½ teaspoon pepper in large bowl. Pat fish dry with paper towels, add to spice mixture, and toss gently to coat. Thread fish, limes, and onion evenly onto four 12-inch metal skewers, in alternating pattern.

2A. FOR A CHARCOAL GRILL: Open bottom vent completely. Light large chimney starter filled with charcoal briquettes (6 quarts). When top coals are partially covered with ash, pour evenly over grill. Set cooking grate in place, cover, and open lid vent completely. Heat grill until hot, about 5 minutes.

2B. FOR A GAS GRILL: Turn all burners to high, cover, and heat grill until hot, about 15 minutes. Turn all burners to medium-high.

3. Clean cooking grate, then repeatedly brush grate with well-oiled paper towels until black and glossy, 5 to 10 times. Place skewers on grill. Cook (covered if using gas), turning as needed, until fish is opaque and flakes apart when gently prodded with paring knife, 5 to 8 minutes.

4. Transfer skewers to platter, tent loosely with aluminum foil, and let rest for 5 minutes. Combine remaining 2 tablespoons oil, cilantro, and shallot in bowl and season with salt and pepper to taste. Brush skewers with oil mixture before serving.

TEST KITCHEN TIP

CUTTING UP SWORDFISH FOR SKEWERS

1. Using sharp knife, trim skin and dark lines from flesh.

2. Cut trimmed flesh into 1¼-inch pieces.

Grilled Whole Red Snapper with Orange, Lime, and Cilantro Vinaigrette

Serves 4

✔ **WHY THIS RECIPE WORKS:** Snapper is one of the most popular fish in Mexican cooking, and it's often grilled whole. The grill gives the mild fish plenty of smoky depth, and keeping the fish whole leaves the fish juicier than fillets would be: The skin protects the fish and seals in flavor while the bones keep the fish moist. We made shallow diagonal slashes on the skin on both sides to ensure even cooking and seasoning. Slashing also had the added benefit of enabling us to gauge the doneness more easily. After cooking, the fish needed only a few cuts to allow us to neatly lift the meat away from the bones. As a final touch, we created a citrusy vinaigrette, which lent a light acidic counterpoint to the smoky grilled fish. When buying whole fish, look for fish with moist, taut skin, clear eyes, and bright red gills. You can substitute bass, trout, mackerel, or bluefish for the snapper. If your fish are a little larger (between 1½ and 2 pounds), simply grill them a minute or two longer on each side. Fish weighing more than 2 pounds will be hard to maneuver on the grill and should be avoided.

- ¼ **cup orange juice**
- 1 **tablespoon lime juice, plus lime wedges for serving**
- 2 **teaspoons sugar**
- 1 **garlic clove, minced**
  Salt and pepper
- ½ **cup plus 1 tablespoon extra-virgin olive oil**
- 1 **tablespoon chopped fresh cilantro**
  Salt and pepper
- 2 **(1½-pound) whole red snapper, scaled and gutted**

1. Whisk orange juice, lime juice, sugar, garlic, ½ teaspoon salt, and ¼ teaspoon pepper together in medium bowl, then whisk in 6 tablespoons oil. Whisk in cilantro and season with salt and pepper to taste. Pat snapper dry with paper towels. Using sharp knife, make shallow diagonal slashes 1 inch apart through skin on both sides of fish, being careful not to cut into flesh. Rub fish with remaining 3 tablespoons oil, then season thoroughly (including cavities) with salt and pepper.

2A. FOR A CHARCOAL GRILL: Open bottom vent completely. Light large chimney starter filled with charcoal briquettes (6 quarts). When top coals are partially covered with ash, pour evenly over grill. Set cooking grate in place, cover, and open lid vent completely. Heat grill until hot, about 5 minutes.

2B. FOR A GAS GRILL: Turn all burners to high, cover, and heat grill until hot, about 15 minutes. Leave all burners on high.

3. Clean cooking grate, then repeatedly brush grate with well-oiled paper towels until black and glossy, 5 to 10 times. Place fish on grill. Cook (covered if using gas) until both sides are browned and crisp and flesh is no longer translucent in center, 12 to 16 minutes, gently flipping fish over using 2 spatulas halfway through grilling. Transfer to carving board.

4. Working with 1 fish at a time, gently cut through skin and flesh down back of fish, from head to tail, without cutting through bones. Gently cut through skin and flesh just behind head, from top to bottom, without cutting through bones. Starting at head and working toward tail, gently run metal spatula between bones and flesh to separate, then gently lift entire fillet from skeleton in single piece. Repeat on second side of fish. Drizzle fish with vinaigrette and serve with lime wedges.

LEARN HOW **GRILLED WHOLE RED SNAPPER**

A whole grilled fish possesses deeper flavor than fillets or steaks. To achieve crispy skin and moist meat, we grilled whole snapper (a popular fish in Mexican cuisine) over high heat, making sure to thoroughly oil the grill to prevent sticking. A few simple cuts made our snapper easy to serve.

1. SLASH SKIN: Using a sharp knife, make shallow diagonal slashes 1 inch apart through the skin on both sides of the fish, being careful not to cut into the flesh. Slashing the fish ensures that it is thoroughly seasoned throughout.

2. OIL GRILL: Clean the cooking grate, then repeatedly brush the grate with well-oiled paper towels until the grate is black and glossy, 5 to 10 times. Oiling the grill well is especially important when grilling delicate fish.

3. GRILL FISH: Grill the fish on a hot grill until both sides are browned and crisp and the flesh is no longer translucent in the center, 12 to 16 minutes. Halfway through grilling, gently flip the fish using two spatulas. A hot fire ensures that the fish has time to pick up plenty of flavorful char before the interior overcooks.

4. SEPARATE FISH FROM BONES: Gently cut through the skin and flesh down the back of the fish, from head to tail, without cutting through the bones. This detaches the bones from the meat and allows you to serve attractive whole fillets rather than small flakes of fish.

5. SEPARATE FILLET FROM HEAD: Gently cut through the skin and flesh just behind head, from top to bottom, without cutting through the bones. Be careful not to cut through the bones, since they can easily leave small shards in the fish.

6. LIFT OFF FILLET: Starting at the head and working toward the tail, gently run a metal spatula between the bones and flesh to separate, then gently lift off the entire fillet in a single piece. Repeat steps 4 through 6 on the second side. Using a large, flat spatula is the key to keeping the fish intact.

HUARACHES WITH POBLANOS, BELL PEPPERS, AND QUESO FRESCO

Vegetarian Mains

Cheesy Stuffed Poblanos

Serves 4 to 6

✔ **WHY THIS RECIPE WORKS:** Poblano peppers are perfect for stuffing; their relatively large size makes them easy to fill, and their grassy, vegetal flavor pairs well with bold ingredients. We set out to create a simple recipe for poblanos stuffed with a cheesy filling. To make the poblanos pliable enough to fill, we microwaved them briefly. To improve our filling's flavor and to anchor the cheese in the peppers, we added a couple of cans of pinto beans (half of which we mashed), corn, garlic, onion, and spices to a combination of Monterey Jack and cheddar cheeses. Roasting the stuffed peppers tenderized them and deepened their flavor. Fresh tomato salsa nicely balanced the rich, cheesy peppers.

2	(15-ounce) cans pinto beans, rinsed
1	cup water
1	tablespoon vegetable oil
1	onion, chopped fine
4	garlic cloves, minced
1	tablespoon ground cumin
1	tablespoon minced fresh oregano or 1 teaspoon dried
1	teaspoon chili powder
1	teaspoon grated lime zest plus 1 tablespoon juice
	Salt and pepper
⅛	teaspoon cayenne pepper
2	cups fresh or thawed frozen corn
4	ounces Monterey Jack cheese, shredded (1 cup)
4	ounces sharp cheddar cheese, shredded (1 cup)
¼	cup minced fresh cilantro
8	large poblano chiles
1	recipe Fresh Tomato Salsa (page 19)

1. Adjust oven racks to upper-middle and lower-middle positions and heat oven to 425 degrees. Line 2 rimmed baking sheets with aluminum foil and set wire rack in each. Using potato masher, mash half of beans with water in bowl until mostly smooth.

2. Heat oil in 12-inch nonstick skillet over medium heat until shimmering. Add onion and cook until softened, about 5 minutes. Stir in garlic, cumin, oregano, chili powder, lime zest, ½ teaspoon salt, and cayenne and cook until fragrant, about 30 seconds. Add mashed bean mixture and cook, stirring constantly, until nearly all liquid has evaporated, 3 to 5 minutes.

3. Stir in corn and remaining beans and cook until warmed through, about 2 minutes. Off heat, stir in Monterey Jack, cheddar, cilantro, and lime juice. Season with salt and pepper to taste.

4. Leaving stem intact, cut slit lengthwise down 1 side of each poblano. Microwave poblanos in covered bowl until just pliable, about 2½ minutes. Gently pry open poblanos, remove seeds, and stuff evenly with bean-cheese mixture. Lay poblanos, stuffed side up, on prepared sheets. Bake until tender, switching and rotating sheets halfway through baking, 30 to 40 minutes. Serve with salsa.

TEST KITCHEN TIP STUFFING POBLANOS

1. Leaving stem intact, cut slit lengthwise down 1 side of poblanos. Microwave poblanos in covered bowl until just pliable.

2. Gently pry open poblanos, remove seeds, and stuff evenly with bean-cheese mixture.

Skillet Rice and Beans with Corn and Tomatoes

Serves 4 to 6

✓ **WHY THIS RECIPE WORKS:** The dish rice and beans is a Mexican staple; it makes the most of basic pantry ingredients for a one-pot meal that's full of flavor. For an aromatic base, we first bloomed onion, garlic, cumin, coriander, and oregano in oil to bring out the full range of their flavors. For a bit of spice and smoky depth, we also added a tablespoon of minced chipotle chile in adobo sauce. Canned black beans made a convenient alternative to dried and soaked beans. Cooking the beans and rice together worked to infuse the beans with flavor as the rice cooked to tenderness. For an extra layer of flavor, we sautéed corn until it was browned and toasty; the deep sweetness of the corn complemented the savory beans nicely. To keep our rice and beans tasting fresh, we tossed together tomatoes (grape tomatoes were the best choice for year-round quality), scallions, cilantro, and lime juice and then sprinkled the mixture over the rice just before serving.

3	tablespoons extra-virgin olive oil
1½	cups fresh or thawed frozen corn
	Salt and pepper
1	onion, chopped fine
4	garlic cloves, minced
1	tablespoon minced canned chipotle chile in adobo sauce
1	teaspoon ground cumin
1	teaspoon ground coriander
½	teaspoon dried oregano
2	(15-ounce) cans black beans, rinsed
2	cups vegetable broth
1	cup long-grain white rice, rinsed
12	ounces grape tomatoes, quartered
5	scallions, sliced thin
¼	cup minced fresh cilantro
1	tablespoon lime juice

1. Heat 1 tablespoon oil in 12-inch nonstick skillet over medium-high heat until shimmering. Add corn and cook, stirring occasionally, until kernels begin to brown and pop, 3 to 5 minutes. Transfer corn to bowl and season with salt and pepper to taste.

2. Add 1 tablespoon oil, onion, and ½ teaspoon salt to now-empty skillet and cook over medium-high heat until softened, about 5 minutes. Stir in garlic, chipotle, cumin, coriander, and oregano and cook until fragrant, about 30 seconds. Stir in beans, broth, and rice and bring to simmer. Cover, reduce heat to low, and simmer gently, stirring occasionally, until liquid is absorbed and rice is tender, about 15 minutes.

3. Meanwhile, combine tomatoes, scallions, cilantro, lime juice, and remaining 1 tablespoon oil in bowl and season with salt and pepper to taste.

4. Off heat, sprinkle corn over rice. Cover and let sit for 5 minutes. Gently fluff rice with fork and season with salt and pepper to taste. Sprinkle tomato mixture over rice and beans and serve.

Zucchini Fritters with Cilantro-Lime Sauce

Serves 4

☑ **WHY THIS RECIPE WORKS:** Zucchini is popular throughout Mexico, used both in sides and in main courses. We wanted to put zucchini in the spotlight by creating flavorful, crispy zucchini fritters. To achieve the crunchiest exteriors on our fritters, we needed dry zucchini; we salted shredded zucchini to draw out some moisture, then squeezed out even more water using a dish towel. Rather than drown the zucchini in a thick, heavy batter, we used just a couple eggs and some flour to allow the delicate zucchini flavor to shine. A cooling, creamy, lime-forward dipping sauce complemented the lightly spicy fritters perfectly. Make sure to squeeze the zucchini until it is completely dry or the fritters will be soggy; once squeezed, don't let the zucchini sit for too long or it will turn brown.

1½   **pounds zucchini, shredded**
      Salt and pepper
½   **cup sour cream**
6   **tablespoons vegetable oil**
¼   **cup minced fresh cilantro**
1   **teaspoon grated lime zest plus
    1 tablespoon juice**
6   **ounces Monterey Jack cheese, shredded
    (1½ cups)**
2   **large eggs, lightly beaten**
2   **jalapeño chiles, stemmed, seeded, and
    minced**
2   **scallions, minced**
1   **tablespoon minced fresh oregano or
    1 teaspoon dried**
1   **teaspoon ground coriander**
1   **garlic clove, minced**
¼   **cup all-purpose flour**

1. Toss shredded zucchini with 1 teaspoon salt and let drain in fine-mesh strainer for 10 minutes. Whisk sour cream, 2 tablespoons oil, 2 tablespoons cilantro, lime zest and juice, ¼ teaspoon salt, and ¼ teaspoon pepper together in bowl; cover and refrigerate until serving.

2. Wrap zucchini in clean dish towel, squeeze out excess liquid, and transfer to large bowl. Stir in Monterey Jack, eggs, jalapeños, scallions, oregano, coriander, garlic, ¼ teaspoon pepper, and remaining 2 tablespoons cilantro. Sprinkle flour over mixture and stir to incorporate.

3. Adjust oven rack to middle position and heat oven to 200 degrees. Set wire rack in rimmed baking sheet and line with triple layer of paper towels. Heat 2 tablespoons oil in 12-inch nonstick skillet over medium heat until shimmering. Drop scant ¼-cup portions of batter into skillet and use back of spoon to press batter into 2½-inch-wide fritters (you should fit about 6 fritters in pan at a time). Cook until well browned and slightly crisp on both sides, about 5 minutes per side.

4. Transfer fritters to prepared rack and keep warm in oven. Wipe skillet clean with paper towels and repeat with remaining 2 tablespoons oil and remaining batter. Serve fritters warm with lime-cilantro sauce.

TEST KITCHEN TIP **SQUEEZING ZUCCHINI DRY**

1. Shred zucchini on large holes of box grater. Toss with salt and let drain in fine-mesh strainer.

2. Squeeze salted zucchini in clean dish towel or several layers of paper towels until dry.

Potato Fritters with Zucchini-Avocado Slaw

Serves 4

✔ **WHY THIS RECIPE WORKS:** In Mexico, bite-size potato fritters are traditionally eaten as an appetizer with salsa and *crema*. We decided to make this appealing dish into a satisfying entrée. We wanted potato cakes with crispy, golden-brown exteriors and soft, creamy interiors; we also wanted a fresh, light slaw to accompany the cakes. To start, we focused on the potatoes. We tried simply boiling them, but the added water prevented the cakes from crisping. Instead, we microwaved the potatoes until they were perfectly tender. We amped up the flavor of the cakes with ground coriander, fresh scallions and cilantro, and salty, tangy Cotija cheese. An egg helped bind the cakes. For the slaw, we decided to use zucchini as our base. To preserve the zucchini's fresh flavor, we opted to skip cooking and instead shredded the squash and marinated it in a flavorful, citrusy dressing. Creamy avocado and crunchy red bell pepper provided pleasant flavor and texture contrasts.

2½   **pounds russet potatoes, unpeeled**
1   **pound zucchini, shredded**
1   **avocado, halved, pitted, and cut into ½-inch pieces**
1   **red bell pepper, stemmed, seeded, and chopped**
6   **tablespoons minced fresh cilantro**
2   **scallions, white parts minced and green parts sliced thin**
1   **jalapeño chile, stemmed, seeded, and minced**
1   **teaspoon grated lime zest plus 2 tablespoons juice**
1   **garlic clove, minced**
   Salt and pepper
8   **ounces Cotija cheese, crumbled (2 cups)**
1   **large egg, lightly beaten**
½   **teaspoon ground coriander**
1   **cup vegetable oil**

1. Prick potatoes all over with fork, place on plate, and microwave until tender, 18 to 25 minutes, turning potatoes over after 10 minutes. Cut potatoes in half and let cool slightly. Scoop flesh into large bowl and mash with potato masher until no lumps remain; let cool for 10 minutes.

2. Meanwhile, wrap zucchini in clean dish towel and squeeze out excess liquid. Combine dried zucchini, avocado, bell pepper, ¼ cup cilantro, scallion whites, jalapeño, lime zest and juice, garlic, ¼ teaspoon salt, and ¼ teaspoon pepper in bowl; cover and refrigerate until serving.

3. Stir Cotija, egg, coriander, remaining 2 tablespoons cilantro, scallion greens, ½ teaspoon salt, and ¼ teaspoon pepper into cooled potato. Divide mixture into 8 equal portions and lightly pack into ¾-inch-thick patties, about 3 inches wide.

4. Adjust oven rack to middle position and heat oven to 200 degrees. Set wire rack in rimmed baking sheet and line with triple layer of paper towels. Heat oil in 12-inch nonstick skillet over medium heat until shimmering. Carefully lay 4 patties in oil and cook until golden brown and crisp on both sides, about 3 minutes per side, adjusting heat as needed so oil bubbles around edges of patties.

5. Transfer fritters to prepared rack and keep warm in oven. Repeat with remaining fritters using oil left in pan. Serve fritters warm with zucchini-avocado slaw.

TEST KITCHEN TIP FRYING POTATO FRITTERS

Carefully lay 4 patties in hot oil and cook until golden brown on both sides, adjusting heat as needed so oil bubbles around patties.

Black Bean Burgers with Chipotle and Corn

Serves 6

✔ **WHY THIS RECIPE WORKS:** Too often, bean-based burgers are dense, bland, and dry. We wanted to create great black bean burgers full of bold Mexican flavor. We started with the most important ingredient: the beans. For burgers that were neither too soft nor too dense and pasty, we mashed most of the beans but left some whole. Adding two eggs and some panko bread crumbs ensured that the burgers would hold together once cooked. To bring a little freshness to the canned beans, we added corn and cilantro. Cumin offered a subtle, earthy flavor, while chipotle chile in adobo sauce brought some much-needed heat and smokiness. As an added bonus, our burgers came together effortlessly: We simply mixed the ingredients, shaped the patties, and cooked them in a skillet until nicely browned on both sides. Serve on hamburger buns with slices of red onion, tomato, avocado, and your favorite cheese, or alongside a simple salad. Avoid over-mixing the bean mixture or the burgers will have a mealy texture.

6	tablespoons vegetable oil
¾	cup fresh or thawed frozen corn
2	(15-ounce) cans black beans, rinsed
2	large eggs
1	tablespoon minced canned chipotle chile in adobo sauce
1	teaspoon ground cumin
½	teaspoon salt
1	cup panko bread crumbs
¼	cup finely chopped red bell pepper
¼	cup minced fresh cilantro
1	shallot, minced

1. Heat 1 tablespoon oil in 12-inch nonstick skillet over medium-high heat until shimmering. Add corn and cook, stirring occasionally, until kernels begin to brown and pop, 3 to 5 minutes; let cool slightly.

2. Meanwhile, mash 2½ cups beans in large bowl with potato masher until mostly smooth. In separate bowl, whisk eggs, chipotle, cumin, salt, and 1 tablespoon oil together. Stir egg mixture, corn, panko, bell pepper, cilantro, shallot, and remaining beans into mashed beans until combined. Divide mixture into 6 equal portions and lightly pack into 1-inch-thick burgers.

3. Adjust oven rack to middle position and heat oven to 200 degrees. Heat 2 tablespoons oil in now-empty skillet over medium heat until shimmering. Carefully lay 3 burgers in skillet and cook until well browned on both sides, 4 to 5 minutes per side.

4. Transfer burgers to paper towel–lined plate and keep warm in oven. Repeat with remaining 2 tablespoons oil and 3 burgers. Serve.

TEST KITCHEN TIP

MAKING BLACK BEAN BURGERS

1. Mash 2½ cups beans in large bowl with potato masher until smooth. Gently stir in remaining ingredients.

2. Divide mixture into 6 equal portions and lightly pack into 1-inch-thick burgers.

Chickpea Cakes with Chipotle-Lime Cream

Serves 6

✔ **WHY THIS RECIPE WORKS:** Chickpeas were brought to Mexico by Arab immigrants, and they're now a popular ingredient in soups and other dishes. To bring this versatile ingredient into the spotlight, we decided to create savory chickpea cakes that would be crisp on the outside and tender and flavorful on the inside. To give our cakes extra layers of flavor, we added some complementary ingredients to the chickpea base. We liked the sweetness provided by corn and decided to toast the kernels to deepen their flavor. Some garlic, ground coriander, and a combination of fresh cilantro and scallions helped further boost the flavor of the cakes. Sour cream provided welcome richness and a bit of tang. To bind the cakes together, we used panko bread crumbs and two eggs, which gave the mixture a malleable texture that was easy to form into cakes. Pan-frying for 3 to 5 minutes on both sides gave the cakes perfectly crisp, nicely browned exteriors with tender, creamy interiors. To take our chickpea cakes one step further, we created a cool, creamy sauce made with sour cream, lime zest, lime juice, and chipotle. Avoid overmixing the chickpea mixture or the cakes will have a mealy texture. Serve with a simple salad, slaw, or rice.

1	cup sour cream
1	tablespoon minced canned chipotle chile in adobo sauce
½	teaspoon grated lime zest plus 1 tablespoon juice
	Salt and pepper
7	tablespoons vegetable oil
1	cup fresh or thawed frozen corn
2	teaspoons ground coriander
1	garlic clove, minced
2	(15-ounce) cans chickpeas, rinsed
2	large eggs
¾	cup panko bread crumbs
4	scallions, sliced thin
3	tablespoons minced fresh cilantro

1. Whisk ½ cup sour cream, chipotle, lime zest and juice, and ¼ teaspoon salt in bowl; cover and refrigerate until serving.

2. Heat 1 tablespoon oil in 12-inch nonstick skillet over medium-high heat until shimmering. Add corn and cook, stirring occasionally, until kernels begin to brown and pop, 3 to 5 minutes. Stir in coriander and garlic and cook until fragrant, about 30 seconds; let cool slightly.

3. Pulse chickpeas in food processor to coarse paste, about 12 pulses. Whisk eggs, 1 teaspoon salt, and 2 tablespoons oil together in medium bowl. Stir in panko, scallions, cilantro, remaining ½ cup sour cream, cooked corn, and processed chickpeas until combined. Divide mixture into 6 equal portions and lightly pack into 1-inch-thick patties.

4. Adjust oven rack to middle position and heat oven to 200 degrees. Heat 2 tablespoons oil in now-empty skillet over medium heat until shimmering. Carefully lay 3 patties in skillet and cook until well browned on both sides, 3 to 5 minutes per side.

5. Transfer patties to paper towel–lined plate and keep warm in oven. Repeat with remaining 2 tablespoons oil and 3 patties. Serve with chipotle-lime cream sauce.

Corn and Black Bean Tortilla Tart

Serves 4 to 6

✓ **WHY THIS RECIPE WORKS:** Our simple, flavorful tortilla tart tastes as good as it looks: Savory layers of mashed, spiced black beans, sautéed corn, fresh tomatoes, and cheese are layered between crisped flour tortillas. For a boldly flavored base element, we combined black beans with onion, garlic, jalapeño, cumin, and vegetable broth; we mashed the beans for a spreadable texture. Sautéed corn, diced tomatoes, lime juice, scallions, and cilantro made for a bright, fresh layer. We liked cheddar cheese for its sharp full flavor, along with *queso fresco* for contrasting tangy saltiness. We lightly oiled the tortillas to help them crisp without burning. The melty cheese glued the layers together for a cohesive final dish. We prefer the taste and texture of fresh corn, but frozen, thawed corn kernels can be used.

¼	cup extra-virgin olive oil
2½	cups fresh or thawed frozen corn
2	large plum tomatoes, cored and cut into ¼-inch pieces
4	scallions, sliced thin
2	tablespoons minced fresh cilantro
1	teaspoon lime juice
	Salt and pepper
1	onion, chopped fine
1	jalapeño chile, stemmed, seeded, and minced
3	garlic cloves, minced
1	teaspoon ground cumin
1	(15-ounce) can black beans, rinsed
¾	cup vegetable broth
4	(10-inch) flour tortillas
6	ounces cheddar cheese, shredded (1½ cups)
2	ounces queso fresco, crumbled (½ cup)

1. Adjust oven rack to middle position and heat oven to 400 degrees. Heat 1 tablespoon oil in 12-inch nonstick skillet over medium-high heat until shimmering. Add corn and cook, stirring occasionally, until kernels begin to brown and pop, 3 to 5 minutes. Transfer to large bowl and let cool slightly. Stir in tomatoes, scallions, 1 tablespoon cilantro, and lime juice, and season with salt and pepper to taste.

2. Wipe skillet clean with paper towels. Add 1 tablespoon oil and onion to skillet and cook over medium heat until softened, 3 to 5 minutes. Stir in jalapeño, garlic, and cumin and cook until fragrant, about 30 seconds. Stir in beans and broth and cook until liquid has nearly evaporated, 5 to 7 minutes. Transfer mixture to large bowl and mash beans with potato masher until mostly smooth. Season with salt and pepper to taste.

3. Line rimless or inverted baking sheet with parchment paper. Lightly brush both sides of tortillas with remaining 2 tablespoons oil. Place 1 tortilla on prepared sheet. Spread one-quarter of mashed beans over top, leaving ½ inch border around edge. Sprinkle with one-quarter of corn mixture, one-quarter of cheddar, and one-quarter of queso fresco. Repeat with remaining tortillas, beans, corn, cheddar, and queso fresco to make layered tart.

4. Bake tart until cheese is melted and slightly brown, 20 to 25 minutes. Let cool on baking sheet for 5 minutes, then slide onto cutting board using parchment; discard parchment. Sprinkle remaining 1 tablespoon cilantro over top. Cut into wedges and serve.

TEST KITCHEN TIP

ASSEMBLING TORTILLA TART

Spread mashed beans onto prepared tortilla; leave ½-inch border around edge. Sprinkle with corn mixture and cheese. Place next tortilla on top; repeat.

Huaraches with Poblanos, Bell Peppers, and Queso Fresco

Makes 6 huaraches; serves 4 to 6

✔ **WHY THIS RECIPE WORKS:** A popular dish in Mexico City, *huaraches* are thick, oblong masa cakes crisped on the outside and topped with ingredients like refried beans, salsa, cheese, and sometimes meat. We decided to create an entree-worthy, vegetarian version of this street-food favorite. For the huarache bases, we started by making a soft dough from masa harina and water. We let the dough rest for a few minutes to ensure that the masa harina was fully hydrated, then pressed it into oblong cakes and cooked it on both sides to create golden-brown, crisp exteriors. As for the toppings, we first layered on rich, creamy refried beans. We sautéed sweet red bell peppers along with slightly spicy poblano chiles for a fresh, flavorful vegetable layer. Quick pickled shallots and radishes provided the perfect crispness that we needed for textural contrast, plus their fresh, bright lime flavor cut through the richness of the beans below. A sprinkle of queso fresco was the perfect finish. You can use canned vegetarian refried pinto beans or make your own (see the recipe on page 293). See the photo on page 236.

- 3 tablespoons vegetable oil
- 2 poblano chiles, stemmed, seeded, and cut into ¼-inch-wide strips
- 2 red bell peppers, stemmed, seeded, and cut into ¼-inch-wide strips
  Salt
- 2 cups (8 ounces) masa harina
- 1¾ cups hot tap water
- ¾ cup vegetarian refried pinto beans, warmed
- 1½ ounces queso fresco, crumbled (⅓ cup)
- ¾ cup Mexican crema
- 1 recipe Pickled Shallot and Radishes (recipe follows)

1. Heat 1 tablespoon oil in 12-inch nonstick skillet over medium-high heat until shimmering. Add poblanos, bell peppers, and ½ teaspoon salt and cook, stirring occasionally, until peppers are softened and lightly browned, 10 to 12 minutes; transfer to bowl and cover to keep warm. Wipe skillet clean with paper towels.

2. Meanwhile, mix masa harina and 1 teaspoon salt in medium bowl, then stir in water with rubber spatula. Using your hands, knead mixture in bowl until soft, sticky dough forms, 1 to 2 minutes. Cover dough with damp dish towel and let sit for 5 minutes.

3. Adjust oven rack to middle position, set wire rack in rimmed baking sheet, set sheet on oven rack, and heat oven to 200 degrees. Line second baking sheet with parchment paper. Transfer dough to clean counter, form into ball, then divide evenly into 6 pieces. Roll each piece into 5-inch-long rope, place on parchment-lined sheet, and cover with damp dish towel.

4. Cut sides of 1-quart zipper-lock bag, leaving bottom seam intact. Place 1 piece dough on 1 side of plastic bag and fold other side over top. Press dough into ⅛-inch-thick oval using pie plate. Remove plastic, return shaped dough to sheet, and cover with damp towel. Repeat with remaining 5 pieces dough.

5. Add 2 teaspoons oil to now-empty skillet and place over medium-high heat until shimmering. Lay 2 pieces dough in single layer in skillet and cook until dark spotty brown on first side, 4 to 6 minutes. Flip dough and continue to cook until crisp on second side, 2 to 4 minutes. Transfer huaraches to wire rack in oven and repeat with remaining 4 teaspoons oil and 4 pieces dough in 2 more batches.

6. Spread refried beans evenly over huaraches, leaving ¼-inch border around edge. Top evenly with pepper mixture, sprinkle evenly with queso fresco, and drizzle with crema. Serve with Pickled Shallot and Radishes.

Pickled Shallot and Radishes
MAKES ABOUT 1 CUP

5	radishes, trimmed and sliced thin
1	shallot, sliced thin
¼	cup lime juice (2 limes)
1	teaspoon sugar
⅛	teaspoon salt

Combine all ingredients in bowl. Refrigerate for up to 2 days.

LEARN HOW **HUARACHES**
These oblong, masa-based tarts are made with some simple shaping techniques.

1. ROLL DOUGH INTO ROPES: Form the dough into a ball, then portion the dough evenly into six pieces. Roll each piece into a 5-inch-long rope, and place on the prepared baking sheet. Cover the dough with a damp dish towel. It is important to keep the dough covered so it doesn't dry out and crack.

2. PRESS DOUGH INTO FLAT OVALS: Working with one piece of dough at a time, press the dough flat into a ⅛-inch thick oval in the prepared zipper-lock bag using a pie plate. This creates the traditional oblong shape.

3. COOK DOUGH: Cook the huaraches in a lightly oiled non-stick skillet until spotty brown and crisp on both sides, 6 to 10 minutes. The dough is cooked before the toppings are added to achieve a crisp crust.

Vegetarian Tamale Pie

Serves 6 to 8

✓ **WHY THIS RECIPE WORKS:** Loaded with beans, vegetables, and cheese and topped with a cornmeal crust, this vegetarian take on tamale pie is rich, hearty, and packed with Mexican flavor. For a deep, boldly flavored sauce, we used the traditional Mexican technique of roasting the main ingredients (canned diced tomatoes, onion, and garlic) until nicely browned and then simply blended them with chipotle chile, chili powder, and lime juice. We combined the sauce with two types of canned beans, corn, zucchini, and fresh cilantro in a baking dish and topped it with a layer of cheese, then a quick cornmeal batter. The pie emerged from the oven with a beautifully browned crust and an ultraflavorful filling.

2 (28-ounce) cans diced tomatoes, drained with 2 cups juice reserved
1 onion, chopped coarse
4 garlic cloves, chopped coarse
1 tablespoon vegetable oil
  Salt and pepper
1 tablespoon minced canned chipotle chile in adobo sauce
1 tablespoon chili powder
4 teaspoons lime juice
2 (15-ounce) cans black beans, rinsed
1 (15-ounce) can pinto beans, rinsed
1½ cups fresh or thawed frozen corn
1 zucchini, cut into ½-inch cubes
¼ cup minced fresh cilantro
1 teaspoon dried oregano
8 ounces Monterey Jack cheese, shredded (2 cups)
4 cups water
1½ cups coarse-ground cornmeal

1. Adjust oven rack to middle position and heat oven to 475 degrees. Line rimmed baking sheet with aluminum foil. Toss tomatoes, onion, garlic, oil, and ½ teaspoon salt together in bowl, then spread onto prepared sheet. Roast vegetables, stirring occasionally, until edges are dark brown, 35 to 40 minutes.

2. Remove vegetables from oven and reduce oven temperature to 375 degrees. Transfer roasted vegetables and any accumulated juices to blender. Add chipotle, chili powder, lime juice, and reserved tomato juice and process until sauce is slightly chunky, 8 to 10 seconds. Season sauce with salt and pepper to taste. Combine sauce, black beans, pinto beans, corn, zucchini, cilantro, and oregano in 13 by 9-inch baking dish and top evenly with Monterey Jack.

3. Bring water to boil in large saucepan over high heat. Add ¾ teaspoon salt, then slowly pour in cornmeal, whisking vigorously to prevent lumps from forming. Reduce heat to medium-high and cook, whisking constantly, until cornmeal begins to soften and mixture thickens, about 3 minutes. Off heat, season with salt and pepper to taste. Spread warm cornmeal mixture evenly over casserole with rubber spatula, pushing it to edges of baking dish.

4. Cover dish with foil and bake for 30 minutes. Remove foil and continue to bake until crust is beginning to brown and filling is bubbling, 30 to 35 minutes. Let cool for 10 minutes before serving.

TEST KITCHEN TIP   TOPPING TAMALE PIE

Spread warm cornmeal mixture evenly over filling using rubber spatula. Push topping to edges of baking dish.

Sopa Seca with Spinach and Chickpeas

Serves 4

✔ **WHY THIS RECIPE WORKS:** This enticing Mexican specialty literally translates as "dry soup," but *sopa seca* is really a cheesy, comforting pasta dish. Traditionally, *fideos*—thin, coiled strands of pasta that are toasted until golden—are cooked in a flavorful sauce of tomatoes and chiles. When we couldn't find fideos at our local supermarket, we substituted vermicelli and toasted it for a pleasantly nutty flavor. Using water as the liquid component resulted in a bland dish; vegetable broth offered a more savory backbone. Onion, ancho chile powder, cumin, and oregano gave the sauce more flavor without making it spicy. We added hearty curly-leaf spinach and chickpeas to make our sopa seca into a complete, satisfying meal. To keep the dish bright and fresh tasting, we cooked the spinach only briefly and then stirred in fresh tomatoes off the heat. Two types of cheese and a liberal amount of fresh herbs completed our satisfying entrée.

8	ounces vermicelli, broken in half
3	tablespoons vegetable oil
1	onion, chopped fine
	Salt and pepper
3	garlic cloves, minced
1	tablespoon ancho chile powder
2	teaspoons minced fresh oregano or ½ teaspoon dried
½	teaspoon ground cumin
2½	cups vegetable broth
1	(15-ounce) can chickpeas, rinsed
1	pound curly-leaf spinach, stemmed and chopped coarse
2	tomatoes, cored and cut into ½-inch pieces
4	ounces Monterey Jack cheese, shredded (1 cup)
2	ounces queso fresco, crumbled (½ cup)
2	tablespoons minced fresh cilantro

1. Toast pasta and 1 tablespoon oil in Dutch oven over medium-high heat, stirring constantly, until most of pasta is browned, 4 to 6 minutes; transfer to paper towel–lined plate.

2. Add remaining 2 tablespoons oil, onion, and ¼ teaspoon salt to now-empty pot and cook over medium heat until softened, about 5 minutes. Stir in garlic, chile powder, oregano, and cumin and cook until fragrant, about 30 seconds.

3. Stir in broth, chickpeas, toasted pasta, ¼ teaspoon salt, and ½ teaspoon pepper. Increase heat to medium and bring to vigorous simmer. Cover and cook, stirring often, until pasta is just tender, 8 to 10 minutes.

4. Uncover, stir in spinach 1 handful at a time, and cook until spinach is mostly wilted, 4 to 6 minutes. Off heat, stir in tomatoes. Sprinkle Monterey Jack over top, cover, and let sit until cheese is melted, about 3 minutes. Sprinkle with queso fresco and cilantro and serve.

TEST KITCHEN TIP **BREAKING PASTA**

1. Loosely wrap vermicelli in kitchen towel, keeping pasta flat, not bunched.

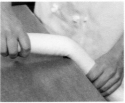

2. Center bundle over edge of counter and push down to break pasta neatly in half.

HUEVOS RANCHEROS

Eggs

Bricklayer's Eggs
Serves 4

☑ **WHY THIS RECIPE WORKS:** *Huevos al albañil*, or bricklayer's eggs, is a traditional dish of fried eggs that are topped with a spicy tomatillo salsa and served with corn tortillas. For our version, we made a quick roasted tomatillo salsa with fresh chiles and aromatics. Since we wanted our recipe to feed four people, we needed to make eight fried eggs. To do this, we cracked the eggs into small bowls so we could add them to the pan all at once, guaranteeing that they would cook at the same rate. Removing the pan from the heat partway through cooking allowed the eggs to cook through gently in the residual heat. Serve with rice, refried beans, and warmed tortillas.

- 4 ounces tomatillos, husks and stems removed, rinsed well, dried, and quartered
- 1 large poblano chile, stemmed, seeded, and chopped
- ½ small onion, chopped coarse
- 1 jalapeño chile, stemmed and halved
- 5 teaspoons vegetable oil
- 2 garlic cloves, peeled and smashed
- 2 teaspoons minced fresh oregano or ½ teaspoon dried
- 1 teaspoon ground coriander
  Salt and pepper
- ¼ cup warm water
- ¼ cup fresh cilantro leaves
- 2 teaspoons lime juice
- 8 large eggs
- 1 tablespoon unsalted butter, cut into 4 pieces and chilled

1. Adjust oven rack 6 inches from broiler element and heat broiler. Line rimmed baking sheet with aluminum foil. Toss tomatillos, poblano, onion, jalapeño, 1 tablespoon oil, garlic, oregano, coriander, ¼ teaspoon salt, and ¼ teaspoon pepper together, then spread onto prepared sheet. Broil vegetables until browned, 10 to 12 minutes, stirring occasionally.

2. Transfer broiled vegetables to food processor. Add warm water, cilantro, and lime juice and pulse until coarsely ground, 10 to 15 pulses. Season with salt and pepper to taste. (Sauce can be refrigerated for up to 2 days; reheat in microwave and adjust consistency with extra water as needed before continuing.)

3. Heat remaining 2 teaspoons oil in 12- or 14-inch nonstick skillet over low heat for 5 minutes. Meanwhile, crack eggs into 2 small bowls (4 eggs per bowl) and season with salt and pepper.

4. Increase heat to medium-high and heat until oil is shimmering. Add butter and quickly swirl to coat skillet. Working quickly, pour 1 bowl of eggs in 1 side of skillet and second bowl of eggs in other side. Cover and cook for 2 minutes.

5. Remove skillet from heat and let stand, covered, about 2 minutes for runny yolks (white around edge of yolk will be barely opaque), about 3 minutes for soft but set yolks, and about 4 minutes for medium-set yolks. Slide eggs onto warm plates and top with sauce. Serve immediately.

TEST KITCHEN TIP FRYING EGGS

1. While skillet heats, crack eggs into 2 small bowls.

2. Working quickly, pour 1 bowl of eggs in 1 side of skillet and second bowl of eggs in other side. Cover skillet and cook for 2 minutes.

Migas

Serves 4

✓ **WHY THIS RECIPE WORKS:** Traditional *migas*, which literally translates as "crumbs," is an appealing dish of fluffy scrambled eggs with onions, chiles, cheese, and crushed tortilla chips, which soften in the eggs to a pleasantly chewy texture. Although most of the recipes we found for this dish used fried chips, we found that they gave the eggs an off-flavor and made the dish overly greasy. We got better results from baked tortilla chips, which had a clean corn flavor. Softening the vegetables before adding them to the eggs helped to drive off excess moisture and keep the egg and tortilla mixture light and fluffy. A handful of pepper Jack cheese and cilantro finished off our creamy, flavorful scramble with a bit of punch. If you'd like to make your own baked tortilla chips, see the recipe on page 21.

2　tablespoons unsalted butter
1　onion, chopped fine
1　red bell pepper, stemmed, seeded, and chopped fine
1　jalapeño chile, stemmed, seeded, and minced
3　garlic cloves, minced
8　large eggs
2　ounces baked tortilla chips, broken into ½-inch pieces (1 cup)
　Salt and pepper
3　ounces pepper Jack cheese, shredded (¾ cup)
2　tablespoons minced fresh cilantro

1. Melt 1 tablespoon butter in 12-inch nonstick skillet over medium heat. Add onion, bell pepper, and jalapeño, cover, and cook until softened and lightly browned, about 8 minutes. Stir in garlic and cook, uncovered, until fragrant, about 30 seconds; transfer to bowl.

2. Beat eggs, tortilla chips, ¼ teaspoon salt, and pinch pepper together with fork in bowl until thoroughly combined; do not overbeat. Wipe out skillet with paper towels, add remaining 1 tablespoon butter, and melt over medium heat. Add egg mixture and, using heat-resistant rubber spatula, constantly and firmly scrape along bottom and sides of skillet until eggs begin to clump and spatula leaves trail on bottom of skillet, 1½ to 2½ minutes.

3. Reduce heat to low and gently but constantly fold eggs until clumped and slightly wet, 30 to 60 seconds. Off heat, gently fold in pepper Jack, cilantro, and vegetable mixture; if eggs are still underdone, return skillet to medium heat for no longer than 30 seconds. Season with salt and pepper to taste. Serve immediately.

TEST KITCHEN TIP **SCRAMBLING EGGS**

1. Add egg mixture to pan; use rubber spatula to scrape bottom and sides of skillet until eggs begin to clump and spatula leaves trail.

2. Reduce heat to low and gently but constantly fold eggs until clumped and slightly wet, 30 to 60 seconds.

Scrambled Eggs with Tomato, Onion, and Jalapeño

Serves 6

✔ **WHY THIS RECIPE WORKS:** *Huevos a la Mexicana* is a traditional scrambled egg dish that features the colors of the Mexican flag: fresh red tomatoes, bold white onions, and spicy green jalapeños. To keep the scramble light and fluffy, we had to eliminate as much moisture as we could from the vegetables. We first decided to sauté the vegetables and then remove them from the pan before adding the eggs. This only partially worked; the tomato still left the eggs weepy and wet. To solve this problem, we opted not to cook the tomato at all and instead drew out the tomato's excess moisture by salting it and letting it drain before sprinkling it over the finished eggs. We knew that some dairy mixed into the eggs would help give them a soft texture; milk made the eggs runny, while richer half-and-half produced substantial eggs that stayed soft without being wet. With the moisture level under control, we shifted our focus to the flavor. Although the vegetables gave the scramble some flavor, we wanted more. Incorporating *queso fresco* and cilantro added additional freshness to the dish while also keeping the red, white, and green colors vibrant. For a hearty variation, we sautéed deeply flavorful chorizo with the onion and jalapeño.

1   **tomato, cored and cut into ¼-inch pieces**
     Salt and pepper
2   **tablespoons unsalted butter**
1   **small onion, chopped fine**
1   **jalapeño chile, stemmed, seeded,**
     and minced
12   **large eggs**
6   **tablespoons half-and-half**
3   **ounces queso fresco, crumbled (¾ cup)**
2   **tablespoons chopped fresh cilantro**

1. Toss tomato with ⅛ teaspoon salt in bowl, then transfer to paper towel–lined plate and let drain for 15 minutes.

2. Meanwhile, melt 1 tablespoon butter in 12-inch nonstick skillet over medium heat. Add onion and jalapeño, cover, and cook until softened and lightly browned, 6 to 8 minutes; transfer to bowl.

3. Beat eggs, half-and-half, ¾ teaspoon salt, and ¼ teaspoon pepper together with fork in bowl until thoroughly combined and mixture is pure yellow; do not overbeat. Wipe out skillet with paper towels, add remaining 1 tablespoon butter, and melt over medium heat. Add egg mixture and, using heat-resistant rubber spatula, constantly and firmly scrape along bottom and sides of skillet until eggs begin to clump and spatula leaves trail on bottom of skillet, 1½ to 2½ minutes.

4. Reduce heat to low and gently but constantly fold eggs until clumped and slightly wet, 30 to 60 seconds. Off heat, gently fold in vegetable mixture and ½ cup queso fresco; if eggs are still underdone, return skillet to medium heat for no longer than 30 seconds. Sprinkle with drained tomato, remaining ¼ cup queso fresco, and cilantro. Season with salt and pepper to taste. Serve immediately.

Scrambled Eggs with Chorizo, Onion, and Jalapeño

Omit tomato and step 1. Substitute 8 ounces Mexican-style chorizo sausage, casings removed, for butter in step 2. Cook chorizo in skillet over medium heat, breaking up meat with wooden spoon, until well browned, 8 to 10 minutes, before adding onion and jalapeño. Substitute shredded cheddar cheese for queso fresco and 2 thinly sliced scallions for cilantro.

Spicy Chilaquiles with Fried Eggs
Serves 4

✓ **WHY THIS RECIPE WORKS:** The traditional Mexican breakfast food known as *chilaquiles* began as a way to use up leftover tortillas and sauce: The tortillas would be lightly fried, then simmered in the sauce and served with fried eggs on top. But most of the recipes we found produced soggy tortillas and bland sauce. We wanted a fresher take on this Mexican classic. We started by baking our tortillas with a little oil to ensure they crisped up. We then made a quick chile sauce using plenty of aromatics, deeply flavored chili powder, and smoky chipotle in adobo. Using canned tomato sauce was far easier and faster than using raw tomatoes. We borrowed a technique from our recipe for Bricklayer's Eggs (page 258) to perfectly fry eight eggs at once. We quickly discovered that proper timing was crucial; the crisp tortillas could not sit for too long without losing their crunchy texture, but our fried eggs cooled down quickly. To solve both problems, we made sure to coat the crisped tortillas in the sauce just as the eggs finished cooking. A final sprinkle of tangy queso fresco and fresh cilantro rounded out the dish nicely. For the best texture, we prefer to use 100 percent corn tortillas in this recipe.

16 (6-inch) corn tortillas, cut into 8 wedges
6   tablespoons plus 2 teaspoons extra-virgin olive oil
    Salt and pepper
1   onion, chopped fine
2   tablespoons chili powder
3   garlic cloves, minced
1   teaspoon minced canned chipotle chile in adobo sauce
2   (8-ounce) cans tomato sauce
1½ cups chicken broth
8   large eggs
1   tablespoon unsalted butter, cut into 4 pieces and chilled
4   ounces queso fresco, crumbled (1 cup)
2   tablespoons chopped fresh cilantro

1. Adjust oven racks to upper-middle and lower-middle positions and heat oven to 425 degrees. Spread tortillas evenly over 2 rimmed baking sheets. Drizzle each sheet with 2 tablespoons oil and ¼ teaspoon salt and toss until evenly coated. Bake, stirring occasionally, until tortillas are golden brown and crisp, 15 to 20 minutes, switching sheets halfway through baking.

2. Heat 2 tablespoons oil in Dutch oven over medium heat until shimmering. Add onion and cook until softened, about 5 minutes. Stir in chili powder, garlic, and chipotle and cook until fragrant, about 30 seconds. Add tomato sauce and broth, bring to simmer, and cook, stirring occasionally, until flavors meld, about 10 minutes. Remove pot from heat.

3. Heat remaining 2 teaspoons oil in 12- or 14-inch nonstick skillet over low heat for 5 minutes. Meanwhile, crack eggs into 2 small bowls (4 eggs per bowl) and season with salt and pepper.

4. Increase heat to medium-high and heat until oil is shimmering. Add butter and quickly swirl to coat skillet. Working quickly, pour 1 bowl of eggs in 1 side of skillet and second bowl of eggs in other side. Cover and cook for 2 minutes.

5. Remove skillet from heat and let stand, covered, about 2 minutes for runny yolks (white around edge of yolk will be barely opaque), about 3 minutes for soft but set yolks, and about 4 minutes for medium-set yolks.

6. While eggs finish cooking, return sauce to brief simmer over medium-high heat. Off heat, stir in toasted tortillas, cover, and let sit until tortillas have softened slightly, 2 to 5 minutes. Divide tortilla mixture among individual plates and sprinkle with queso fresco. Slide eggs on top, sprinkle with cilantro, and serve immediately.

Green Chile and Potato Frittata

Serves 6

✔ **WHY THIS RECIPE WORKS:** This south-of-the-border take on frittata combines light, fluffy eggs with spicy poblano chiles and tender Yukon Gold potatoes for a hearty, Mexican-inspired breakfast. To ensure that every element was perfectly cooked at the same time, we jump-started the cooking of the potatoes in the microwave. As the potatoes parcooked, we sautéed onions and poblano peppers to soften them and mellow their flavors. Garlic, oregano, cumin, and chipotle provided subtle background flavors; we found that the best way to guarantee even distribution of the spices was to mix them into the vegetables. After stirring some chopped cilantro into our beaten eggs for freshness and color, we poured them into the pan with the spiced vegetables. We stirred the eggs as they scrambled to ensure that they cooked evenly, but cooked them only partially so that we could broil the frittata to crisp the top. Before sliding the skillet under the broiler, we scattered cheese evenly over the top; cubing the cheese (rather than shredding it) created cheesy pockets in the finished frittata. We took the pan out of the oven when the eggs in the center were still slightly underdone, allowing the gentle residual heat to finish the cooking. You will need a 10-inch ovensafe nonstick skillet for this recipe. Because broilers vary in intensity, watch the frittata carefully as it cooks.

1 **pound Yukon Gold potatoes, unpeeled, cut into ½-inch pieces**

2 **tablespoons extra-virgin olive oil**
 Salt and pepper

12 **large eggs**

3 **tablespoons half-and-half**

3 **tablespoons chopped fresh cilantro**

2 **poblano chiles, stemmed, seeded, and cut into ½-inch pieces**

1 **onion, chopped fine**

3 **garlic cloves, minced**

2 **teaspoons minced fresh oregano or ½ teaspoon dried**

2 **teaspoons minced canned chipotle chile in adobo sauce**

½ **teaspoon ground cumin**

4 **ounces Monterey Jack cheese, cut into ¼-inch pieces (1 cup)**

1. Adjust oven rack 6 inches from broiler element and heat broiler. Toss potatoes, 1 tablespoon oil, and ¼ teaspoon salt together in bowl. Cover and microwave until potatoes are translucent around edges, 5 to 7 minutes, stirring halfway through microwaving.

2. Meanwhile, beat eggs, half-and-half, cilantro, ¾ teaspoon salt, and ½ teaspoon pepper together with fork in bowl until thoroughly combined; do not overbeat.

3. Heat remaining 1 tablespoon oil in 10-inch ovensafe nonstick skillet over medium heat until shimmering. Add poblanos and onion and cook until softened, about 8 minutes. Stir in hot potatoes, then stir in garlic, oregano, chipotle, and cumin and cook until fragrant, about 30 seconds.

4. Add egg mixture and, using heat-resistant rubber spatula, constantly and firmly scrape along bottom and sides of skillet until large curds form and spatula leaves trail on bottom of skillet, but eggs are still very wet, about 3 minutes. Shake skillet to distribute eggs evenly. Sprinkle with Monterey Jack and gently press into eggs with spatula.

5. Broil until frittata has risen and surface is puffed and spotty brown, 2 to 3 minutes; when cut into with paring knife, eggs should be slightly wet and runny. Remove skillet from oven and let frittata rest for 5 minutes. Using oven mitts (skillet handle will be hot), run spatula around skillet edge to loosen frittata, then carefully slide it out onto serving plate. Serve warm or at room temperature.

Huevos Rancheros

Serves 4

✓ **WHY THIS RECIPE WORKS:** *Huevos rancheros*, or "ranch-style eggs," is a hearty yet simple Mexican breakfast dish. Versions vary from cook to cook based on the available ingredients, but the basic formula is almost always the same: Fried eggs are draped with a fresh, spicy tomato salsa and served with warm tortillas. We wanted a streamlined recipe that would feed four people. For a simple salsa with big flavor, we roasted canned diced tomatoes with green chiles, onion, chili powder, and garlic. To make sure our salsa wasn't too dry, we combined the roasted vegetables with some of the liquid from the canned tomatoes. Although many traditional recipes call for fried eggs, we opted to take an easier approach: we poached our eggs right in the flavorful tomato sauce. The eggs picked up lots of flavor from the salsa, and we could easily cook eight at a time. Serve with refried beans. See the photo on page 256.

2	(28-ounce) cans diced tomatoes
1	tablespoon packed brown sugar
1	tablespoon lime juice
1	onion, chopped
½	cup chopped canned green chiles
¼	cup extra-virgin olive oil
3	tablespoons chili powder
4	garlic cloves, sliced thin
	Salt and pepper
4	ounces pepper Jack cheese, shredded (1 cup)
8	large eggs
1	avocado, halved, pitted, and diced
3	scallions, sliced thin
⅓	cup minced fresh cilantro
8	(6-inch) corn tortillas, warmed

1. Adjust oven rack to middle position and heat oven to 500 degrees. Line rimmed baking sheet with parchment paper. Drain tomatoes in fine-mesh strainer set over bowl, pressing with rubber spatula to extract 1¾ cups tomato juice; discard extra juice. Whisk sugar and lime juice into tomato juice.

2. In separate bowl, combine onion, chiles, oil, chili powder, garlic, ½ teaspoon salt, and drained tomatoes. Spread tomato mixture evenly over prepared sheet. Roast until charred in spots, 35 to 40 minutes, stirring halfway through baking. (Tomato juice mixture and roasted vegetables can be refrigerated separately for up to 24 hours; reheat vegetables in microwave for 45 seconds and bring juice to room temperature before continuing.)

3. Reduce oven temperature to 400 degrees. Combine roasted vegetables and tomato juice in 13 by 9-inch baking dish, season with salt and pepper to taste, and sprinkle evenly with pepper Jack. Using spoon, make 8 indentations (2 to 3 inches wide) in tomato mixture. Crack 1 egg into each indentation and season eggs with salt and pepper.

4. Bake until egg whites are just beginning to set but still have some movement when dish is shaken, 13 to 16 minutes. Transfer dish to wire rack, tent with aluminum foil, and let sit for 5 minutes. Sprinkle with avocado, scallions, and cilantro. Serve immediately with warm tortillas.

LEARN HOW **HUEVOS RANCHEROS**

Huevos rancheros is a traditional Mexican breakfast, but many recipes overcomplicate this simple morning meal. We simplify and streamline by swapping fresh tomatoes for canned diced tomatoes and poaching the eggs right in the salsa.

1. DRAIN TOMATOES: Pour the tomatoes into a fine-mesh strainer set over a large bowl. Press with a rubber spatula to extract 1¾ cups of juice; discard any extra juice. Whisk brown sugar and lime juice into the reserved tomato liquid. Using canned diced tomatoes is faster and easier than using fresh.

2. ROAST VEGETABLES FOR SALSA: Combine the diced tomatoes, onion, green chiles, garlic, and chili powder with oil and spread the mixture on a rimmed baking sheet. Roast in a 500-degree oven until slightly charred. Roasting intensifies the flavor of the tomatoes and other salsa ingredients.

3. MAKE SALSA: Reduce the oven temperature to 400 degrees. Combine the roasted vegetables with the reserved tomato liquid in a 13 by 9-inch baking dish. The tomato liquid ensures that the salsa isn't too dry and gives the salsa a brighter flavor.

4. SPRINKLE WITH CHEESE: Sprinkle the pepper Jack cheese evenly over the top of the tomato mixture. Not only does pepper Jack melt well, its flavor and mild bite meld nicely with the other elements of the dish.

5. MAKE INDENTATIONS IN SALSA AND BAKE EGGS: Using a spoon, make eight indentations in the salsa. Crack one egg into each indentation and bake until the egg whites are just set. Poaching the eggs in the salsa in the oven makes it easy to cook eight eggs at once.

6. FINISH AND SERVE: Transfer the baking dish to a wire rack, tent with aluminum foil, and let sit for 5 minutes. Sprinkle with avocado, scallions, and cilantro and serve with warm tortillas. Letting the eggs set in the residual heat ensures that they don't overcook.

Tomato and Corn Tostadas with Baked Eggs

Serves 4

✔ **WHY THIS RECIPE WORKS:** For a unique and flavorful breakfast dish with Mexican flair, we decided to pair crunchy, crisp corn tostadas with soft, rich eggs and flavorful roasted vegetables. We started by roasting cherry tomatoes, corn, and onion with smoky chipotle and aromatic spices. To avoid dirtying another pan, we baked the eggs in divots we made in the vegetable mixture. A slather of warm, creamy refried beans and a sprinkle of queso fresco and cilantro finished off our tostadas perfectly. Any type of refried beans will work well here; if you want to make your own, see the recipes on page 293.

1½	pounds cherry tomatoes, halved
1½	cups fresh or thawed frozen corn
1	onion, halved and sliced thin
2	tablespoons plus ¾ cup vegetable oil
3	garlic cloves, minced
2	teaspoons minced canned chipotle chile in adobo sauce
2	teaspoons minced fresh oregano or ½ teaspoon dried
1	teaspoon ground cumin
½	teaspoon ground coriander
	Salt and pepper
8	(6-inch) corn tortillas
8	large eggs
1	cup refried beans, warmed
2	ounces queso fresco, crumbled (½ cup)
3	tablespoons chopped fresh cilantro

1. Adjust oven rack to middle position and heat oven to 500 degrees. Line rimmed baking sheet with aluminum foil. Toss tomatoes, corn, onion, 2 tablespoons oil, garlic, chipotle, oregano, cumin, coriander, ½ teaspoon salt, and ¼ teaspoon pepper together, then spread onto prepared sheet. Roast vegetables, stirring occasionally, until tomatoes are softened and skins begin to shrivel, 10 to 15 minutes. Remove sheet from oven.

2. Meanwhile, using fork, poke center of each tortilla 3 or 4 times (to prevent puffing and allow for even cooking). Heat remaining ¾ cup oil in 8-inch heavy-bottomed skillet over medium heat to 350 degrees. Line second rimmed baking sheet with several layers of paper towels.

3. Working with 1 tortilla at a time, add to hot oil and place metal potato masher on top to keep tortilla flat and submerged in oil. Fry until crisp and lightly browned, 45 to 60 seconds (no flipping is necessary). Transfer fried tortilla to paper towel–lined sheet. Repeat with remaining tortillas. Sprinkle with salt.

4. Using spoon, make 8 indentations (2 to 3 inches wide) in tomato mixture. Crack 1 egg into each indentation and season eggs with salt and pepper. Bake until egg whites are just set and yolks are still runny, 5 to 7 minutes, rotating sheet halfway through baking.

5. Spread 2 tablespoons warm refried beans over each tostada, then top with vegetables and eggs. Sprinkle with queso fresco and cilantro and serve immediately.

TEST KITCHEN TIP BAKING EGGS

1. Using back of large spoon, make 8 large indentations in surface of vegetable mixture, 2 to 3 inches wide.

2. Crack 1 egg into each indentation and season with salt and pepper. Bake until egg whites are just set and yolks are still runny, 5 to 7 minutes.

Sweet Potato and Chorizo Hash

Serves 4

☑ **WHY THIS RECIPE WORKS:** Chorizo with potatoes is a popular Mexican taco filling; the hearty combination is both savory and satisfying. Inspired by these flavors, we set out to create a simple breakfast hash. Although russet potatoes crisp up beautifully, we also wanted to include sweet potatoes—not only are they a popular Mexican staple, but we thought their earthy sweetness would give our hash depth of flavor. Tests revealed that an equal amount of sweet and russet potatoes produced the best results: While using just sweet potatoes left the hash with a soft and mushy consistency, a balanced combination of the two created a well-rounded and flavorful hash that crisped nicely. Cubing and microwaving the potatoes shortened their cooking time considerably. For the meat, we chose Mexican-style chorizo for its intense flavor. Onion, garlic, chipotle, thyme, and cumin gave our hash an aromatic backbone. We discovered that the key to achieving crisp hash was getting good browning on the potatoes. Once we added the potatoes to the skillet, we packed them down to ensure good contact with the hot pan and cooked them for a couple of minutes without stirring. We then flipped browned portions of the mixture and packed everything down again to encourage additional browning. As for the eggs, we kept the recipe streamlined by poaching them right in the hash: We made indentations in the potato mixture, cracked the eggs into the divots, and then covered the pan and cooked them over low heat. If you notice that the potatoes aren't getting brown in step 3, turn up the heat.

1 **pound russet potatoes, peeled and cut into ½-inch pieces**
1 **pound sweet potatoes, peeled and cut into ½-inch pieces**
1 **tablespoon vegetable oil**
   Salt and pepper

8 **ounces Mexican-style chorizo sausage, casings removed**
1 **onion, chopped fine**
3 **garlic cloves, minced**
1½ **teaspoons minced canned chipotle chile in adobo sauce**
¾ **teaspoon minced fresh thyme or ¼ teaspoon dried**
½ **teaspoon ground cumin**
½ **cup heavy cream**
8 **large eggs**
1 **tablespoon minced fresh chives**

1. Toss russet potatoes, sweet potatoes, oil, ½ teaspoon salt, and ¼ teaspoon pepper together in bowl. Cover and microwave until potatoes are translucent around edges, 7 to 9 minutes, stirring halfway through microwaving.

2. Meanwhile, cook chorizo in 12-inch nonstick skillet over medium-high heat, breaking up meat with wooden spoon, until beginning to brown, about 5 minutes. Stir in onion and cook until onion is softened and lightly browned, 5 to 7 minutes. Stir in garlic, chipotle, thyme, and cumin and cook until fragrant, about 30 seconds.

3. Stir in cream and hot potatoes. Using back of spatula, gently pack potatoes into skillet and cook undisturbed for 2 minutes. Flip hash, 1 portion at a time, and lightly repack into skillet. Repeat flipping process every few minutes until potatoes are nicely browned, 6 to 8 minutes.

4. Off heat, use spoon to make 4 indentations (2 to 3 inches wide) in hash, pushing hash up into center and around edges of skillet (bottom of skillet should be exposed in each divot). Crack 2 eggs into each indentation and season with salt and pepper. Cover and cook over medium-low heat until whites are just set and yolks are still runny, 4 to 8 minutes. Sprinkle with chives and serve immediately.

Breakfast Burritos

Serves 6

✓ **WHY THIS RECIPE WORKS:** Egg-filled breakfast burritos are a flavorful, fun-to-eat morning meal. We set out to develop the ultimate version. We started by perfecting the filling. Half-and-half made our eggs ultrarich and creamy. Tasters liked the complementary combination of red peppers and onion, along with a jalapeño chile for spice. Chorizo sausage made the burritos more satisfying and offered meaty, garlicky bites. Cheddar cheese and scallions rounded out the flavor of the filling. We softened the tortillas in the microwave to make them pliable enough to roll. Serve with hot sauce or salsa, sour cream, and sliced avocado.

6	ounces Mexican-style chorizo sausage, casings removed
1	red onion, chopped fine
1	red bell pepper, stemmed, seeded, and chopped
1	jalapeño chile, stemmed, seeded, and minced
8	large eggs
¼	cup half-and-half
	Salt and pepper
1	tablespoon unsalted butter
6	ounces cheddar cheese, shredded (1½ cups)
3	scallions, sliced thin
6	(10-inch) flour tortillas

1. Cook chorizo in 12-inch nonstick skillet over medium-high heat, breaking up meat with wooden spoon, until beginning to brown, about 5 minutes. Add onion, bell pepper, and jalapeño and cook until vegetables are softened, about 5 minutes; transfer to bowl.

2. Beat eggs, half-and-half, ½ teaspoon salt, and ⅛ teaspoon pepper together with fork in bowl until thoroughly combined and mixture is pure yellow; do not overbeat. Wipe out skillet with paper towels, add butter, and melt over medium heat. Add egg mixture and, using heat-resistant rubber spatula, constantly and firmly scrape along bottom and sides of skillet until eggs begin to clump and spatula leaves trail on bottom of skillet, 1½ to 2½ minutes.

3. Reduce heat to low and gently but constantly fold eggs until clumped and slightly wet, 30 to 60 seconds. Off heat, gently fold in cheddar, scallions, and chorizo mixture; if eggs are still underdone, return skillet to medium heat for no longer than 30 seconds.

4. Wrap tortillas in damp dish towel and microwave until warm and pliable, about 1 minute. Lay warm tortillas on counter. Mound egg mixture across center of tortillas, close to bottom edge. Working with 1 tortilla at a time, fold sides then bottom of tortilla over filling, pulling back on it firmly to tighten it around filling, then continue to roll tightly into burrito. Serve immediately.

TEST KITCHEN TIP

ASSEMBLING A BREAKFAST BURRITO

1. Mound egg mixture across center of tortillas, close to bottom edge.

2. Fold sides then bottom of tortilla over filling, pulling back on it firmly to tighten it around filling, then continue to roll tightly into burrito.

Mexican Breakfast Sandwiches

Serves 4

✔ **WHY THIS RECIPE WORKS:** A *torta de huevo* is Mexico's answer to the breakfast sandwich: A crusty roll called a *talera* is stuffed with eggs and a host of other Mexican ingredients. For our version, we opted for kaiser rolls, which made a good substitute for the traditional taleras. We made a quick chipotle mayonnaise by combining mayo with a small amount of smoky and spicy chipotle chile in adobo. Beans are a frequent addition to these Mexican sandwiches; we decided to combine refried beans with fresh tomato, avocado, and a bit of pickled jalapeño brine for brightness. Coating our vegetables with the creamy beans helped prevent them from falling out of the sandwiches. We toasted the buns under the broiler and coated the bottom halves with our bean mixture and the top halves with the spicy chipotle mayo. As for the eggs, we knew that perfectly frying four eggs at a time can be a bit of a challenge; cracking our eggs ahead of time meant they could be poured into the pan all at once, rather than one at a time. We crisped up a few pieces of bacon to lend a salty crunch to the sandwiches, and reserved some of the bacon fat for cooking our eggs. Once the eggs were perfectly fried, we slid them onto the buns and finished off our sandwiches with tangy pickled jalapeños and the crisp bacon. Any type of refried beans will work well here; if you want to make your own, see the recipes on page 293.

- 4   kaiser rolls
- ¼   cup mayonnaise
- 1   teaspoon minced canned chipotle chile in adobo sauce
- ⅓   cup refried beans
- 1   avocado, halved, pitted, and cut into ½-inch pieces
- 1   plum tomato, cored and diced into ½-inch pieces
- ¼   cup jarred sliced jalapeños, plus 2 teaspoons brine
- 6   slices bacon
- 4   large eggs
-      Salt and pepper

1. Adjust oven rack 6 inches from broiler element and heat broiler. Arrange rolls split side up on rimmed baking sheet. Combine mayonnaise and chipotle in bowl. In separate bowl, gently combine refried beans, avocado, tomato, and jalapeño brine.

2. Cook bacon in 12-inch nonstick skillet over medium heat until crisp, 7 to 9 minutes. Transfer to paper towel–lined plate, let cool slightly, then break each slice in half.

3. Broil rolls until golden brown, 1 to 3 minutes, rotating sheet halfway through broiling. Flip rolls and broil until just crisp on second side, 1 to 2 minutes.

4. Crack eggs into 2 small bowls (2 eggs per bowl) and season with salt and pepper. Pour off all but 1 tablespoon fat from skillet and heat over medium heat until shimmering. Working quickly, pour 1 bowl of eggs in 1 side of skillet and second bowl of eggs in other side. Cover and cook for 1 minute. Remove skillet from heat, and let sit, covered, 15 to 45 seconds for runny yolks (white around edge of yolk will be barely opaque), 45 to 60 seconds for soft but set yolks, and about 2 minutes for medium-set yolks.

5. Spread chipotle mayonnaise on roll tops and refried bean mixture on roll bottoms. Slide 1 egg onto each bottom. Top with bacon, sliced jalapeños, and bun tops. Serve immediately.

MEXICAN STREET CORN

Sides

Simple Rice Dishes

Each serves 4

✔ **WHY THIS RECIPE WORKS:** Brought to Mexico by the Spanish during the colonial period, rice is a staple of the midday *comida*, the main meal of the day. Pilaf-style rice is traditional, which means the rice is toasted before being simmered in liquid. While our Classic Mexican Rice (page 278) is the ultimate example of a rice side dish, we wanted to develop some simpler sides that could be made any night of the week. We set out to create several versatile, flavorful recipes that could accompany a wide variety of main dishes. First, we needed to get the method just right. Rinsing the rice washed away some of the starches that would otherwise cause the rice to clump, and toasting the rice kept the grains tender and separate. Letting the rice sit for 10 minutes after cooking, with a folded dish towel placed under the lid of the pot, ensured fluffy, fully cooked rice. With our method down, we turned to flavorings. We started with a basic, go-with-everything white rice brightened with lime juice. For our second recipe, we seasoned the rice with a quick cilantro puree, which gave the dish an intense herb flavor. In a final variation, we combined robust ancho chile powder and spicy chipotle chile in adobo to give the rice some kick.

Lime Rice

Basmati, jasmine, or Texmati rice can be substituted for the long-grain rice.

1	tablespoon unsalted butter
1½	cups long-grain white rice, rinsed
2¼	cups water
	Salt and pepper
1	teaspoon grated lime zest plus 2 tablespoons juice
2	scallions, sliced thin (optional)

1. Melt butter in large saucepan over medium heat. Add rice and cook, stirring often, until edges begin to turn translucent, about 2 minutes. Stir in water and 1 teaspoon salt and bring to boil. Reduce heat to low, cover, and simmer until liquid is absorbed and rice is tender, 16 to 20 minutes.

2. Off heat, lay clean folded dish towel underneath lid, and let rice sit for 10 minutes. Add lime zest and juice and scallions, if using, and fluff rice with fork to incorporate. Season with salt and pepper to taste. Serve.

Cilantro Rice

Basmati, jasmine, or Texmati rice can be substituted for the long-grain rice.

2¼	cups chicken broth
1½	cups fresh cilantro leaves, plus 2 tablespoons minced
2	tablespoons unsalted butter
1	small onion, chopped fine
2	garlic cloves, minced
1½	cups long-grain white rice, rinsed
	Salt and pepper

1. Process broth and cilantro leaves in blender until cilantro is finely chopped, about 15 seconds. Melt butter in large saucepan over medium heat. Add onion and cook until softened, about 5 minutes. Stir in garlic and cook until fragrant, about 30 seconds. Add rice and cook, stirring often, until edges begin to turn translucent, about 2 minutes. Stir in broth mixture and 1 teaspoon salt and bring to boil. Reduce heat to low, cover, and simmer until liquid is absorbed and rice is tender, 16 to 20 minutes.

2. Off heat, lay clean folded dish towel underneath lid, and let rice sit for 10 minutes. Add minced cilantro and fluff rice with fork to incorporate. Season with salt and pepper to taste. Serve.

Chile Rice

Basmati, jasmine, or Texmati rice can be substituted for the long-grain rice.

2   tablespoons unsalted butter
1   small onion, chopped fine
2   garlic cloves, minced
2   teaspoons ancho chile powder
1   teaspoon minced canned chipotle chile in adobo sauce
1½   cups long-grain white rice, rinsed
2½   cups chicken broth
    Salt and pepper

1. Melt butter in large saucepan over medium heat. Add onion and cook until softened, about 5 minutes. Stir in garlic, chile powder, and chipotle and cook until fragrant, about 30 seconds. Add rice and cook, stirring often, until edges begin to turn translucent, about 2 minutes. Stir in broth and ¾ teaspoon salt and bring to boil. Reduce heat to low, cover, and simmer until liquid is absorbed and rice is tender, 16 to 20 minutes.

2. Off heat, lay clean folded dish towel underneath lid, and let rice sit for 10 minutes. Fluff rice with fork and season with salt and pepper to taste. Serve.

LEARN HOW **SIMPLE RICE DISHES**

For perfectly tender, separate grains of rice, we toast the rice and cook it gently over low heat.

1. RINSE RICE: Place the rice in a fine-mesh strainer and rinse under cold water until the water runs clear. Let the rice drain well before cooking. Rinsing washes away excess starches that would otherwise make the rice sticky and gummy.

2. TOAST RICE: Melt the butter and cook any aromatics until softened. Stir in the rinsed and drained rice and cook, stirring often, until the edges of the grains turn translucent. Toasting the rice highlights its nutty flavor and helps it cook up fluffy and light.

3. ADD LIQUID AND SIMMER, THEN STEAM OFF HEAT: Stir in the liquid and bring to a simmer. Reduce the heat to low, cover, and continue to simmer until the rice is tender. Remove the pot from the heat and lay a folded dish towel under the lid. The dish towel absorbs moisture and prevents the rice from becoming gummy.

Classic Mexican Rice

Serves 6 to 8

✓ **WHY THIS RECIPE WORKS:** Traditional Mexican rice is a cornerstone of Mexican cuisine, and it's easy to understand why: Nutty, tender rice is perfectly complemented by plenty of aromatic ingredients, and the dish has an appealing, clean, grassy spice from fresh chiles. The rice is usually fried until golden, which gives it its signature nutty flavor; tomatoes, onions, garlic, and chicken broth add complexity and savory flavors. This versatile side can accompany any number of Mexican dishes, from enchiladas to moles and beyond. But many versions we tried turned out soupy, oily, or one-note. We wanted a version with clean, balanced flavor and tender rice that wasn't greasy or watery. Traditionally, the liquid component in this dish is a mix of chicken broth and pureed fresh tomatoes; we settled on equal parts of each for the most balanced flavor. For an appealing red color we added tomato paste, which, although nontraditional, boosted flavor as well. Sautéing the rice in just ⅓ cup of oil (rather than deep-frying it, as some recipes suggested) made for a less oily final dish, and cooking the rice until golden helped develop deep, toasty notes. Moving the cooking from the stovetop to the even heat of the oven ensured that the rice cooked uniformly. A bit of fresh cilantro, fresh minced jalapeño, and a squeeze of lime juice provided brightness and complemented the rich rice. To make this dish vegetarian, substitute vegetable broth for the chicken broth.

- 2   tomatoes, cored and quartered
- 1   onion, chopped coarse
- 3   jalapeño chiles, stemmed
- ⅓   cup vegetable oil
- 2   cups long-grain white rice, rinsed
- 4   garlic cloves, minced
- 2   cups chicken broth
- 1   tablespoon tomato paste
- 1½   teaspoons salt
- ½   cup minced fresh cilantro
-      Lime wedges

1. Adjust oven rack to middle position and heat oven to 350 degrees. Process tomatoes and onion in food processor until smooth, about 15 seconds. Transfer mixture to 4-cup liquid measuring cup and spoon off excess as needed until mixture measures 2 cups. Remove ribs and seeds from 2 jalapeños and discard; mince flesh and set aside. Mince remaining 1 jalapeño, including ribs and seeds; set aside.

2. Heat oil in Dutch oven over medium-high heat for 1 to 2 minutes. Drop 3 or 4 grains rice in oil; if grains sizzle, oil is ready. Add rice and cook, stirring frequently, until light golden and translucent, 6 to 8 minutes.

3. Reduce heat to medium. Add garlic and reserved seeded jalapeños and cook, stirring constantly, until fragrant, about 1½ minutes. Stir in pureed tomato-onion mixture, broth, tomato paste, and salt and bring to boil. Cover, transfer pot to oven, and bake until liquid is absorbed and rice is tender, 30 to 35 minutes, stirring well after 15 minutes.

4. Remove pot from oven and fold in cilantro and reserved jalapeño with seeds to taste. Serve with lime wedges.

TEST KITCHEN TIP FRYING RICE

Heat oil in Dutch oven over medium-high heat for 1 to 2 minutes. Add rice and fry, stirring often, until rice is light golden and translucent, 6 to 8 minutes.

Baked Brown Rice with Black Beans and Cilantro

Serves 4 to 6

✔ **WHY THIS RECIPE WORKS:** Considering rice's popularity in Mexican cooking, we decided to develop a preparation for nutty, chewy brown rice inspired by Mexican flavors. But brown rice can be tricky to cook well: when cooked on the stovetop, the long cooking time translates to an inedibly dry, crusty bottom layer. Although the microwave can speed up the cooking process, the rice tends to cook unevenly in the apppliance's unpredictable heat. While rice cookers deliver excellent results, not everyone has one; to simulate the consistent, indirect heat of a rice cooker, we decided to bake the rice in a covered baking dish in the oven. This method eliminated scorching and guaranteed perfect, evenly cooked rice every time. Next we moved on to flavorings. Since brown rice has a distinct flavor of its own, pairing it with the right ingredients can make or break the final dish. We wanted to bump up the flavor of the rice (but not mask it) while also complementing its chewy texture. We quickly realized that, with our additions, we would need more space than we had in our small baking dish; since we would be sautéing vegetables anyway, we decided to streamline the recipe and move the whole process to a Dutch oven. As for flavorings, we first decided to swap out some of the water for chicken broth to boost savory flavor. We caramelized an onion and a green pepper to deepen their flavors. Once the rice was cooked, we stirred in a can of black beans, which added both complementary flavor and texture, and cilantro for a burst of freshness. A squeeze of lime brightened the rice nicely. Medium-grain or short-grain brown rice can be substituted for the long-grain rice.

4 teaspoons extra-virgin olive oil
1 onion, chopped fine
1 green bell pepper, stemmed, seeded, and chopped fine
3 garlic cloves, minced
2¼ cups water
1 cup chicken broth
1½ cups long-grain brown rice
1 teaspoon salt
1 (15-ounce) can black beans, rinsed
¼ cup minced fresh cilantro
¼ teaspoon pepper
Lime wedges

1. Adjust oven rack to middle position and heat oven to 375 degrees. Heat oil in Dutch oven over medium heat until shimmering. Add onion and bell pepper and cook, stirring occasionally, until softened and well browned, 12 to 14 minutes. Stir in garlic and cook until fragrant, about 30 seconds.

2. Stir in water and broth and bring to boil. Off heat, stir in rice and salt. Cover, transfer pot to oven, and bake until liquid is absorbed and rice is tender, 1 hour 5 minutes to 1 hour 10 minutes.

3. Remove pot from oven, add beans, and fluff rice with fork to incorporate. Replace lid and let rice sit for 5 minutes. Fold in cilantro and pepper. Serve with lime wedges.

Quinoa, Black Bean, and Mango Salad

Serves 6

✔ **WHY THIS RECIPE WORKS:** For a fresh-tasting salad featuring nutty quinoa, we combined the tiny seeds with a variety of fresh Mexican ingredients like mango, bell pepper, and avocado. Black beans made the salad heartier, and a simple but intense lime dressing gave the dish some bite. We like the convenience of prewashed quinoa; if you buy unwashed quinoa, rinse it and then spread it out over a clean dish towel to dry for 15 minutes before cooking.

1½   cups prewashed white quinoa
2¼   cups water
       Salt and pepper
5   tablespoons lime juice (3 limes)
½   jalapeño chile, stemmed, seeded, and chopped
¾   teaspoon ground cumin
½   cup extra-virgin olive oil
⅓   cup fresh cilantro leaves
1   red bell pepper, stemmed, seeded, and chopped
1   mango, peeled, pitted, and cut into ¼-inch pieces
1   (15-ounce) can black beans, rinsed
2   scallions, sliced thin
1   avocado, halved, pitted, and sliced thin

1. Toast quinoa in large saucepan over medium-high heat, stirring often, until quinoa is very fragrant and makes continuous popping sound, 5 to 7 minutes. Stir in water and ½ teaspoon salt and bring to simmer. Reduce heat to low, cover, and simmer gently until most of water has been absorbed and quinoa is nearly tender, about 15 minutes. Spread quinoa onto rimmed baking sheet and let cool for 20 minutes; transfer to large bowl.

2. Process lime juice, jalapeño, cumin, and 1 teaspoon salt in blender until jalapeño is finely chopped, about 15 seconds. With blender running, add oil and cilantro; continue to process until smooth and emulsified, about 20 seconds.

3. Add bell pepper, mango, beans, scallions, and lime-jalapeño dressing to cooled quinoa and toss to combine. Season with salt and pepper to taste. Serve, topping individual portions with avocado.

TEST KITCHEN TIP PREPARING A MANGO

1. Cut thin slice from 1 end of mango and rest mango on trimmed bottom. Cut off skin in thin strips, top to bottom.

2. Cut down along each side of flat pit to remove flesh.

3. Trim around pit to remove any remaining flesh. Cut or slice flesh as directed in recipe.

Mango, Jícama, and Orange Salad

Serves 4 to 6

✓ **WHY THIS RECIPE WORKS:** Jícama, with its crisp, apple-like texture and mild flavor, is well suited to raw applications like salads. We decided to combine this unique ingredient with fresh mangos and oranges, which boasted nuanced sweetness that complemented the jícama nicely. To bring the salad together, we made a spicy lime syrup dressing, which mellowed the jícama's tough crunch and infused it with flavor. Make sure that the syrup has cooled before pouring it over the fruit.

3   tablespoons sugar
¼   teaspoon grated lime zest plus
     3 tablespoons juice (2 limes)
¼   teaspoon red pepper flakes
     Pinch salt
12 ounces jícama, peeled and cut into
     ¼-inch pieces (1½ cups)
2   oranges
2   mangos, peeled, pitted, and cut into
     ½-inch pieces

1. Bring sugar, lime zest and juice, pepper flakes, and salt to simmer in medium saucepan over medium heat, stirring constantly, until sugar is dissolved, about 2 minutes. Off heat, stir in jícama and let syrup cool for 20 minutes.

2. Meanwhile, cut away peel and pith from oranges. Slice oranges into ½-inch-thick rounds, then cut rounds into ½-inch pieces. Place oranges and mangos in large bowl.

3. When syrup is cool, pour over oranges and mangos and toss to combine. Refrigerate for 15 minutes before serving.

Shaved Zucchini Salad with Pepitas

Serves 4 to 6

✓ **WHY THIS RECIPE WORKS:** In Mexico, zucchini is consumed in almost every conceivable preparation, including raw in salads. For our version, we shaved the zucchini into long ribbons using a vegetable peeler and then tossed it with a simple vinaigrette that wouldn't mask the zucchini's delicate flavor. Tangy *queso fresco*, crunchy toasted pepitas, and fresh cilantro provided flavor and textural contrast. Using in-season zucchini and good olive oil is crucial in this dish. Look for small zucchini, which are younger and have thinner skins. Be ready to serve this dish quickly after it is assembled.

1½ pounds zucchini
½   teaspoon grated lime zest plus
     1 tablespoon juice
1   garlic clove, minced
     Salt and pepper
2   tablespoons extra-virgin olive oil
½   cup chopped fresh cilantro
2   ounces queso fresco, crumbled (½ cup)
¼   cup pepitas, toasted

Using vegetable peeler, slice zucchini lengthwise into very thin ribbons. Whisk lime zest and juice, garlic, ¾ teaspoon salt, and ¼ teaspoon pepper together in large bowl. Whisking constantly, slowly drizzle in oil until incorporated. Add zucchini, cilantro, and queso fresco and toss to combine. Season with salt and pepper to taste. Sprinkle with pepitas and serve immediately.

Cherry Tomato and Avocado Salad

Serves 4 to 6

✔ **WHY THIS RECIPE WORKS:** This simple salad combines bright tomatoes, creamy avocado, and grassy poblanos. For big tomato flavor, we salted the tomatoes to draw out their juice, then reduced the liquid with aromatic ingredients to make a flavorful dressing. If you don't have a salad spinner, wrap the bowl with plastic wrap after the salted tomatoes have sat; gently shake to remove seeds and excess liquid. Strain the liquid and proceed with the recipe as directed. If you have less than ½ cup of juice after spinning, use the entire amount of juice and reduce it to 3 tablespoons as directed.

1½ pounds cherry tomatoes, quartered
½ teaspoon sugar
    Salt and pepper
1 tablespoon red wine vinegar
1 garlic clove, minced
½ teaspoon ground coriander
2 tablespoons extra-virgin olive oil
2 avocados, halved, pitted, and cut into ½-inch pieces
1 poblano chile, stemmed, seeded, and cut into 2-inch-long matchsticks
½ cup fresh cilantro leaves

1. Toss tomatoes, sugar, and ¼ teaspoon salt in large bowl and let sit for 30 minutes. Transfer tomatoes and any accumulated juices to salad spinner and spin until seeds and excess liquid have been removed, 45 to 60 seconds, stopping to redistribute tomatoes several times during spinning. Return tomatoes to bowl. Strain ½ cup tomato liquid through fine-mesh strainer into 2-cup liquid measuring cup; discard any extra liquid.

2. Bring tomato liquid, vinegar, garlic, and coriander to simmer in small saucepan over medium heat and cook until reduced to 3 tablespoons, about 5 minutes. Transfer to small bowl and let cool to room temperature, about 5 minutes. Whisking constantly, slowly drizzle in oil until incorporated.

3. Add avocados, poblano, and cilantro to bowl with tomatoes. Drizzle with dressing and gently toss to combine. Season with salt and pepper to taste. Serve.

Cabbage-Carrot Slaw

Serves 4 to 6

✔ **WHY THIS RECIPE WORKS:** For a brightly flavored slaw that would go well with rich braised meats, we tossed shredded cabbage with flavorful ingredients and let it meld in the refrigerator for 1 hour.

1 cup cider vinegar
½ cup water
1 tablespoon sugar
1½ teaspoons salt
1 teaspoon dried oregano
½ head green cabbage, cored and sliced thin (6 cups)
1 onion, halved and sliced thin
1 large carrot, peeled and shredded
1 jalapeño chile, stemmed, seeded, and minced
1 cup chopped fresh cilantro

Whisk vinegar, water, sugar, salt, and oregano together in large bowl until sugar is dissolved. Add cabbage, onion, carrot, and jalapeño and toss to combine. Cover and refrigerate for at least 1 hour or up to 24 hours. Drain slaw, return to bowl, and stir in cilantro. Serve.

Roasted Winter Squash with Chipotle and Lime

Serves 4 to 6

☑ **WHY THIS RECIPE WORKS:** Squash is a popular vegetable in Mexican cooking, used in soups, stews, and side dishes. For an easy-to-prepare roasted squash dish with tons of deep flavor, we turned to delicately sweet butternut squash. First, we tossed our sliced butternut squash with melted butter and spices to create a savory crust when roasted. To encourage the squash slices to caramelize, we used a hot 425-degree oven, placed the squash on the lowest oven rack, and baked the squash for nearly an hour to ensure that all the excess moisture had evaporated. Finally, we put together a sweet and spicy vinaigrette, using lime juice and chipotle as our base. A bit of honey rounded out the tangy, spicy ingredients with an earthy sweetness, while some minced cilantro offered a burst of freshness. Once the squash was cooked, we drizzled it with our simple vinaigrette for a splash of bold flavor, brightness, and visual appeal. This dish can be served warm or at room temperature. For the best texture it's important to remove the fibrous flesh just below the squash's skin.

1   **(2½- to 3-pound) butternut squash**
3   **tablespoons unsalted butter, melted**
1   **teaspoon ground cumin**
1   **teaspoon ground coriander**
    Salt and pepper
2   **tablespoons extra-virgin olive oil**
1   **tablespoon minced fresh cilantro**
2   **teaspoons honey**
2   **teaspoons lime juice**
½   **teaspoon minced canned chipotle chile in adobo sauce**

1. Adjust oven rack to lowest position and heat oven to 425 degrees. Using sharp vegetable peeler or chef's knife, peel squash until completely orange with no white flesh remaining (roughly ⅛ inch deep). Halve squash lengthwise and scrape out seeds. Place squash cut side down on cutting board and slice crosswise ½ inch thick.

2. Toss squash with melted butter, cumin, coriander, ½ teaspoon salt, and ½ teaspoon pepper. Arrange on rimmed baking sheet in single layer. Roast squash until side touching sheet toward back of oven is well browned, 25 to 30 minutes. Rotate sheet and continue to bake until side touching sheet toward back of oven is well browned, 6 to 10 minutes. Remove squash from oven and use metal spatula to flip each piece. Continue to roast until squash is very tender and side touching sheet is browned, 10 to 15 minutes longer.

3. Whisk oil, cilantro, honey, lime juice, and chipotle together in bowl and season with salt and pepper to taste. Transfer squash to serving platter, drizzle with vinaigrette, and serve.

TEST KITCHEN TIP

PREPARING SQUASH FOR ROASTING

1. Drive tip of chef's knife into center of squash; steady with dish towel. Drive knife down through squash. Rotate squash and repeat to cut in half.

2. Scrape out seeds using spoon, then place squash flat side down on cutting board and slice crosswise into ½-inch-thick pieces.

Mashed Spiced Pumpkin

Serves 4 to 6

✔ **WHY THIS RECIPE WORKS:** Pumpkins are native to Mexico, and are used both for their seeds and for their sweet, bright orange flesh. We set out to create a side dish that made pumpkin the star ingredient. Sugar pumpkins are best for cooking; they are more flavorful than larger pumpkins, and their drier, denser flesh cooks more quickly. We started by cutting a pumpkin in half; leaving the skin on made it easy to scoop out the softened flesh after cooking. We tried roasting the pumpkin halves cut side up, but the flesh dried out too quickly. Instead, we roasted the pumpkin halves cut side down to allow them to steam slightly, then turned the pumpkin over for the last 30 minutes of roasting to eliminate extra moisture and provide deep, caramelized flavor. Our next move was to puree the flesh in a food processor, but the silky smooth texture reminded tasters of baby food. Instead, we decided to go with a more rustic-textured mash, which we achieved by simply mashing the pumpkin with a potato masher. A simple combination of butter, brown sugar, and warm spices rounded out the flavor of the dish.

- 1 (4- to 4½-pound) sugar pumpkin, halved lengthwise and seeded
- 4 tablespoons unsalted butter
- 1 onion, chopped fine
  Salt and pepper
- 1 garlic clove, minced
- ¾ teaspoon ground cumin
- ¾ teaspoon ground coriander
- ¼ teaspoon ground cinnamon
- ⅛ teaspoon cayenne pepper
- 3 tablespoons packed brown sugar

1. Adjust oven rack to middle position and heat oven to 375 degrees. Line rimmed baking sheet with aluminum foil and place pumpkin halves cut side down on sheet. Roast until flesh can be easily pierced with a skewer, 45 minutes to 1 hour.

2. Flip pumpkin and continue to roast for 30 minutes. Let pumpkin cool slightly, then scoop flesh into bowl; discard skins. Mash pumpkin with potato masher until almost smooth.

3. Melt butter in large saucepan over medium heat. Add onion and ¾ teaspoon salt and cook until softened, about 5 minutes. Stir in garlic, cumin, coriander, cinnamon, and cayenne and cook until fragrant, about 30 seconds. Add sugar and mashed pumpkin and cook, stirring frequently, until mixture is heated through, about 2 minutes. Adjust consistency with water as needed. Season with salt and pepper to taste. Serve.

TEST KITCHEN TIP

PREPARING A PUMPKIN FOR ROASTING

1. Remove stem; set pumpkin stemmed side down on damp dish towel to hold in place.

2. Position chef's knife on top of pumpkin and strike with mallet to drive it into pumpkin. Continue to hit knife with mallet until it cuts through pumpkin.

Mexican Street Corn

Serves 6

✔ **WHY THIS RECIPE WORKS:** At Mexican street food stalls, grilled corn on the cob is served slathered with a creamy sauce and sprinkled with a crumbly cheese like queso fresco. To duplicate this dish at home, we tossed the corn with chili powder–spiked oil before grilling to keep it from drying out and to infuse it with flavor. For the topping, we combined mayonnaise and sour cream with cilantro, garlic, lime juice, chili powder, and cheese. If both queso fresco and Cotija are unavailable, substitute ½ cup grated Pecorino Romano. See the photo on page 274.

2 ounces queso fresco or Cotija cheese, crumbled (½ cup)
¼ cup mayonnaise
3 tablespoons sour cream
3 tablespoons minced fresh cilantro
4 teaspoons lime juice
1 garlic clove, minced
¾ teaspoon chili powder
¼ teaspoon pepper
¼ teaspoon cayenne pepper (optional)

4 teaspoons vegetable oil
¼ teaspoon salt
6 large ears corn, husks and silk removed

1. Combine queso fresco, mayonnaise, sour cream, cilantro, lime juice, garlic, ¼ teaspoon chili powder, pepper, and cayenne, if using, in large bowl. In second large bowl, combine oil, salt, and remaining ½ teaspoon chili powder, then add corn and toss to coat.

2A. FOR A CHARCOAL GRILL: Open bottom vent completely. Light large chimney starter filled with charcoal briquettes (6 quarts). When top coals are partially covered with ash, pour evenly over half of grill. Set cooking grate in place, cover, and open lid vent completely. Heat grill until hot, about 5 minutes.

2B. FOR A GAS GRILL: Turn all burners to high, cover, and heat grill until hot, about 15 minutes. Leave all burners on high.

3. Clean and oil cooking grate. Place corn on grill (on hot side if using charcoal). Cook (covered if using gas), turning as needed, until corn is lightly charred on all sides, 7 to 12 minutes. Transfer corn to bowl with mayonnaise mixture and toss to coat. Serve.

Toasted Corn with Epazote

Serves 4 to 6

✔ **WHY THIS RECIPE WORKS:** *Esquites,* a sautéed corn dish sold by street vendors in Mexico City, gets its unique flavor from fresh epazote, which has a savory, citrusy flavor. If you can't find fresh epazote, substitute a combination of 2 tablespoons minced fresh cilantro and 1 tablespoon minced fresh oregano.

4 tablespoons unsalted butter
6 ears corn, kernels cut from cobs (5 cups)

1 serrano chile, stemmed, seeded, and minced
   Salt and pepper
3 tablespoons chopped fresh epazote

Melt butter in 12-inch nonstick skillet over medium-high heat. Add corn, serrano, and ½ teaspoon salt and cook, stirring occasionally, until corn is lightly browned, 10 to 15 minutes. Off heat, stir in epazote and season with salt and pepper to taste. Serve.

Restaurant-Style Black Beans

Serves 4 to 6

☑ **WHY THIS RECIPE WORKS:** At Mexican restaurants, saucy, slightly spicy black beans are a popular side dish. We wanted to re-create this dish at home, but many recipes rely on long-cooked dried beans. While this method produces flavorful, creamy beans, we wanted something easier and quicker that we could make any night of the week. Using canned black beans was an obvious starting point; our next challenge was to infuse the canned beans with deep, rich flavor. Bacon, which tasters preferred over salt pork, added smoky, meaty depth and a fresh jalapeño added a spicy, grassy kick. Onion, garlic, and cumin provided an aromatic backbone, while a splash of lime juice counterbalanced the deep flavors with a burst of bright freshness. To get the right consistency, we processed a portion of the beans into a coarse, chunky base, which helped thicken the mixture without dulling the flavor of the beans. After about 15 minutes of simmering, the bean-sauce base had the perfect consistency. For extra flavor and textural contrast, we topped our beans with queso fresco and chopped fresh cilantro. Serve with hot sauce.

- 2 **(15-ounce) cans black beans, rinsed**
- 1½ **cups chicken broth, plus extra as needed**
- 2 **slices bacon, chopped**
- 1 **onion, chopped fine**
- 1 **jalapeño chile, stemmed, seeded, and minced**
- 3 **garlic cloves, minced**
- 1 **teaspoon ground cumin**
- 1 **tablespoon lime juice**
  Salt and pepper
- 2 **ounces queso fresco, crumbled (½ cup)**
- 2 **tablespoons chopped fresh cilantro**

1. Process 1½ cups beans and broth in food processor to coarse paste, about 20 seconds, scraping down sides of bowl as needed. Cook bacon in medium saucepan over medium heat, stirring occasionally, until crisp, 5 to 8 minutes. Using slotted spoon, transfer bacon to paper towel–lined bowl and set aside.

2. Add onion and jalapeño to fat left in saucepan and cook over medium heat until onion is softened, about 5 minutes. Stir in garlic and cumin and cook until fragrant, about 30 seconds. Stir in processed beans and remaining whole beans and cook, stirring often, until well combined and thickened slightly, 15 to 20 minutes.

3. Off heat, stir in lime juice and crisp bacon and season with salt and pepper to taste. Adjust consistency with extra hot broth as needed. Transfer beans to serving bowl and sprinkle with queso fresco and cilantro. Serve.

TEST KITCHEN TIP **RINSING CANNED BEANS**

To ensure bright, clean flavor, rinse canned beans in a fine-mesh strainer before using.

Refried Beans

Makes 3 cups; serves 4 to 6

☑ **WHY THIS RECIPE WORKS:** No Mexican meal is complete without beans, and rich, creamy, refried beans are one of the most common preparations in Mexico. Since this dish is an integral part of the cuisine, we wanted a foolproof method for perfect refried beans. The food processor made quick work of achieving a supple, silky base. We reserved a cup of beans, which we pulsed into the puree until the mixture was just slightly chunky.

- ½ cup chicken broth, plus extra as needed
- 2 (15-ounce) cans pinto beans, rinsed
- 1 tablespoon vegetable oil
- 3 ounces salt pork, rind removed, chopped fine
- 1 onion, chopped fine
- 1 poblano chile, stemmed, seeded, and chopped fine
- 1 jalapeño chile, stemmed, seeded, and minced
  Salt and pepper
- 3 garlic cloves, minced
- ½ teaspoon ground cumin
- 1 tablespoon minced fresh cilantro
- 2 teaspoons lime juice

1. Process broth and all but 1 cup beans in food processor until smooth, about 30 seconds, scraping down sides of bowl as needed. Add remaining beans and pulse until coarsely ground, about 5 pulses.

2. Heat oil in 12-inch nonstick skillet over medium heat until shimmering. Add salt pork and cook, stirring occasionally, until rendered and well browned, 10 to 15 minutes; discard pork, leaving fat behind in skillet.

3. Add onion, poblano, jalapeño, and ¼ teaspoon salt to fat left in skillet and cook over medium heat until vegetables are softened and beginning to brown, about 8 minutes. Stir in garlic and cumin and cook until fragrant, about 30 seconds. Stir in processed beans and cook, stirring often, until well combined and thickened slightly, about 5 minutes. Off heat, stir in cilantro and lime juice and season with salt and pepper to taste. Adjust consistency with extra hot broth as needed. Serve.

Vegetarian Refried Beans

To make these beans less spicy, omit the jalapeño.

Subtitute 1 cup water for ½ cup broth; add all of water to processor in step 1. Omit salt pork and add vegetables to pan when oil is shimmering. Add 2 tablespoons tomato paste, ½ teaspoon dried oregano, and ½ teaspoon chipotle chile powder to pan with garlic and cumin. Adjust consistency with extra hot water as needed before serving.

TEST KITCHEN TIP MAKING REFRIED BEANS

1. Process broth and all but 1 cup beans until smooth, then add remaining beans and pulse until coarsely ground.

2. After sautéing aromatics, add bean puree and cook until thickened slightly, about 5 minutes.

Drunken Beans

Serves 8 to 10

✓ **WHY THIS RECIPE WORKS:** *Frijoles borrachos*, or drunken beans, are a northern Mexican staple. This satisfying, brothy dish is simple, humble, and utterly comforting: Pinto beans are cooked with a bit of pork or lard, a few herbs and aromatics, and either beer or tequila. We set out to create a recipe for creamy, intact beans in a lightly thickened broth with multidimensional flavor. We started with dried beans, since a full-flavored bean cooking liquid was essential. We soaked the beans in salt water before cooking them, which helped to soften their skins. Bacon gave the dish smoky, savory depth, and doubled as a crisp garnish. We sautéed our aromatics—traditional onion, poblano chiles, and garlic—in the rendered bacon fat for deep flavor. A combination of tequila (added at the beginning of cooking) and light beer (added at the end) created good depth of flavor with subtle malty notes. To underscore the fresh and sweet flavors in the beans, we added a bundle of cilantro stems, reserving the leaves for garnish. Although the gentle heat of the oven worked to ensure the beans cooked evenly, using the oven alone left us with a broth that was thin and watery. Simmering the pot uncovered on the stovetop at the end of cooking allowed some of the liquid to evaporate, producing a perfect, brothy pot of beans. You'll get fewer blowouts if you soak the beans overnight as directed, but if you are pressed for time you can quick-salt-soak your beans. In step 1, combine the salt, water, and beans in a large Dutch oven and bring to a boil over high heat. Remove the pot from the heat, cover, and let stand for 1 hour. Drain and rinse the beans and proceed with the recipe. Our favorite Mexican lager is Tecate. Queso fresco can be substituted for the Cotija.

  Salt
1 **pound (2½ cups) dried pinto beans, picked over and rinsed**
30 **sprigs fresh cilantro (1 bunch)**

4 **slices bacon, cut into ¼-inch pieces**
1 **onion, chopped fine**
2 **poblano chiles, stemmed, seeded, and chopped fine**
3 **garlic cloves, minced**
½ **cup tequila**
2 **bay leaves**
1 **cup Mexican lager**
¼ **cup tomato paste**
2 **limes, quartered**
2 **ounces Cotija cheese, crumbled (½ cup)**

1. Dissolve 3 tablespoons salt in 4 quarts cold water in large bowl or container. Add beans and soak at room temperature for at least 8 hours or up to 24 hours. Drain and rinse well.

2. Adjust oven rack to lower-middle position and heat oven to 275 degrees. Pick leaves from 20 cilantro sprigs (reserve stems), mince, and refrigerate until needed. Using kitchen twine, tie remaining 10 cilantro sprigs and reserved stems into bundle.

3. Cook bacon in Dutch oven over medium heat until crisp, 5 to 8 minutes; transfer to paper towel–lined plate. Add onion, poblanos, and garlic to fat left in pot and cook over medium heat until softened, 5 to 7 minutes. Off heat, add tequila and let sit until evaporated, 3 to 4 minutes. Stir in 3½ cups water, beans, cilantro bundle, 1 teaspoon salt, and bay leaves and bring to boil over high heat. Cover, transfer pot to oven, and bake until beans are just soft, 45 minutes to 1 hour.

4. Remove pot from oven. Discard bay leaves and cilantro bundle. Stir in beer and tomato paste and bring to vigorous simmer over medium-low heat. Cook, stirring frequently, until liquid is thick and beans are fully tender, about 30 minutes. Season with salt to taste. Serve, passing lime wedges, Cotija, minced cilantro, and reserved crisp bacon separately.

Enfrijoladas

Serves 4 to 6

✓ WHY THIS RECIPE WORKS: *Enfrijoladas* are straightforward Mexican comfort food: Corn tortillas are coated with refried beans, folded into quarters, placed in a baking dish, topped with cheese, and baked. For the best flavor, we made quick homemade "refried" black beans. We made sure our bean mixture was thick enough to cling to the tortillas, then thinned the rest of the mixture with broth and poured it over the top of the dish for extra bean flavor. Monterey Jack cheese melted perfectly; scallions and cilantro provided freshness. We prefer the flavor and texture of our winning corn tortillas (page 7) in this recipe since they retain their structure and chew.

 2 **(15-ounce) cans black beans, rinsed**
 2 **cups chicken broth**
 1 **tablespoon vegetable oil**
 1 **onion, chopped fine**
 1 **jalapeño chile, stemmed, seeded, and minced**
 ½ **teaspoon salt**
 3 **garlic cloves, minced**
 2 **teaspoons chili powder**
 2 **teaspoons minced fresh oregano or ½ teaspoon dried**
 1 **teaspoon ground cumin**
 2 **tablespoons tomato paste**
 12 **(6-inch) corn tortillas**
    Vegetable oil spray
 4 **ounces Monterey Jack cheese, shredded (1 cup)**
 2 **scallions, sliced thin**
 2 **tablespoons minced fresh cilantro**

1. Adjust oven rack to middle position and heat oven to 400 degrees. Process 2 cups beans and 1 cup broth in food processor until smooth, about 30 seconds, scraping down sides of bowl as needed. Add remaining beans and pulse until coarsely ground, about 5 pulses.

2. Heat oil in 12-inch nonstick skillet over medium heat until shimmering. Add onion, jalapeño, and salt and cook until onion is softened, about 5 minutes. Stir in garlic, chili powder, oregano, and cumin and cook until fragrant, about 30 seconds. Stir in tomato paste and cook for 1 minute. Stir in processed beans and cook, stirring often, until well combined and thickened slightly, about 3 minutes. Let bean mixture cool slightly.

3. Spray both sides of tortillas with oil spray. Stack tortillas, wrap in damp dish towel, and place on plate; microwave until warm and pliable, about 1 minute.

4. Working with 1 tortilla at a time, dip into bean mixture to coat both sides and fold into quarters; shingle folded tortillas in 3 columns widthwise in 13 by 9-inch baking dish.

5. Whisk remaining 1 cup broth into remaining bean mixture and pour over tortillas. Sprinkle with Monterey Jack and bake until tortillas are heated through and cheese is melted, about 10 minutes. Sprinkle with scallions and cilantro and serve.

TEST KITCHEN TIP MAKING ENFRIJOLADAS

1. Dip tortilla into bean mixture to coat both sides, then fold into quarters.

2. Shingle folded tortillas in 3 columns across length of 13 by 9-inch baking dish.

Conversions & Equivalents

Some say cooking is a science and an art. We would say that geography has a hand in it, too. Flour milled in the United Kingdom and elsewhere will feel and taste different from flour milled in the United States. So we cannot promise that the loaf of bread you bake in Canada or England will taste the same as a loaf baked in the States, but we can offer guidelines for converting weights and measures. We also recommend that you rely on your instincts when making our recipes. Refer to the visual cues provided. If the bread dough hasn't "come together in a ball," as described, you may need to add more flour—even if the recipe doesn't tell you to. You be the judge.

The recipes in this book were developed using standard U.S. measures following U.S. government guidelines. The charts below offer equivalents for U.S., metric, and imperial (U.K.) measures. All conversions are approximate and have been rounded up or down to the nearest whole number.

EXAMPLE:

| 1 teaspoon | = | 4.9292 milliliters, rounded up to 5 milliliters |
| 1 ounce | = | 28.3495 grams, rounded down to 28 grams |

VOLUME CONVERSIONS

U.S.	METRIC
1 teaspoon	5 milliliters
2 teaspoons	10 milliliters
1 tablespoon	15 milliliters
2 tablespoons	30 milliliters
¼ cup	59 milliliters
⅓ cup	79 milliliters
½ cup	118 milliliters
¾ cup	177 milliliters
1 cup	237 milliliters
1¼ cups	296 milliliters
1½ cups	355 milliliters
2 cups (1 pint)	473 milliliters
2½ cups	591 milliliters
3 cups	710 milliliters
4 cups (1 quart)	0.946 liter
1.06 quarts	1 liter
4 quarts (1 gallon)	3.8 liters

WEIGHT CONVERSIONS

OUNCES	GRAMS
½	14
¾	21
1	28
1½	43
2	57
2½	71
3	85
3½	99
4	113
4½	128
5	142
6	170
7	198
8	227
9	255
10	283
12	340
16 (1 pound)	454

CONVERSIONS FOR INGREDIENTS COMMONLY USED IN BAKING

Baking is an exacting science. Because measuring by weight is far more accurate than measuring by volume, and thus more likely to achieve reliable results, in our recipes we provide ounce measures in addition to cup measures for many ingredients. Refer to the chart below to convert these measures into grams.

INGREDIENT	OUNCES	GRAMS
1 cup all-purpose flour*	5	142
1 cup cake flour	4	113
1 cup whole-wheat flour	5½	156
1 cup granulated (white) sugar	7	198
1 cup packed brown sugar (light or dark)	7	198
1 cup confectioners' sugar	4	113
1 cup cocoa powder	3	85
4 tablespoons butter† (½ stick, or ¼ cup)	2	57
8 tablespoons butter† (1 stick, or ½ cup)	4	113
16 tablespoons butter† (2 sticks, or 1 cup)	8	227

* U.S. all-purpose flour, the most frequently used flour in this book, does not contain leaveners, as some European flours do. These leavened flours are called self-rising or self-raising. If you are using self-rising flour, take this into consideration before adding leavening to a recipe.

† In the United States, butter is sold both salted and unsalted. We generally recommend unsalted butter. If you are using salted butter, take this into consideration before adding salt to a recipe.

OVEN TEMPERATURES

FAHRENHEIT	CELSIUS	GAS MARK (IMPERIAL)
225	105	¼
250	120	½
275	135	1
300	150	2
325	165	3
350	180	4
375	190	5
400	200	6
425	220	7
450	230	8
475	245	9

CONVERTING TEMPERATURES FROM AN INSTANT-READ THERMOMETER

We include doneness temperatures in many of the recipes in this book. We recommend an instant-read thermometer for the job. Refer to the above table to convert Fahrenheit degrees to Celsius. Or, for temperatures not represented in the chart, use this simple formula:

Subtract 32 degrees from the Fahrenheit reading, then divide the result by 1.8 to find the Celsius reading.

EXAMPLE:

"Roast chicken until thighs register 175 degrees."
To convert:

175°F – 32 = 143°
143° ÷ 1.8 = 79.44°C, rounded down to 79°C

Index

Note: Page references in *italics* indicate photographs.